D1457548

OXFORD CLASSICAL AND PHILOSOPHICAL
MONOGRAPHS

*Published under the supervision of a Committee of the
Faculty of Literae Humaniores in the University of Oxford*

SIKYON

Audrey Griffin

CLARENDON PRESS · OXFORD
1982

Oxford University Press, Walton Street, Oxford OX2 6DP

London Glasgow New York Toronto
Delhi Bombay Calcutta Madras Karachi
Kuala Lumpur Singapore Hong Kong Tokyo
Nairobi Dar es Salaam Cape Town
Melbourne Auckland

and associate companies in
Beirut Berlin Ibadan Mexico City

Published in the United States by
Oxford University Press, New York
© Audrey Griffin 1982

British Library Cataloguing in Publication
Griffin, Audrey
Sikyon. – (Oxford classical and philosophical monographs)
1. Sikyon, Greece – Antiquities
I. Title
938   DF261.S5
ISBN 0-19-814718-X

Set by Hope Services, Abingdon
and printed in Great Britain
at the University Press, Oxford
by Eric Buckley
Printer to the University

Acknowledgements

I have received much valuable help and support from various sources during the production of this work, both recently and in the period 1971 to 1976, when I was writing its original version as a D. Phil. thesis. First of all, I should name my supervisors, George Forrest and John Boardman, who have been most helpful both in the preparation of the original thesis and in its transition into publishable form. Professor C. M. Robertson has also read the chapters on Sikyonian art, and has made various valuable suggestions. My thanks must also go to Miss L. H. Jeffery, who, as my tutor in Greek History when I was an undergraduate, helped me to develop my interest in Sikyon and encouraged me to study the subject in depth.

Part of my research was necessarily done on the site at Sikyon, and in the course of this I have enjoyed the hospitality and help of the British School at Athens (I am especially grateful to the former Secretary, Mrs Jane Rabnett). Several of my journeys to Greece and other expenses have been generously supported by an award from the Craven Committee.

In addition, I have been greatly assisted at various times and in various ways by the following: Professor A. Andrewes, Professor R. M. Cook, Dr Kern, Dr J. Lazenby, Dr Maetzke, Dr Olga Palagia. Particular thanks are due to Professor A. K. Orlandos and the Greek Archaeological Service, for permission to photograph published objects in the Sikyon Museum and to use some of my photographs here. I should also mention the custodians of the Sikyon Museum, who were extremely co-operative and appeared to enjoy having visitors.

Finally, a special acknowledgement to my husband (or, as the Greek Archaeological Service will have it, my wife), Michael Gray. His powers of observation have been much exploited at Sikyon and other sites, and many of the arguments contained in this work are the better for having been exposed to his constructive criticism. Any value which the final product may have is to his credit as much as mine.

Contents

Plates

(at end)

Figures

Abbreviations

AA	*Archäologischer Anzeiger*
ADelt.	Ἀρχαιολογικὸν Δελτίον
AJA	*American Journal of Archaeology*
AM	*Mitteilungen des deutschen archäologischen Instituts, Athenische Abteilung*
AZ	*Archäologische Zeitung*
BCH	*Bulletin de correspondance hellénique*
BICS	*University of London Institute of Classical Studies, Bulletin*
Boll. Fil. Class.	*Bollettino di filologia classica*
BSA	*Annual of the British School at Athens*
CP	*Classical Philology*
CQ	*Classical Quarterly*
CR	*Classical Review*
DAA	Raubitschek, *Dedications from the Athenian Akropolis*
EAA	*Enciclopedia dell' arte antica*
FdD	*Fouilles de Delphes*
Hesp.	*Hesperia*
JHS	*Journal of Hellenic Studies*
LSAG	Jeffery, *Local Scripts of Archaic Greece*
LSJ	Liddell and Scott, rev. Stuart Jones, *Greek–English Lexicon*
NC	Payne, *Necrocorinthia*
ÖJh.	*Jahreshefte des österreichischen archäologischen Institutes in Wien*
PAE	Πρακτικὰ τῆς ἐν Ἀθήναις Ἀρχαιολογικῆς Ἑταιρείας
RA	*Revue archéologique*
RE	Pauly-Wissowa, *Real-Encyclopädie der classischen Altertumswissenschaft*
REA	*Revue des études anciennes*
Rhein. Mus.	*Rheinisches Museum für Philologie*
Riv. Fil.	*Rivista di filologia*
SEG	*Supplementum Epigraphicum Graecum*
TAPA	*Transactions and Proceedings of the American Philological Association*
VS	Johansen, *Les vases sicyoniens*

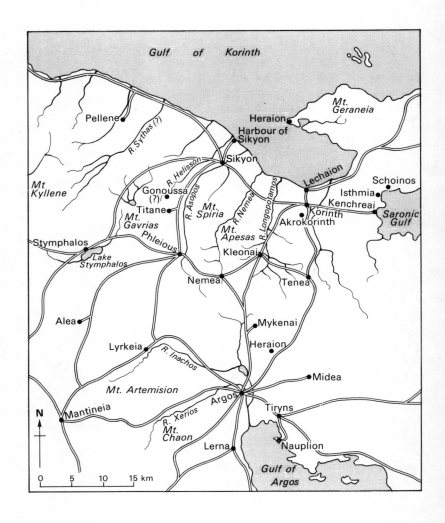

Fig. 1. Map of the North-east Peloponnese (derived from Roux, *Pausanias en Corinthie*).

Introduction

The study of Greek history, especially that of the fifth and fourth centuries BC, frequently appears to confine itself to the activities of the most important states, Athens and Sparta, and later Thebes and Macedon. Other states are occasionally allowed to become prominent, but usually only when they are involved in the affairs of their larger neighbours and thus are drawn into what may be called the mainstream of the subject.

Such a view of Greek history is encouraged by the nature of the surviving ancient sources, which concentrate on the major states largely to the exclusion of the minor ones, and thus make the study of the latter extremely difficult for sheer lack of material. However, it remains both possible and desirable to attempt such a study; possible, because a shortage of material, though inconvenient and sometimes infuriating, is not the same thing as a total absence of it, and desirable, in order to correct the distorted view of Greek history which will otherwise be produced by excessive emphasis on the major states.

The smaller Greek states have the merit, from the historian's point of view, that it is possible to study any one of them over a fairly long period and in all aspects of its life, without producing a work of unmanageable size. The political history, so far as it can be recovered, can be set alongside the topography of the site as it is known from ancient sources and modern excavation, and the evidence of descriptions and finds for economic, artistic, and religious activity, to give a comprehensive account of the state in question. Because of the deficiencies of the sources, this account is likely to be somewhat fragmentary, but the different aspects will, it is to be hoped, throw some light on each other and thus help to fill in the gaps. In the case of Sikyon, there is an abundance of information about the non-political aspects, which makes it likely that such an approach will be particularly rewarding. The general conclusion can also be drawn that the all-too-common treatment of, for instance, 'history' on the one hand and 'art and archaeology' on the other as strictly separate subjects is likely to lead to a serious loss of understanding. Although for the sake of clarity they may have to be placed under separate chapter-headings, they must be looked upon as intimately interconnected.

The history of Sikyon, as it appears in ancient sources, is very largely art history. On the political side, apart from a brief period of success under the tyrants, especially Kleisthenes, Sikyon seems to have been a distinctly minor power, and consequently tends to figure in the sources only as a contributor of contingents to armies, or in other ways playing a subsidiary role. The resulting history is inevitably extremely scrappy—in fact not a history of Sikyon as such, but an account of her dealings with Athens, Sparta, Thebes, and so on, and not a connected account at that, but a series of isolated incidents whose significance is often obscured by their very isolation. In order to put these events together in a coherent narrative, and to relate them from the point of view of Sikyon herself rather than from that of the major powers in whose affairs she occasionally became involved, a large amount of guesswork is required, and in many cases it will prove necessary to leave a blank in the narrative, with the admission that there is not enough solid fact at these points to support even a guess.

One event in the history of Sikyon about which we are certain is that in 303 BC Demetrios Poliorketes, having captured the city, decided to rebuild it on a new site. It was this Hellenistic city which Pausanias saw and which has been the object of modern excavations, and although both Pausanias' account and the excavated remains suggest that this site had been in use before 303, the exact location of the earlier city and how far, if at all, it overlapped with its successor remains uncertain. Consequently we have little archaeological evidence about archaic and classical Sikyon, and must derive our information about it from the description given by Pausanias of such parts of it as still survived in his day. Unfortunately, the usefulness of his account is considerably diminished by the fact that he saw the city in a desolate and depopulated state after being severely damaged by an earthquake, which he himself says had destroyed many of its most noteworthy features. Many of the temples he mentions were abandoned or ruined, and although several ancient works of art still survived it is probable that many more had perished. Hence Pausanias' description of Sikyon leaves several important topographical questions unanswered, and is not as informative as might have been hoped about works by Sikyonian artists.

It is its schools of sculpture and painting which give Sikyon its chief claim to fame, since many major artists originated here, and the city also claimed to have been the scene of much of the early development of painting and sculpture. Even if not all these claims were well-founded, it is significant that Sikyon enjoyed a sufficiently high artistic reputation to justify making them at all. Because of the misfortunes of survival already mentioned, it is not possible to be certain to what extent Sikyonian artists actually worked in their native city, and thus were more intimately connected with it than by the mere fact of birth and citizenship; most of their known works were located elsewhere. But it is known that Hellenistic Sikyon possessed a public collection of paintings, which, it may reasonably be assumed, consisted largely, if not entirely, of works by local artists. Much of the artistic activity of archaic Sikyon may plausibly be associated with the tyrant Kleisthenes, including the building of the Tholos and

'Monopteros' at Delphi. If the site of archaic Sikyon is ever excavated, it may yield further evidence of his activity, especially in the field of public building. Such excavations might also help to solve other questions about archaic Sikyon, such as the existence of the local pottery industry, which for the time being must be left unanswered for lack of evidence.

A more general question, but again insoluble in the present state of our knowledge, concerns the reason for Sikyon's being so rich in artists of various kinds (in the fields of literature and music as well as the visual arts). Were political conditions there particularly favourable to the pursuit of an artistic career, if only by their stability? This seems not to have been the case during the fourth and early third centuries BC, when artistic activity was at a high point, but the internal affairs of Sikyon were often extremely confused and unstable. Was the city a particularly fertile source of patronage, whether public or private? The instances quoted above suggest that this may have been so, at least at certain periods.

The best-attested and most interesting period in the history of Sikyon runs from approximately the middle of the seventh century BC to the end of the third. Sikyonia is relatively rich in Bronze Age sites, including one near the Hellenistic city, and the king-list given, in somewhat differing forms, by Pausanias and Eusebios purports to record something of the history of this period, but the Dark Ages are completely blank, archaeologically as well as in other respects. The history of Sikyon begins again with the rise of the Orthagorid tyranny, and it was probably under this dynasty that the city first became prominent as the home of artists. In the middle of the third century BC Sikyon came under the rule of Aratos and joined the Achaian League, and her history from then on can hardly be separated from that of the League as a whole. The schools of sculpture and painting are known to have remained active until late in the century, but then appear to have come to an end. Sikyon's history from then on, especially after the Roman conquest, is largely one of decline, completed by the earthquake whose effects Pausanias saw. Although there seem to have been some subsequent attempts at recovery, his visit effectively marks the end of Sikyon's history.

PART I: TOPOGRAPHICAL AND ARCHAEOLOGICAL QUESTIONS

1. The Names of Sikyon

A. Aigialeia

Pausanias, drawing on Sikyonian local tradition, says that the city was originally called Aigialeia after Aigialeus, its founder and first king, who also gave the name Aigialos to the area of the Peloponnese which he ruled. Similar information is given by other authors; Strabo makes Aigialeis the original name of the city, and Eustathios Aigialoi.[1] Hesychios applies the name Aigialeis to 'the Ionians who went on Agamemnon's expedition, and now the Achaians at Sikyon'.[2] Stephanos of Byzantion makes Aigialos a place between Sikyon and Bouprasion[3] − not, therefore, identical with Sikyon itself. The name Aigialeus reappears as that of a son of Adrastos, after whom, according to Herodotos, the non-Dorian tribe at Sikyon was named after the abolition of the Kleisthenic tribe-names.[4] Aigialeis or Aigialos is also a name commonly used of the coastal strip of Achaia, while Eusebios applies it to the whole of the Peloponnese.[5]

B. Sikyon

This name for the city, and Sikyonia for its territory, according to Pausanias, were derived from a later king Sikyon,[6] but a botanical derivation, from the plant *sikyos*, is also possible.[7] In the archaic local alphabet the name was spelt 'Sequwon', and the spelling with Se- rather than Si- continued in use until the end of the fifth century BC.[8] The city was known by this name throughout most of its history.

---

[1] Paus. ii.5.6; cf. ii.6.5, where the name is given as Aigiale, and vii.1.1, where he says that the Sikyonians claimed that Achaia was originally called Aigialos, and its inhabitants Aigialeis, after Aigialeus (cf. Hdt. vii.94); Strabo, viii.382; Eustath. *ad Il.* 291.22 ff.   [2] Hesych. s.v. Αἰγιαλεῖς.
[3] Steph. Byz. s.v. Αἰγιαλός.   [4] Hdt. v.68.2.
[5] e.g. *Iliad*, ii.575, Paus. vii.1.1, Strabo, viii.383, Eustath, *ad Il.* 292.20 ff.; Euseb. *Chron.* i (ed. Schoene), 173.   [6] Paus. ii.6.5.
[7] Eustath, *ad Il.* 291.34 ff., 1302.19 ff.; Hesych. s.v. σικυώνια.
[8] Cf. e.g. the graffito from Delphi *LSAG* 143, No. 2, Pl. 23.

C. Mekone

Various sources state that Sikyon once bore this name, which was supposed to have been derived from the fact that Demeter discovered the poppy (*mekon*) there.[9] A poppy was one of the attributes of the cult-statue of Aphrodite by Kanachos at Sikyon.[10] Hesiod relates that Mekone was the scene of the trick played on the gods by Prometheus, who induced them to accept the inferior parts of the sacrificial victims and leave the rest to men.[11] Kallimachos makes it the scene of the division of honours between the gods after the battle with the Giants.[12] The name was apparently unknown to Pausanias, who mentions only the change from Aigialeia to Sikyon.

D. Telchinia

Eustathios and Stephanos of Byzantion give this as a former name of Sikyon,[13] Eustathios adding the explanation that it was so called because the Telchines had once lived there. These 'Kunstdaimonen' are obviously appropriate inhabitants for a city which became famous as an artistic centre, but they are usually located in Krete, Rhodes, or Kypros.[14] The name Telchis or Telchin appears in the Sikyonian king-lists,[15] and the place-name Telchinia could have been derived from this, though again it is not mentioned by Pausanias.

E. Demetrias

This was the name given by the Sikyonians to the new city founded by Demetrios Poliorketes. However, like the rest of the honours paid to him, it soon fell into disuse,[16] and the city is referred to as 'Sikyon' throughout the Hellenistic and Roman periods. However, the name appears to have been remembered and revived during the Middle Ages, since it is found in the Byzantine historian Nikephoros Gregoras,[17] applied to 'this city, formerly called Sikyon'.

---

[9] Strabo, viii.382, Steph. Byz. s.v. Σικυών, Eustath. *ad Il.* 291.22 ff., Schol. Pind. *Nem.* ix.123b. Cf. also *Etym. Mag.* s.v. Μηκώνη.

[10] Paus. ii.10.5.

[11] *Theog.* 535 ff.

[12] Fr. 119 (Pf.) 1-3. Schol. B on *Il.* xv.21 places the incident at Sikyon (κλῆρος ὁ μυθευόμενος ἐν Σικυῶνι).

[13] Eustath. *ad Il.* 291.28 ff., Steph. Byz. s.v. Σικυών and Τελχίς.

[14] Cf. J. Overbeck, *Die antiken Schriftquellen zur Geschichte der bildenden Kunst bei den Griechen* (Leipzig, 1868), 40-55.

[15] Paus. ii.5.6, Euseb. *Chron.* i (ed. Schoene), 173-4.

[16] Diod. xx.102.3, Plut. *Dem.* 25.3.

[17] Nik. Greg. iv.9 (i, p. 116.19 ff.), with reference to the moving of the site by Demetrios. Cf. Schol. Tzetz. *Chil.* viii.410.

2. The City of Sikyon

A. *The visible remains of Sikyon*

Excavation at Sikyon has been largely confined to the plateau on which
the Hellenistic city stood, apart from a few graves and other occasional
finds in the coastal plain. The plateau is roughly triangular, its sides facing
approximately east, south, and north-west, and consists of two 'steps',
the western one being the higher. Such 'steps' may be found all along the
eastern part of the northern coast of the Peloponnese, between the coastal
plain and the mountainous areas behind. The coastal plain narrows from
east to west, being at its broadest in Korinthia, while in parts of Achaia
it is totally lacking, and the mountains run right down to the sea. At
Sikyon the plain is still relatively broad, the distance from Kiato on the
coast to Vasiliko on the seaward edge of the plateau being 4 km. The
accounts of Demetrios' re-foundation of Sikyon show that the archaic
and classical city lay somewhere in this plain,[1] and there is some evidence
that its harbour was at Kiato. The plain is exceedingly fertile, and is at
present mainly given over to the cultivation of apricots. There is a gradual
slope up from the coast to the foot of the plateau, which then rises in a
steep cliff cut on the east (seaward) side by several gullies up which run
paths; the main road to Vasiliko also uses one of these. The other two
sides of the plateau are equally precipitous, the south being apparently
completely inaccessible, the north-west having one path up, which may or
may not correspond to an ancient entrance to the Hellenistic akropolis. At
the west end there is a relatively gentle slope down from the plateau,
which is followed by the road to ancient Titane. The length of the plateau
from Vasiliko to its western tip is about 2.5 km. The north-west and south
sides of the plateau are bounded by the valleys of the Helisson and the
Asopos respectively — that of the Helisson being relatively narrow and
having steep cliffs on the other side, while that of the Asopos is broader
and its other side less steep.[2]

The western section of the plateau served as the akropolis of the Hellenistic city; the theatre and stadium are cut into the fairly steep slope
separating it from the lower 'step', and the main part of the city was

---

[1] Diod. xx.102.2–4; Plut. *Dem.* 25.3; Paus. ii.7.1.
[2] See map, Fig. 2. It should be noted that many descriptions of the site are based
on the assumption that the seaward side of the plateau faces north, whereas in fact
it more nearly faces east. This often leads to difficulty in identifying parts of the
plateau to which they refer.

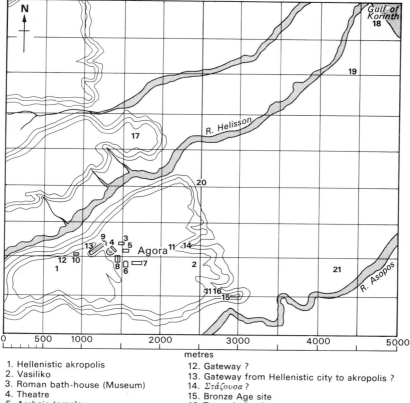

Fig. 2. Map of Sikyon (derived from Pharaklas, Σικυώνια, Fig. 31).

1. Hellenistic akropolis
2. Vasiliko
3. Roman bath-house (Museum)
4. Theatre
5. Archaic temple
6. Bouleuterion
7. Stoa
8. Gymnasium
9. Stadium
10. Site of building ?
11. Section of wall
12. Gateway ?
13. Gateway from Hellenistic city to akropolis ?
14. Στάζουσα ?
15. Bronze Age site
16. Tower built of reused material
17. Tsagriza
18. Kiato
19. Tragana
20. Moulki
21. ʻWest of Asoposʼ site

situated on this lower level. The excavated buildings all lie fairly close to the slope between the two levels, and if they have been correctly identified with buildings mentioned by Pausanias it seems that the Agora was situated here. The modern village (now officially renamed Sikyon; formerly, and still popularly, Vasiliko) lies at the eastern edge of the plateau, where the road ascends from the coastal plain, and abundant architectural fragments can be seen lying about in the area between the village and the site. The first ancient building one comes to when approaching from this direction is a Roman bath-house, now

restored and used as the museum.[3] After this, the most conspicuous
structure is the theatre.[4]

This is placed on an ideal natural site — not only does the slope of
the akropolis provide the site for the auditorium, but large portions of the
stage-structure are cut out of outcrops of rock in front of the main slope.
When first excavated these were well preserved; they are now somewhat
eroded, so our knowledge of this part of the theatre depends largely on
earlier reports and photographs.[5] The most conspicuous features of the
auditorium are the two vaulted tunnels giving direct access from outside
into the lower *diazoma*. The auditorium has not been fully explored, but
seems likely to have been one of the largest in mainland Greece.[6] The
lower part at least was divided into fifteen sections — an unusually large
number. The upper rows of seats were rock-cut. Among the rock-cut
parts of the stage-building were ramps leading up to the stage on either
side. (See Plate 1.) The presence of these, and of undisturbed rock filling
much of the lower part of the stage-building, strongly suggests that the
stage was from the first raised on top of the *proskenion*. There are two
ramps each side, separated by a wall; those nearer the auditorium presumably gave access to the stage, while those behind, which rose somewhat
higher, perhaps led to an upper floor within the stage-building.[7] Access
to the *parodoi* and front ramps was by double gateways, similar to those
at Epidauros. The original *proskenion* was built of poros, and decorated
with engaged Ionic half-columns; the *paraskenia* were shallow, being
purely ornamental.[8] Later, this poros *proskenion* appears to have been
replaced by one of marble, and later still this was demolished to make
way for a Roman-type low, deep stage. Even in its original form, however,
the *orchestra* was less than circular. Around it runs a semicircular water-

---

[3] Fig. 2, No. 3; *PAE* 1935, pp. 78–83 (excavation of bath-house, with finds of
sculpture); N. Pharaklas, Σικυώνια, Athens Technological Organization/Athens
Center of Ekistics, 1971, Fig. 39.

[4] Fig. 2, No. 4; W. J. McMurtry and M. L. Earle, 'Excavations at the Theatre of
Sicyon: i General Report of the Excavations: ii Supplementary Report of the Exca-
vations: iii A Sicyonian statue', *AJA* v (1889), 267–303; Earle, *AJA* vii (1891), 281–
2, viii (1893), 388–96; C. L. Brownson and C. H. Young, 'Further Excavations at the
Theatre of Sicyon in 1891', *AJA* viii (1893), 397–409; A. Fossum, 'The Theatre at
Sicyon', *AJA* (2nd series) ix (1905), 263–76; W. Fiechter, *Das Theater in Sikyon*
(Stuttgart, 1931); A. Orlandos, ''Ανασκαφαὶ Σικυῶνος', *PAE* 1952, pp.393–4; G.
Roux, *Pausanias en Corinthie*, Annales de l'Université de Lyon (Paris, 1958), 134–42;
Pharaklas, Fig. 38.

[5] Best illustrated Fiechter, Figs. 1–2 and 13.

[6] Fossum, 264 calculates that there is room for sixty tiers of seats.

[7] The stage-structure in general is closely paralleled by that at Isthmia, where too
the high stage was enforced by the shape of the ground (E. R. Gebhard, *The Theater
at Isthmia* (Chicago and London, 1973), 17 ff.) and was probably approached by
ramps (ibid., 51 f.).

[8] But Gebhard, 55 f. n. 42 holds that the poros sill supported a wooden *proskenion*, and that the poros capital assigned to it by Fiechter does not belong.

channel, bridged by slabs opposite each staircase of the auditorium, and emptying at its central point into a drain which runs away under *orchestra* and stage. Apparently this was originally constructed as a drain pure and simple, but later, probably at the time when the marble *proskenion* was erected, converted for use as an underground passage. This runs from the 'tank' beneath the centre of the *orchestra* to a flight of steps just behind the *proskenion*, and has been compared to the similarly constructed 'Charonian Steps' at Eretria.[9] At Sikyon, however, there is no trace of steps at the *orchestra* end, and a fairly large gap was left between the bottom step of the flight behind the *proskenion* and the floor of the passage, in order not to obstruct the flow of water in the drain; the passage would therefore have been rather inconvenient for actors to use, and its function must remain uncertain. The interior of the stage-building, where not occupied by rock, was divided into a number of rooms; along the back, facing the exterior, was a stoa flanked by large square rooms, one of which was later converted into a fountain.

A statue found in the theatre was identified as a Dionysos, and tentatively ascribed to Thoinias, a late member of the school of Lysippos. A base signed by Thoinias was found reused in the stylobate of the marble *proskenion*.[10] Presumably this belonged to a statue which stood in or near the theatre, but had disappeared by the time the marble *proskenion* was built. The lettering of the inscription (which lists the athletic victories of one Kallistratos), plus what is known of Thoinias' career, suggests a date in the third quarter of the third century BC. Some of the other blocks in the marble stylobate were there being used for the third time, since they bear two sets of masons' marks surviving from earlier uses. The first set apparently dates from the third century BC, the second from the second century BC; from the second set may be reconstructed a small square building, but the original use is quite uncertain.[11]

The *terminus ante quem* for the construction of the theatre is 251 BC,

[9] The tunnel at Eretria, Brownson, *AJA* vii (1891), 275 ff., compared with the Sikyon arrangement, ibid., 280. But cf. C. H. Skalet, *Ancient Sicyon, with a Prosopographia Sicyonia* (Baltimore, 1928), 13 n. 55 (quoting Fossum's opinion that the tunnel at Sikyon was only a drain). There is a similar central drain in the theatre at Isthmia (Gebhard, 73) dating from at least the first Roman period (mid-1st century AD), but this never seems to have been anything but a drain. But Gebhard (12 n. 6) accepts that the Sikyon passage was used by actors, and refers to a similar arrangement at Segesta.

[10] The Dionysos, Earle, *AJA* v (1889), 292–303, Pl. viii; now Athens 256. Roux, 142 suggests an alternative identification as one of the Dioskouroi. Kallistratos base, McMurtry, *AJA* v (1889), 283 ff., No. 2; *IG* iv, No. 428; L. Moretti, *Inscrizioni agonistiche grece* (Rome, 1953), 103 ff., No. 40; *SEG* xiv, No. 311; J. Marcadé, *Receuil des signatures de sculpteurs grecs* (Paris, 1953 and 1957), ii, 129, Pl. xlvii, 6. Still *in situ*, but the signature has disappeared.

[11] For the masons' marks and possible reconstruction, see Fiechter, op. cit., 16 f.

when the inhabitants of Sikyon gathered there in the confusion following Aratos' capture of the city.[12] The most likely date is about 303, but an earlier date has been suggested, largely on the grounds of certain resemblances of design to the theatre at Epidauros, which might suggest that the architect of the theatre at Sikyon was experimenting with features which were later carried out more successfully at Epidauros.[13] However, these features may just as well be regarded as imitating those at Epidauros, and in one important respect — the raised stage — Sikyon appears definitely later, since at Epidauros this was not part of the original design, but the result of a later alteration. It seems more probable, therefore, that the theatre was built as part of Demetrios' new city. If any earlier theatre existed at Sikyon (as is likely, since dramatic performances are known to have taken place there), no trace of it has been found.

The other excavated buildings at Sikyon lie on the lower level of the plateau, to the right as one looks down from the theatre. This area can be identified as the Agora from Pausanias' description,[14] and the temple which has been excavated here is identified variously as that of Artemis Limnaia which Pausanias passed on his way from the theatre to the Agora, or that of Apollo which stood in the Agora itself. This temple was said to have been founded by Proitos, so the original building must have been ancient, but by Pausanias' time this had been burnt down and rebuilt by one Pythokles, whose identity and date are uncertain. The history of the excavated temple is at least consistent with its having been the temple of Apollo, since it was an archaic foundation rebuilt in the Hellenistic period.[15] The surviving foundations are entirely Hellenistic, but the archaic ground-plan was evidently retained in the rebuilding. (See Plate 2.) It is rather long and narrow (approximately 38 m. × 11.50 m.), giving a length:width proportion somewhat greater than 3:1. Such proportions (which were apparently deliberately chosen by the architect, not forced on him by any peculiarity of the site) are paralleled in the early archaic

[12] Plut. *Arat.* 8.6.

[13] Fossum, op. cit., 271–4 suggests an early or middle 4th–century date on these grounds. But a Hellenistic date for the theatre is taken for granted by Fiechter and others.

[14] Largely through the identification of the Bouleuterion mentioned by Paus. ii.9.6 as the building described below, pp. 11 f.

[15] Philadelpheus, Ἀνασκαφαὶ Σικυῶνος', *ADelt.* x (1926), 46–50; Orlandos, *PAE* 1937, pp. 94–6; Roux, 143 f; Pharaklas, Fig. 36. Here Fig. 2, No. 5. Orlandos favours the identification of the temple as that of Artemis Limnaia, while Roux makes it that of Apollo. Pythokles is sometimes identified with the 2nd–century BC sculptor Pythokles mentioned by Pliny, *NH* xxxiv.52, but this is totally uncertain. The name Ti. Claudius Pythokles appears in an inscription in the Sikyon Museum, dating from the Roman Imperial period; if this is the rebuilder of the temple of Apollo, the date appears to exclude the identification of this with the excavated temple.

temples at Isthmia and Thermon,[16] but unlike these the temple at Sikyon appears to have had an entablature entirely of stone. The terracotta palmette antefixes suggest a date in the third quarter of the sixth century BC. It may be that the ground-plan was derived from a yet earlier building on the same site, but there is no evidence that one existed.

In the Hellenistic temple, and presumably also in its predecessor, there was a rather deep *pronaos* and *opisthodomos*. Part of a circular base, presumably from the cult-statue, was found *in situ* against the west wall of the *cella*. Some slabs of the *cella* floor were also found *in situ*, bearing masons' marks. Dark-on-light palmette antefixes and fragments of the entablature of the archaic temple were found, and from the Hellenistic temple some fragments of a light-on-dark terracotta sima, and roof-tiles stamped δαμ (οσία).[17] The temple was later rebuilt as a Christian church;[18] if it was the temple of Artemis Limnaia, it was already in ruins when Pausanias saw it.

The existence of a stoa or similar structure to the west of the temple is reported,[19] but this has never been thoroughly excavated, and its date and nature remain uncertain.

Some distance south of the temple are the foundations of a large hypo-style hall, which is identified as the Bouleuterion in the Agora mentioned by Pausanias.[20] It is on the basis of this identification that the topography of Hellenistic Sikyon is worked out, since it fixes the position of the Agora. The building is almost square (41.15 m. × 40.50 m.), with sixteen internal Ionic columns, the lower parts of two of which were found *in situ*. The main entrance was on the north side, presumably facing the Agora, and here there was a porch. In the original excavation, considerable traces of banked-earth seats were found, but these have now largely disappeared. Some stone seats which appear to have been used in the Bouleuterion were also found.[21] The area between the central four pillars

[16] *Hesp.* xxviii (1959), 301 n.3.

[17] Base, *ADelt.* x (1926), 47; masons' marks, *PAE* 1937, p. 94; archaic entabla-ture and antefixes, *PAE* 1937, p. 96, Figs. 3–4; Hellenistic sima, *ADelt.* x (1926), 48–50, Figs. 4–5; tiles, *PAE* 1937, p. 94.

[18] *ADelt.* x (1926), 47; *PAE* 1937, p. 96.

[19] *PAE* 1938, p. 121. Shown on the map Pharaklas, Fig. 32, to the north of the Gymnasium. At present it is only a mound with no visible traces of the structure. It shows up well in the aerial photograph, R. V. Schoder, *Ancient Greece from the Air* (London, 1974), 197.

[20] Philadelpheus, 'Note sur le Bouleuterion (?) de Sicyone', *BCH* 1 (1926), 174–82; Orlandos, *PAE* 1938, pp. 120–1, 1939, pp. 100–2, 1941–4, pp. 56–9, 1951, pp. 187 f. and 191, 1953, pp. 184–8; W. A. McDonald, *The Political Meeting-places of the Greeks* (Baltimore, 1943), 240 ff., Pl. xiii; Roux, 146 ff.; Pharaklas, Fig. 35. Here Fig. 2, No. 6. Cf. Paus. ii.9.6.

[21] Banked-earth seats, *BCH* 1 (1926), 177 ff., Figs. 3–4; Skalet, Fig. 17. Some still survived in 1953 (*PAE* 1953, pp. 184 ff.), but none are now visible. Stone seats, *PAE* 1939, p. 102.

was evidently surrounded on three sides by a balustrade, the stone foundation of which still survives.[22] In the building were found fragments of terracotta simas with light-on-dark decoration, at least one of which presumably belonged to the Bouleuterion itself, fragments of a lion-head spout, and a relief palmette antefix.[23] In the late Roman period the building was converted into a bath-house, and two large stone tubs were sunk in the floor.[24]

The Stoa lies to the east of the Bouleuterion and likewise faces north; the two together may therefore reasonably be taken as marking the south side of the Hellenistic Agora. Little of the Stoa survives apart from the foundations, but its ground-plan is traceable, and it can be seen to have had a double row of columns, of which the outer, at least, were probably Doric, and rooms behind. There were probably forty-seven columns in the outer row, twenty-four in the inner (including the end ones), and three at each end, and twenty rooms. It is quite large (105.30 m. × 16 m.), and has been compared to the Stoa of Attalos in the Agora at Athens for its dimensions and layout.[25] So far as can be made out from the surviving remains, and from the finding of third-century BC coins within it, it was an entirely Hellenistic structure. Its function is not known.

The last building of the group around the Hellenistic Agora is the Gymnasium.[26] It lies against the slope of the Hellenistic akropolis, occupying two terraces; such architectural remains as have been found suggest that we have the original buildings only on the lower terrace (the one nearer the Agora), and that those on the upper level are of a later date, probably comprehensively rebuilt after an earthquake or similar disaster.[27]

The entire structure is supported by a massive retaining wall, and a similar wall separates the two terraces within it. The only entrance seems to have been at the north-west corner of the lower level, where there was an elaborate *propylon*. The upper terrace was approached by three stairways,

[22] *BCH* 1 (1926), 177, *PAE* 1953, pp. 186 f. (with inscriptions of the early Roman period).

[23] *BCH* 1 (1926), 180, 181, Fig. 5. Fragments of several simas were found, and it is uncertain which actually belonged to the building.

[24] *BCH* 1 (1926), 177 ff., *PAE* 1938, pp. 120 f.

[25] Philadelpheus, *ADelt.* x (1926), 49; Orlandos, *PAE* 1939, p. 102, 1951, pp. 188 f., 1952, pp. 387–91; Roux, 148 f.; Pharaklas, Fig. 34; here Fig. 2, No. 7.

[26] *PAE* 1932, pp. 63–70, 1934, pp. 116–22, 1935, pp. 73–5, 1936, pp. 86–90, 1952, pp. 391 ff., 1953, pp. 188 f.; Roux, 149 ff.; Pharaklas, Fig. 37; here Fig. 2, No. 8.

[27] Orlandos, *PAE* 1953, p. 188 seems to take the surviving buildings on the upper terrace as constituting a later extension of the Gymnasium on to this level, but elsewhere (*PAE* 1936, pp. 88 ff.) he distinguishes architectural fragments belonging to the rebuilt upper level from others which appear comparable in workmanship to those from the lower level, and which therefore probably belong to contemporary buildings on the upper level.

one at each end and one in the centre of the dividing wall. The lower terrace was surrounded on its three outer sides by Ionic colonnades with rooms behind. One room on the eastern side was somewhat larger than the rest, and had two columns at the entrance instead of a simple doorway; this has been identified at the *ephebeion*. Quite considerable remains of the colonnades have been found, and they have now been partly re-erected. (See Plate 3.) By the southern outer wall were found small columns and capitals which apparently came from windows. Other finds included roof-tiles with painted floral decoration, part of a pedimental sima (from which it is concluded that there were pediments at the narrow ends of the colonnades) and coins, probably of the third century BC, which suggest that the Gymnasium was built at this time.[28] The upper terrace also had colonnades on three sides, but no rooms behind them; both the original structure and that which replaced it were Doric. On both levels, a water-channel ran in front of the colonnades to catch rain-water running off the roofs. Water from the upper channel appears simply to have run down grooves in the terrace-wall into the lower. At a later date the courtyard of the lower terrace appears to have been extended on the short sides by pushing back the colonnades to a position close in front of the walls of the rooms, but the drains were left in their original position.[29]

The most interesting feature of the Gymnasium is the pair of fountains, which are built into the terrace-wall dividing the two levels on either side of the central staircase. They are well preserved, especially the southern one, and a fair degree of reconstruction has been possible. (See Plates 4 and 5.) In their external appearance they were almost identical, each having two Doric columns *in antis* at the entrance, and a further pair of columns *in antis* built into the front wall of the cistern. The roof was presumably flat, level with the ground-line of the upper terrace. Where the fountains differ is in their internal arrangements; the northern one received its water through three spouts, whose attachment–holes remain in the back wall, while the southern one had two vaulted reservoirs cut back under the upper terrace, and the water entered through a single hole in the back wall. The reservoirs were lined with hard cement, on which traces of painted decoration were found, and floored with a simple pebble-mosaic. Above the water-inlet of the southern fountain is a rectangular hole in the back wall, possibly a niche for a statue.[30] A small area outside the western wall of the upper terrace, between it and the slope of the akropolis, where there is a spring and some rock-cut niches, was probably a sanctuary of the Nymphs.[31]

[28] *PAE* 1935, p. 75.　　　　　　　　　　[29] *PAE* 1952, pp. 392 f.
[30] Northern fountain, *PAE* 1932, pp. 66 f., *AJA* xxxviii (1934), 153–7, Pl. xvi; southern fountain, *PAE* 1934, pp. 119 ff.
[31] Skalet, Fig. 8; *PAE* 1953, p. 189; Roux, 152. There is a lozenge-shaped cistern in front of it.

The Stadium lies to the west of the theatre, and like it is cut into the slope of the akropolis, the length being made up by artificial terracing.[32] It has not been excavated, and Pausanias does not mention it.

No excavation has taken place on the Hellenistic akropolis, but during the theatre excavations some late sixth-century BC architectural terracottas were found, which had apparently fallen from a building on the upper level.[33] Remains of a building, perhaps that from which the terracottas came, are reported in the area by earlier visitors to the site, but are now no longer visible.[34] There are other traces of foundations in the area between the Stadium and the north-west side of the plateau.

The walls of the Hellenistic city have never been systematically investigated, and since the site is so strongly naturally fortified it is quite possible that it never had walls all the way round. Remains of walls are visible in some places, but in others there appears a vertical rock-face at the top of the cliff, which was perhaps artificially shaped to take the place of a built wall. There is a possible gateway to the Hellenistic akropolis on the north-west side of the plateau, where a steep path runs down through a gap in the cliffs to the Helisson valley. Also at this side of the plateau, near the Stadium, is what appears to have been an entrance to the akropolis from the lower city. There seems to be no trace of a wall separating the two levels.

The existence of an archaic temple in the area of the Hellenistic Agora shows that this site was to some extent in use before 303 BC, but the main part of the archaic and classical city undoubtedly lay in the plain below. From here we have only occasional archaeological finds to supplement the indications given by Pausanias and other sources. The most striking of these are the fifth- and fourth-century BC mosaic floors.[35] which were mostly found near the foot of the plateau. Also from the plain comes a bronze plaque bearing the epitaph of Iphinoe, one of the daughters of Proitos, who was said to have died at Sikyon; the lettering is fourth-century, and the sense of the inscription requires that it stood in the Agora, but unfortunately the point at which it was found is not at all well defined, so it

[32] Skalet, 14 f.; here Fig. 2, No. 9.

[33] *AJA* v (1889), 281; E. D. Van Buren, *Greek Fictile Revetments in the Archaic Period* (London, 1926), 89, No. 70, 127, No. 33, 151, No. 36, 196 f., No. 135; *Corinth*, iv 1, p. 9.

[34] Shown on the map, G. A. Blouet, *Expédition scientifique de Morée; architecture, sculptures, inscriptions et vues du Peloponèse, des Cyclades, et de l'Attique* (Paris, 1831–8), iii, Pl. 81, M and N; Skalet, 4 n. 13, Figs. 1a and 5; Roux (137 f.) was unable to find it.

[35] *PAE* 1935, pp. 82 f.; 1938, pp. 122 f.; 1941–4, pp. 59 f.; also *ADelt.* xxi (1966), B 124 ('West of Asopos' site, in the coastal plain by the new Korinth–Patras road) and *ADelt.* xxii (1967), B 165, *BCH* c (1976), 575–88 (at Kokkinia, in the plain south of the Asopos).

is not as useful as might have been hoped for fixing the location of the classical Agora.[36] Other pre-Hellenistic finds from the plain have mostly been of graves,[37] which presumably lay outside the city. Since the plain is intensively cultivated, opportunities for large-scale excavation are unlikely to arise,[38] so information about the archaic and classical city will probably continue to be derived only from casual finds.

B. Pausanias' visit to Sikyon

Pausanias approached Sikyon from Korinth; within Sikyonia, but before reaching the city, he saw a number of noteworthy grave-monuments, and the Olympion beside the Asopos. 'By the gate', presumably that by which he entered the city, he saw a spring, which was called Στάζουσα because the water dripped from the roof of a cave instead of rising from the ground in the usual way.[1] Various attempts have been made to identify this; one promising candidate is in a gully on the east side of the plateau to the north of Vasiliko, and consists of a fairly large cave with tunnels coming in from the back and sides. Beside it are the ruins of a building, apparently of Roman brick.[2]

On entering the city, Pausanias first visited the Hellenistic akropolis, where he saw temples of Tyche Akraia and the Dioskouroi, both containing wooden statues. A statue of Tyche is represented on coins of the early Hellenistic and Roman Imperial periods,[3] and a statuette and an over-life-size marble head of her were found in the Roman bath.[4] The latter bears a strong resemblance to the Tyche of Antioch by the Sikyonian Eutychides. (See Plate 7.) Of the buildings whose remains have been found on the Hellenistic akropolis, the archaic structure above the theatre is more likely to have been the temple of the Dioskouroi, since the cult of Tyche probably did not exist before the Hellenistic period. The foundation near the north-west edge of the plateau, at the top of a very steep cliff,

---

[36] *PAE* 1952, pp. 394 f., No. 3, Fig. 11; 1953, p. 190; *SEG* xv, No. 195. Found 'in the vineyard (?) of K. Damatopoulos'.

[37] e.g. *PAE* 1936, pp. 91 f. – at a site called 'Graves', apparently near Moulki, and at Tragana in the plain; *ADelt.* xxii (1967), B 164 f. – at Chteri in the plain.

[38] A small but fruitful opportunity was given by the construction of the new Korinth–Patras road, which revealed the 'West of Asopos' site. See *ADelt.* xxi (1966), B 124, xxii (1967), B 164f.

[1] Paus. ii.7.2–4.

[2] This fountain may be identical with the Μικρή Βρύσις mentioned by Earle, *AJA* v (1889), 287 f., though if so, the Turkish wall which he saw in front of it has now disappeared. Frazer, *Pausanias*, iii.48 f. suggests that the Στάζουσα was a spring at the foot of the plateau near where the road ascends to Vasiliko.

[3] E. T. Newell and S. P. Noe, *Alexander Coinage of Sikyon* (New York, 1950), No. 36, p. 30, Pls. xii and xviii (there identified as Demeter); F. Imhoof–Blumer and P. Gardner, *Numismatic Commentary on Pausanias*, 28, No. 2, Pl. H iii.

[4] *PAE* 1935, p. 80, No. 6, 78, Fig. 8; ibid., pp. 82 f., No. 6, 81, Fig. 14.

would have been an appropriate site for the worship of Tyche with the epithet Akraia.

Pausanias descended from the akropolis by the theatre, where he saw a statue said to be of Aratos, and then came to the temple of Dionysos. This contained a chryselephantine statue of the god, and stone figures of Bakchai.[5] Pausanias does not name the sculptor or sculptors of these statues, so no date can be assigned to them or to the temple. It is one of the problems of Pausanias' account of Sikyon that he gives enough instances of buildings and statues surviving from before 303, even on what is thought of as the Hellenistic site, to make it unjustifiable simply to assume that any structure for which he gives no date was Hellenistic or later. In the case of Dionysos, whose cult at Sikyon was associated with dramatic performances from the time of Kleisthenes,[6] it is likely that the temple was always close to the theatre, but this was not necessarily on the same site before and after 303. Pausanias describes an annual festival at which the ancient statues of Dionysos Bakcheios and Lysios were brought in procession from the *kosmeterion* to the temple.[7] The location of the *kosmeterion* is not known, and even the significance of the name is obscure; it is usually translated 'adorning–place'. However, if it was a surviving building of the old city, the procession from it to the temple of Dionysos might represent the removal of the god from his old to his new sanctuary at the time of the change of site.

The next building which Pausanias noticed was a ruined temple of Artemis Limnaia; this may be identical with the excavated temple, and if so must have existed on its later site in the archaic period. The fact that Pausanias saw it in ruins is no guarantee of great antiquity, since its condition might have been the result of the recent earthquake; however, the uncertainty of the local guides about the fate of the cult-statue, which he comments on, might suggest that the temple had been abandoned a long time before. The epithet Limnaia is rather surprising, since one would expect it to be associated with a wet and probably low-lying site, in the plain or one of the river-valleys, from whence the cult might have been transferred to the plateau in 303. However, the extensive drainage arrangements in the theatre and gymnasium of Hellenistic Sikyon suggest that the plateau itself was a fairly wet place; Diodoros mentions its abundant water-supply.[8]

---

[5] Paus. ii.7.5. These statues are represented on coins, *NCP* 28 f., No. 3, Pl. H iv–vii.

[6] Cf. Hdt. v.67.5.

[7] These statues were supposed to date from the Bronze Age, the Bakcheios being supposed to have been set up by Androdamas son of Phleias (the eponymous hero of Phleious, son of Dionysos and son-in-law of Sikyon), and the Lysios to have been brought from Thebes by one Phanes on the orders of the Pythia, at the time of Aristomachos' unsuccessful invasion of the Peloponnese.

[8] Diod. xx.102.4.

At the entrance to the Agora, Pausanias saw a sanctuary of Peitho, to which an interesting story was attached. After killing the Python, Apollo and Artemis came to Aigialeia (as Sikyon was then called) for purification, but were overcome with fear at a place therafter called Phobos, and fled to Krete. After this the Sikyonians were afflicted by a plague, and were instructed to placate Apollo and Artemis. They therefore sent seven boys and seven girls as suppliants to the river Sythas, and the gods were persuaded to return to the akropolis, at a spot which was thereafter consecrated to Peitho. This was the origin of a ceremony still carried out in Pausanias' day, when the boys went in procession to the Sythas (in western Sikyonia) and then brought the gods to the sanctuary of Peitho, and from there to the temple of Apollo. This information is important for the topography of archaic Sikyon, since the equation of the place where Apollo and Artemis entered the akropolis with a sanctuary near the Hellenistic Agora (which, although not stated by Pausanias in so many words, certainly seems to be assumed in his account of the festival) firmly identifies the plateau as the archaic akropolis.[9]

The temple of Apollo, to which Pausanias came next, was certainly of early origin, having supposedly been founded by Proitos after his daughters' recovery from their madness. The original building had been destroyed by fire, along with a collection of objects of mythological interest which had been housed in it. Of these Pausanias mentions Marsyas' flutes and the spear with which Meleager killed the Kalydonian Boar, but Ampelius, who probably used a Hellenistic source and speaks of these objects as if they were still to be seen, gives a longer list,[10] including the cauldron in which Medeia boiled Pelias, the pebble with which Athena voted for Orestes' acquittal, and a chest belonging to Adrastos whose contents nobody knew. Apart from the last, none of these objects has any particular connection with Sikyon; in the case of Marsyas' flutes, Pausanias gives the explanation (presumably derived from local guides) that they were washed down the river Marsyas into the Maiander, and reappeared in the Sikyonian Asopos.[11] If the excavated temple was that of Apollo, perhaps the collection was housed in the large *opisthodomos*.

Having reached the Agora, Pausanias evidently proceeded to walk round it. Near the sanctuary of Peitho was a *temenos* of the Roman emperors, which had originally been the house of the tyrant Kleon, who ruled in

[9] Pharaklas, 40, § 112 takes the sanctuary of Peitho as a Hellenistic structure, and suggests that the ceremony originally took place at the temple of Apollo and Artemis on the old akropolis (Paus. ii.11.1). However, the cult was by its very nature closely tied to a particular spot, so it seems unlikely that it could have survived transplantation. The suppliant boys may be represented on coins, *NCP* 29, No. 4, Pl. H vii–ix.
[10] *Lib. Mem.* 8.5.
[11] The Sikyonian Asopos was supposed to be fed by the Maiander (Paus. ii.5.3).

the early third century BC. In front of it was the *heroon* of Aratos.[12] (At this point Pausanias inserts an account of Aratos' career.)[13] Continuing round the Agora, he next came to the altar of Isthmian Poseidon, which may have dated from the period after the destruction of Korinth in 146 BC, when Sikyon took over the presidency of the Isthmian Games.[14] Near this were aniconic statues of Zeus Meilichios and Artemis Patroa, in the shape of a pyramid and a column respectively; Pausanias comments unfavourably on their workmanship, but gives no indication of date.[15] Next came the Bouleuterion and a stoa dedicated by Kleisthenes from the spoils of the Sacred War. Unless Pausanias was mistaken about its origin, this cannot be identical with the excavated stoa, which is Hellenistic.

In the open part of the Agora stood a bronze Zeus by Lysippos[16] and a gilded Artemis whose sculptor Pausanias does not name. It is possible that the Zeus, at least, was originally set up in the old city, and moved to its position in the Hellenistic Agora after 303. Nearby was a ruined temple of Apollo Lykeios, with a story attached of how the god had helped the Sikyonians to rid themselves of wolves. This was done by poisoning them with the bark of a log which was thereafter kept in the sanctuary, but which had probably disappeared by Pausanias' time, since the Sikyonian guides could not say what kind of tree it came from. There is no information about the date of this temple. After this Pausanias saw a row of bronze female statues which 'they' (presumably the local guides) called the daughters of Proitos, although the inscription which went with the statues said otherwise. Pausanias does not say whom the statues really represented, or how the confusion of identity came about. There may have been statues of the daughters of Proitos in the archaic Agora, since one of them, Iphinoe, was supposed to have been buried there.[17] Finally, Pausanias saw a bronze Herakles by Lysippos, which, like the Zeus, may have stood elsewhere before 303, and a Hermes Agoraios by an unknown sculptor.

At this point Pausanias concludes his description of the Agora, and proceeds to other places of interest in the city. Unfortunately, at this point also his route becomes rather obscure. The problem arises because

[12] The cult of Aratos is described in detail by Plutarch, *Arat.* 53.
[13] Paus. ii.8.2–9.5.
[14] Paus. ii.9.6, cf. ii.2.2.
[15] A. B. Cook, *Zeus: a Study in Ancient Religion* (Cambridge, 1914, 1925, 1940), ii, 1144 ff. suggests that the Zeus-pyramid may have been a royal grave-monument, 'deified', so to speak, as a result of the recurring close connection of the Sikyonian kings with Zeus. This would, of course, make the Zeus-figure at least extremely ancient. But cf. the dedications to Zeus Meilichios from Lebadeia (*BCH* lxiv–lxv (1940–1), 49 ff.), consisting of herm-like square pillars surmounted by an omphalos instead of a bust, which date from *c.* 200 BC.
[16] Shown on coins, *NCP* 29, No. 6, Pl. H x.
[17] Cf. p. 14 and n. 36.

he next turns to the gymnasium 'not far from the Agora', mentions that it contained a Herakles by Skopas, then goes on to describe the sanctuary of Herakles 'elsewhere', then goes 'from here' to the sanctuaries of Asklepios and Aphrodite, and finally from these to the Gymnasium of Kleinias.[18] It appears possible that the move from the gymnasium to the sanctuary of Herakles is a digression on the subject of statues of Herakles rather than a record of Pausanias' actual movements, and that the strictly topographical description recommences at 'from here'. If so, it is not clear from where Pausanias restarted his journey — the Agora or the gymnasium, either of which might plausibly be regarded as the place where he had left off his topographical account, or the sanctuary of Herakles, where his narrative had brought him. The question is further complicated by the possibility that the gymnasium 'not far from the Agora' and the Gymnasium of Kleinias are one and the same — the excavated Gymnasium being both near the Agora and of the right date to have been built by Kleinias, who was Aratos' father and lived in the first half of the third century BC. There is no trace on the ground of any of the sanctuaries mentioned, or of the second gymnasium if there were two, so there is no archaeological evidence to help determine Pausanias' route.

The *peribolos* of the sanctuary of Herakles was known as Παιδιζή. The cult-statue was an extremely ancient wooden one by Laphaes of Phleious, a sculptor otherwise known only from Pausanias' ascription to him of a statue of Apollo at Aigeira, on the basis of its resemblance to the Sikyonian Herakles.[19] Though no precise date can be assigned to Laphaes, it appears clear that he was thought of as a figure of the archaic period at the latest; no date at all is given for the sanctuary building.

The sanctuary of Asklepios, which Pausanias visited next, contained, besides the Asklepieion itself, a building shared between Hypnos and Apollo Karneios. The figure of Hypnos was perhaps quite old, since nothing was left of it in Pausanias' time except the head; the chamber occupied by Apollo Karneios could be entered only by the priests, so Pausanias was unable to see what statue, if any, it contained. The Asklepieion proper contained a chryselephantine cult-statue by Kalamis, probably the younger rather than the older sculptor of that name.[20] According to

[18] Paus. ii.10.1–7.
[19] Paus. vii.26.6.
[20] Paus. x.19.4 — his pupil Praxias made some of the pedimental figures for the 4th-century temple of Apollo at Delphi. Statues of Asklepios on Sikyonian coins, *NCP* 30, No. 9, Pl. H xiii (standing figure, probably bearded), cf. ibid., 158, No. 9 (seated figure, said to be similar to the Epidauros statue). The cult-statue is described as beardless, and so is probably not represented by either of these. A statuette in the Sikyon Museum (*PAE* 1935, p. 79, 77, Figs. 5–6) also shows the god standing and bearded.

Pausianias, the cult was brought from Epidauros by a woman named Nikagora, wife of Echetimos and mother of Agasikles. The giving of these details makes her look like a real rather than a fictitious person, but she is otherwise unknown and it is impossible to date her. However, the fact that she brought the cult from Epidauros suggests a date not much before 400 BC at the earliest.[21] The god arrived in the form of a serpent, and one of the dedications in the Asklepieion was a figure of a woman sitting on a serpent, who was said to be Aristodama, the mother of Aratos, who was reputedly the son of Asklepios. On either side of the entrance were statues of Pan and Artemis.[22] In the stoa were statues of Oneiros and Hypnos Epidotes,[23] and a large bone of a sea-monster.[24] Of these items, only the statuette of Aristodama can be dated, and that must be third-century BC at the earliest.

Next to the sanctuary of Asklepios was that of Aphrodite. This likewise contained a chryselephantine cult-statue, the work of the late archaic Sikyonian sculptor Kanachos.[25] Here, as in the case of the Asklepieion, the cult and the statue dated from before 303, but it is impossible to tell whether the building which housed them did too. Pausanias gives some details of the Aphrodite cult, including the use of the herb *paideros*, which was reputed to grow only in this sanctuary.[26] Also in the sanctuary was a statue, possibly ancient, of Antiope, the mother of Amphion and Zethos. According to Homer, Zeus was their father, but in Sikyonian local legend Zethos at least was the son of the Sikyonian king Epopeus,[27] and hence, as Pausanias says, Antiope herself was claimed as Sikyonian too.

On his way from these two sanctuaries to the Gymnasium of Kleinias, Pausanias passed a sanctuary of Artemis Pheraia on his right. This contained a wooden statue which the Sikyonians claimed had been brought from Pherai. The Argives, who also worshipped this goddess, made a similar claim for their cult-statue.[28] In the Gymnasium of

---

[21] The arrival of Asklepios at Korinth, where he took over a sanctuary of Apollo, appears to have taken place towards the end of the fifth century. At Sikyon too, Apollo Karneios, who had a subsidiary shrine in the Asklepieion, may have been the original healing god superseded by Asklepios.

[22] A statue of Pan is represented on coins (*NCP* 30, No. 8, Pl. H xii) and a statuette was found in the Roman bath (*PAE* 1935, pp. 79, 78, Fig. 7), but both these are standing figures, whereas Pausanias describes the one in the Asklepieion as seated.

[23] Cf. Epidotai Theoi at Epidauros (Paus. ii.27.6).

[24] For such objects in temples cf. Paus. ix.20.4–5 (the Triton in the temple of Dionysos at Tanagra).

[25] For other works by him, see Paus. ix.10.2.

[26] Cf. Athen. xiv.622c for its use by the Sikyonian *phallophoroi*.

[27] *Od.* xi.260–5; Paus. ii.6.1 ff. (quoting Asios, fr. 1 Kinkel). Here Amphion is called δῖος, so he is presumably thought of as the son of Zeus. On the other hand, Paus. ii.10.4 apparently takes them both as sons of Epopeus and hence Sikyonians.

[28] Paus. ii.23.5.

Kleinias Pausanias saw two statues, herm-like figures of Artemis and Herakles.[29]

The Gymnasium of Kleinias is the last building of Hellenistic Sikyon which Pausanias describes. The remainder of his visit to the city was occupied with the archaic akropolis and the temples, likewise ancient, which stood upon it.[30] The most important of these appears to have been that of Athena, which served to define the location of the archaic akropolis.[31] It was supposed to have been founded by Epopeus, who was buried in front of the altar, and to have been, by contemporary standards, a particularly large and splendid building. However, in Pausanias' time only the altar survived, the temple itself having been destroyed by lightning. The way in which Pausanias speaks of this event suggests that it had taken place quite a long time previously, since he says that even the memory of the temple had been lost. Near Epopeus' grave were the Ἀποτρόπαιοι θεοί, of whose cult Pausanias speaks in the present tense, as though it was still kept up in his day; this is in marked contrast to the apparent abandonment of the other shrines in the area. The sanctuary of Artemis and Apollo, also supposed to have been founded by Epopeus, and the Heraion ascribed to Adrastos had both lost their cult-statues. Behind the Heraion were altars of Pan and Helios, also founded by Adrastos. Lower down on the slope of the akropolis was a shrine of Demeter said to have been founded as a thank–offering by Plemnaios, another early king of Sikyon, whose children invariably died at birth until Demeter intervened.[32] There was also in this area a temple of Apollo Karneios, of which only the columns were standing in Pausanias' time. This was perhaps the original site of the cult later housed in the Asklepieion. Finally, there was a ruined temple of Hera Prodromia, said to have been founded by Phalkes son of Temenos, who led the Dorian conquest of Sikyon.[33]

Even without Pausanias' statement that this area was the original akropolis of Sikyon, the presence of so many ancient temples would suggest that it was an important part of the archaic city. It is therefore highly desirable to establish its geographical relationship to the Hellenistic city. Unfortunately, Pausanias is vague on this point, but his statement that the temple of Athena was near the Sacred Gate, which was presumably a gate in the city wall, suggests a location near the edge of the plateau where the wall ran. He also says that Plemnaios' sanctuary of

---

[29] Skopas' Herakles in the gymnasium near the Agora was probably a full-length figure, which may be represented on coins (*NCP* 30, No. 7, Pl. H xi). The fact that the two gymnasia contained different statues is a point in favour of keeping them distinct. The only statues found in the excavated Gymnasium were Roman portraits, which do not help to identify the building.

[30] Paus. ii.11.1–2. [31] Paus. ii.5.6.
[32] Paus. ii.5.8. [33] Paus. ii.6.7.

Demeter was on the slope down to the plain, that is, on the seaward edge of the plateau.

A promising candidate for identification as Pausanias' archaic akropolis is the site of a Bronze Age settlement[34] on a projecting spur at the south-east corner of the plateau. This consists of a steep-sided mound connected to the main part of the plateau by a narrow neck. The vertical rock-face at the sides of the mound shows some signs of having been artificially shaped into a wall-like formation, as elsewhere round the edge of the plateau. However, it was apparently not included within the main line of the city wall, since traces of this can be seen cutting across the junction between the spur and the main part of the plateau. (See Plate 6.) At this point also there is a ruined tower built of reused architectural pieces. The only trace of buildings on the spur itself is on the neck, where the foundations of a wall and some isolated squared blocks can be seen, but the mound is rich in sherds, not only Bronze Age but of later periods, ranging from Geometric to Byzantine. The presence of these suggests that the site was more or less continuously frequented throughout the city's history, and its military advantages — ease of fortification and an excellent view over the coastal plain — make it an obvious site for an akropolis. The Sacred Gate was probably situated at the junction of the spur with the main part of the plateau. A track which leads down from the base of the spur to the plain no doubt had an ancient predecessor, which would have given access first from the ancient city to its akropolis and later to the Hellenistic city by way of the Sacred Gate.

After visiting the ancient akropolis, Pausanias left the city and travelled to Titane and other sites in the inland part of Sikyonia. He then returned to Sikyon and passed through the plain on his way to the harbour-town. In the plain he saw a ruined temple of Hera, said to have been dedicated by Proitos, which had probably stood within the old city. At the harbour itself he saw nothing he considered worth mentioning, but beside the coast road leading west to Aristonautai, the harbour of Pellene, was a temple of Poseidon.[35] This apparently lay between the Sikyonian harbour-town and the mouth of the Helisson, somewhere near the centre of modern Kiato. A large basilica, dated to the fifth century AD, has been excavated at Kiato, and fragments of earlier buildings were found in its foundations.[36] These may have come from one or both of the temples mentioned above, of which no other trace has been found. The harbour itself may have been located near an artificial mound[37] which

---

[34] R. Hope-Simpson and O. T. P. Dickinson, *A Gazetteer of Aegean Civilisation in the Bronze Age, vol. 1: The Mainland and Islands,* (Göteborg, 1972), A76.

[35] Paus. ii.12.2.   [36] *PAE* 1933, pp. 81–90; 1954, pp. 218–31.

[37] Pharaklas, 53 f., § 156 and Fig. 33. He claims to have seen traces of a wharf near the mound, but these are no longer visible.

today lies some distance inland, and well to the east of the modern harbour of Kiato.

C. The problem of the ancient akropolis

Pausanias' remarks about the ancient akropolis of Sikyon are not entirely consistent with each other. On the one hand, he says that Demetrios moved the city on to the old akropolis,[1] thereby suggesting that the latter consisted of the whole of the plateau, or at least the lower part of it where the Hellenistic city was situated. This version is supported by his account of the sanctuary of Peitho in the Hellenistic Agora, since this was supposed to mark the spot where Apollo and Artemis had entered the old akropolis in response to the supplications of the Sikyonians.[2] On the other hand, he also refers to the area where the temple of Athena stood as the akropolis of the city founded by Aigialeus,[3] and the Bronze Age site, which appears to be the area to which he is referring, is a fair distance from the Hellenistic Agora and rather separate from the rest of the plateau. Archaeological evidence does not help us to choose between the two possibilities, since the presence of an archaic temple in the Hellenistic Agora shows that this area was occupied before 303. From a military point of view, however, the Bronze Age site appears much more satisfactory, since it is capable of being fortified independently of the rest of the plateau, which the Hellenistic Agora is not. In order to secure the latter it would have been necessary to occupy the Hellenistic akropolis, which overlooks it, and in that case the distinction between old and new akropolis, on which Pausanias insists so strongly,[4] would have no real foundation.

It is this difficulty of fortifying one part of the plateau separately from the rest, while the plateau as a whole seems excessively large for an akropolis, which gives rise to the theory that the ancient akropolis was not on the plateau of the Hellenistic city at all, but on the smaller flat-topped hill of Tsagriza to the north, on the other side of the Helisson valley, where traces of occupation at the appropriate periods are said to have been found.[5] In this view, archaic Sikyon is seen as a group of *komai* like those which made up Sparta, scattered over the plain between the foot of the plateau and the sea. Such a scattered group of settlements, with a relatively distant akropolis, would have been extremely difficult to fortify, so Demetrios would have had good reason to create his new city on the plateau.

This view of the topography of archaic Sikyon cannot be ruled out by archaeological evidence alone, since this is insufficient to prove or

[1] Paus. ii.7.1; cf. Diod. xx.102.2.   [2] Paus. ii.7.8.   [3] Paus. ii.5.6.
[4] Τῆ νῦν ἀκροπόλει, ii.7.5; τὴν τότε ἀκρόπολιν, ii.7.8.
[5] Pharaklas, 36 ff., § 105 ff., Fig. 31, No. 10. Here Fig. 2, No. 17.

disprove any theory on the subject; but it seems totally incompatible
with the statements of Pausanias and others about the relationship between
the Hellenistic city and its predecessor, which cannot be made to yield
any other interpretation than that the ancient akropolis was somewhere
on the plateau, however difficult it may be to establish its exact location.
Further important evidence about the relationship between city and
akropolis before 303 is given by Diodoros in his account of Demetrios'
capture of Sikyon, and by Xenophon in certain passages of his account
of the career of Euphron.[6] Diodoros relates how Demetrios captured
the city proper by forcing his way inside the walls,[7] and then occupied
the space between the last houses of the city and the foot of the akropolis
in preparation for an attack on the latter. Xenophon makes it clear that
the *polis* of Sikyon was thought of as consisting of three parts, akropolis,
city, and harbour–town; the harbour-town, and even the city itself, could
be held in the face of a hostile garrison on the akropolis, but possession
of the akropolis was considered essential for secure control of the *polis*.[8]
The picture presented by both authors is that of the city in the plain and
the akropolis on the plateau immediately above.

They do not, however, make it clear whether the akropolis occupied
the whole of the plateau or only part of it. I have already indicated that
the Bronze Age site is the part of the plateau which could most easily
be fortified independently of the rest, and would therefore have been the
most useful part for a garrison to occupy. Demetrios' advice to the
Sikyonians, παρὰ τὴν πόλιν οἰκεῖν τὴν πόλιν,[9] may be translated 'settle
the city *beside* the akropolis' (rather than on it), and would thus make
sense if the akropolis was on the Bronze Age site. However, there remain
other passages in which the akropolis is equated with the Hellenistic city-
site, especially that of Pausanias about the sanctuary of Peitho, which cannot
be explained away. It seems that even if the term 'akropolis' was properly
applied only to the Bronze Age site, it could be extended to other parts of
the plateau, and perhaps especially to the area of the Hellenistic Agora,
where there were ancient temples, just as on the akropolis proper. A relatively loose usage no doubt became easier with the passage of time after 303,
as the exact layout of the earlier city was forgotten.

[6] Diod. xx.102.2; Xen. *Hell.* vii.1.44–3.12.

[7] There are several other ancient references to the walls of Sikyon, e.g. Xen. *Hell.*
iv.4.14; Diod. xi.88.2, xiv.91.3; Front. *Strat.* iii.2.10 (walls of the harbour-town);
Polyain. iv.7.3 ('the gates towards Pellene'). Of these, Xenophon's evidence is the
most valuable, since he wrote at a time when the old city was still flourishing. It is
clear that by the 4th century BC Sikyon was a regular walled city.

[8] At one stage of his career, Euphron occupied the harbour–town while his
enemies held the city and the akropolis; later he seized the city as well (τοῦ ἄστεως
ἐκράτει), but with the akropolis still in hostile hands he was not in full control of the
state (τῆς πόλεως κρατεῖν).   [9] Plut. *Dem.* 25.3.

3. Titane and other Sites in Sikyonia

Ancient Sikyonia was a relatively large area, bordering on Korinthia to the east, where the boundary was the river Nemea,[1] and on the territory of Pellene to the west. Here the river Sythas normally formed the boundary,[2] but on occasions Sikyon succeeded in expanding at Pellene's expense. The remaining borders, with Phleiasia and Kleonaia to the south and Arkadia to the south-west, ran through mountainous country. Not surprisingly, the majority of known ancient sites are in the fertile coastal plain, though some, such as Titane, lie inland.

Judging by the prominence which Pausanias gives to it, Titane was the most important site in Sikyonia after the city of Sikyon itself. He was interested in it as a religious centre, with its ancient sanctuaries of Asklepios and Athena. The site has been identified,[3] but there is very little left of the sanctuaries, and no serious excavation has taken place.

Pausanias carefully distinguishes the direct route from Sikyon to Phleious, which lay east of the Asopos, from the road to Titane, which in fact probably continued to Phleious, lying mostly west of the Asopos, but crossing and re-crossing it. This road was too narrow for wheeled traffic, and the distance from Sikyon to Titane was sixty stades. Titane was said to have been founded by Titan, the brother of Helios, and its Asklepieion by Alexanor, son of Machaon, the son of Asklepios. The sanctuary, as Pausanias saw it, stood in a grove of cypresses, and contained very ancient wooden statues of Asklepios and Hygieia. On top of a hill was the sanctuary of Athena, containing an ancient wooden statue of the goddess which was said to have been struck by lightning. Lower down on the slope was an altar of the winds, where yearly rites were performed to bring them under control, which were said to involve the use of Medeia's spells.[4]

It is obvious that in Pausanias' opinion the sanctuaries at Titane were

---

[1] Strabo, viii.382, Livy, xxxiii.15.1.

[2] Paus. vii.27.12. Roux, 144 identifies it as the Trikkalas or Trikkaliotikou, the river of Xylokastro; Pharaklas, 5, § 30 as the Katharoneri, the next river to the east. If Aristonautai, the harbour of Pellene, is correctly placed at Xylokastro (*RE* ii,960, s.v. *Aristonautai*), Pharaklas is probably right; if at Kamari (J. K. Anderson, 'A topographical and historical study of Achaea', *BSA* xlix (1954), 74 n. 19), Roux is probably right.

[3] Roux, 158 ff., Figs. 35–7; Pharaklas, App. ii,15, § 63 and 35 f. n. 34.

[4] Paus. ii.11.3–12.1.

extremely ancient, but most of the remains visible on the site are Hellenistic or Roman, though there is some evidence of occupation during the Bronze Age and the archaic period.[5] The mid-sixth-century BC sculptors Dipoinos and Skyllis made a statue of Athena for Sikyon, which was struck by lightning; this is sometimes thought to have been the one at Titane, but other identifications are also possible.[6] The origin of the cult of Asklepios is extremely doubtful; there are reasons for believing that it was introduced relatively late, despite Pausanias' belief to the contrary.[7] It is possible that Asklepios took over the sanctuary from Alexanor, who retained a subsidiary place in it.

The name Titane itself appears to have links with northern Greece, where there was a Mount Titanos near Krannon in Thessaly. Similar links are to be found in the local cult, since Koronis, the mother of Asklepios, whose statue was kept in the sanctuary of Athena, was supposed to have been a native of the Dotian plain, and the god's birth was frequently located there.[8] Sikyonia as a whole is connected with Thessaly through the Bronze Age king Epopeus, who was supposed to have migrated from Thessaly to Sikyon, and through the place-name Ephyra, which is found both in Sikyonia and as another name for Krannon.[9] Similarly, the family of Kypselos is said to have originated from Gonoussa 'above Sikyon', but his father Aëtion is described as a Lapith, descended from Kaineus.[10] The identification of Ephyra and Gonoussa is extremely uncertain; it would be tempting to put them near Titane and thus define a particular area of Sikyonia as having Thessalian connections, but there seem to be no suitable sites in the area. A location for both towns in northern Sikyonia, north-west of Sikyon itself, has been suggested.[11] The 'Gonoessa' mentioned in the *Catalogue of Ships* is said by Pausanias to have been identical with Donoussa, a town lying between Pellene and Aigeira, which was subject to the Sikyonians and was eventually destroyed by them. This identification, rather than the more obvious one with Gonoussa 'above Sikyon', is supported by the position of 'Gonoessa' in the *Catalogue*,

[5] Cf. Roux, loc. cit., Pharaklas, loc. cit., Hope–Simpson and Dickinson, *Gazetteer*, A73.   [6] Pliny, *NH* xxxvi.10.

[7] E. J. and L. Edelstein, *Asclepius: a Collection and Interpretation of the Testimonies* (Baltimore, 1945), ii, 240 ff.

[8] Mt. Titanos, Hom. *Il.* ii.735, Strabo, ix.438–9, Steph. Byz. s.v. Ἀστέριον and Τίτανα; Dotian plain, Hesiod, fr. 59 (Merk.–West), *Hom. Hymn* xvi.1–3.

[9] Epopeus, Paus. ii.6.1; Ephyra, Strabo, viii.338 (a list of several towns of that name). Cf. M. B. Sakellariou, *Atti e memorie del 1° congresso internazionale di micenologia*, ii, 901–7.

[10] Paus. ii.4.4., v.18.7; Hdt. v.92.β.1.

[11] Pharaklas, 18 f. § 39. However, others, e.g. Roux, 157, place Gonoussa at Liopesi near Titane (Pharaklas's site 141). Ephyra should be looked for near a river, since Strabo places it on the Selleeis (unidentified).

after Hyperesia, which, according to Pausanias, was the original name of Aigeira.[12] The destruction of the town should probably be assigned to the reign of Kleisthenes, when Sikyon attacked Pellene and possibly Aigeira as well. A site near modern Kamari is suggested for Donoussa, which would have been left well inside Achaian territory after the time of Kleisthenes, when the river Sythas became the western boundary of Sikyonia.[13]

Two other sanctuaries mentioned by Pausanias have never been located.[14] These are the grove of Pyraia, where there was a sanctuary of Demeter and Kore, and the sanctuary of the Eumenides. The former is said to have been about ten stades from Sikyon, to the left of the direct road to Phleious, and the latter about twenty stades from the city along the Titane road, on the eastern bank of the Asopos.

The other sites in Sikyonia which are mentioned in ancient sources are chiefly of military importance. These are Epieikia, near the border with Korinthia, where a Spartan garrison was placed during the Korinthian War, Derai, a fortress captured by Dionysios of Syracuse in 369 B C, and Thyamia, on the border between Sikyonia and Phleiasia.[15] Pausanias also mentions the capture by Epameinondas of a Sikyonian town called Phoibia, and Stephanos of Byzantion mentions both this and another town called Bouphia, which is often thought to have been the same place.[16] Attempts have been made to identify all these sites. Derai has been located at Stimanga in south-east Sikyonia, Thyamia nearby at Evangelistria, and Epieikia also nearby at Pournari. The latter identification has, however, been disputed.[17] A site nearer the coast would be more appropriate for Derai, since Dionysios' troops arrived either by sea or along the coastal plain from Korinth, and fought a battle with the Sikyonians in the plain. If the name is derived from δειρή = 'neck', it might be at the point where some river emerges into the plain. Phoibia–Bouphia has also been tentatively

[12] *Il.* ii.573, Paus. vii.26.13. Cf. Paus. vii.26.2.

[13] Pharaklas, App. ii, 16, §67, Fig. 52 top right. His text and maps appear inconsistent. The excavations by Verdelis to which he refers (App. ii, 36 f. n. 37) are still unpublished. Kleisthenes and Pellene, *P. Oxy.* 1241, col. iii, lines 2 ff., Anaxandridas of Delphi, *FGH* 404, F 1, Aelian, *VH* 6.1 (does not name Kleisthenes, but obviously refers to the same occasion); Aigeira, Paus. vii.26.2-3.

[14] Paus. ii.11.3-4.

[15] Epieikia, Xen. *Hell.* iv.2.14, 4.13; Derai, Xen. *Hell.* vii.1.22; Thyamia, Xen. *Hell.* vii.2.1., 2.20-3, 4.11.

[16] Paus. ix.15.4, Steph. Byz. s.v. Φοιβία and Βουφία, which is said to have been mentioned in Ephoros, Bk. 23, which dealt with Epameinondas' campaigns – hence the suggestion that it is identical with Phoibia.

[17] Derai, Pharaklas, App. ii, 17, §71 and 34 n. 14; Thyamia, ibid., 17, §71 and 34 n. 15; Epieikia, ibid., 17, §71 and 33 n. 12. But W. K. Pritchett, *Studies in Ancient Greek Topography* (Berkeley, 1965-9), ii, 81 doubts whether Epieikia can be precisely located.

located in southern Sikyonia, at the twin sites of Kastraki and Chania, close to the border with Phleiasia.[18] Strabo mentions a town in Sikyonia called Plataiai, the birthplace of the poet Mnasalkas. It has been suggested that this was the settlement on top of Tsagriza.[19]

There are a few other sites in Sikyonia which have yielded more or less important archaeological finds, though not usually from organized excavations. Among these are Tzami, between Sikyon and Stymphalos, where an inscribed bronze plaque dating from *c.* 500 BC was found, along with other bronze and terracotta objects suggesting the presence of a sanctuary; Kokkinia in the coastal plain just south of the Asopos, which has yielded a fourth-century BC floral mosaic; Alonia near Poulitsa, between the Nemea and the Asopos, where an inscription, probably of the fifth century BC, has been found; and Stimanga, where there are remains of Hellenistic and Byzantine buildings.[20] There are many other sites where sherds have been noticed on the surface, and there is probably considerable scope for further investigation in the region.

[18]   Pharaklas, App. ii, 17, § 71.
[19]   Strabo, ix.412; Pharaklas, App. ii, 17, § 71.
[20]   Tzami, Orlandos, Ἑλληνικά, x (1937–8), 5 ff. (the inscription, now Athens 16355, *LSAG* 143, No. 8, Pl. 23); also Stikas, *PAE* 1941–4, pp. 61 ff. (remains of watch-tower, with late Hellenistic or early Roman pottery); Kokkinia, *ADelt.* xxii (1967), B 165, *BCH* c (1976), 575–88; Alonia, *BCH* lxxxiii (1959), 607, *REG* lxxiv (1961), 164, No. 299, *SEG* xxiv, No. 271, *Hesp.* xli (1972), 204 f., No. 7, Pls. 35–6, Fig. 1; Stimanga, Alexandri, *ADelt.* xviii (1963), B 74 ff.

4. Industries and Agriculture

The coastal plain of Korinthia and Sikyonia – τὸ μεταξὺ Κορίνθου καὶ Σικυῶνος – was proverbial for its richness and fertility, as several sources attest.[1] Diodoros also remarks that the plateau on which Hellenistic Sikyon stood was sufficiently well watered to support gardens,[2] as it still does. Various agricultural products are mentioned, including a fairly well-reputed wine, the *sikyos* and *sikya* after which, according to Eustathios, the city was named, the *kolokasia* from which was derived the epithet Kolokasia applied to Athena at Sikyon, and plums, known locally as *hamadrya*.[3] There are some references to Sikyonian olive oil, both as an ordinary agricultural product and in the story that it flowed from the ground in front of the temple of Athena in response to Epopeus' prayers. The Latin poets use the epithet *olivifera* of Sikyon, and *Sicyonia baca* of the olive, suggesting that Sikyonia was an important centre of production. The oil was used for medical and cosmetic purposes.[4]

The exact nature of the *sikyos* and *sikya* is a little doubtful; they are mentioned along with the *kolokynte* by Theophrastos, and the account of these vegetables given by Athenaios suggests that the usage of the names was not precise – some authors treated them as interchangeable, others maintained a distinction between them. The Megalopolitans called the *kolokynte sikyonia*, suggesting that it too was grown at Sikyon. In accordance with Athenaios' statement that the Hellespontines called long gourds *sikyai* and round gourds *kolokyntai*, the former term is usually translated 'bottle-gourd', while *sikyos* is translated 'cucumber'.[5] The term *sikya* was also used in medical contexts to mean 'cupping-instrument', which was presumably made from the dried fruit of the *sikya*, and *sikyone* is also used both of a vegetable (probably identical with

---

[1] Ar. *Aves*, 967–8 and Schol., Diod. viii.21.3, Athen. v.219a, Eustath. *ad Il.* 291.29 f., Suda, s.v. εἰ τὸ μέσον κτήσαιο Κορίνθου καὶ Σικυῶνος, Lucian, *Icaromen.* 18 and *Nav.* 20, Liban. *Epist.* 371.3, Zenob. iii.57, Livy, xxvii.31.1, Hygin. *Fab.* 276.4, Schol. Leid. on *Il.* ii.572.　　　[2] Diod. xx.102.4.
[3] Wine, Pliny, *NH* xiv.74 (cf. Athen. i.33.b–c on Sikyonian water); *sikyos* and *sikya*, Eustath. *ad Il.* 291.35 ff., 1302.19 ff.; *kolokasia*, Athen. iii.72b, Eustath. *ad Il.* 948.35 ff.; *hamadrya*, Hesych. s.v. ἀμάδρυα, Phot. p. 85 Reizenstein.
[4] Spring of oil, Paus. ii.6.3, Ampelius, *Lib. Mem.* 8.5; cultivation, Paus. x.32.19, Virgil, *Georg.* ii.519, Ovid, *Ibis* 317, *Epist. ex Pont.* iv.15.10, Stat. *Theb.* iv.50, Symm. *Epist.* iii.23.1; uses, Dioskorides, *Mat. Med.* i.30.5.
[5] Theophr. *Hist. Plant.* i.13.3, Athen. ii.58f–59a; cf. W. T. Thistleton-Dyer, 'On some ancient plant-names', *Jour. Phil.* xxxiv (1918), 297 ff.

the *sikya*, since it is described as 'long') and of a medical instrument
made from it.[6]

As well as these vegetable products, Sikyonia provided good grazing
land for horses. The earliest reference to this is in the *Iliad*, where
Agamemnon is said to have accepted the mare Aithe from Echepolos of
Sikyon in return for permission not to take part in the expedition to
Troy. (King Agesilaos of Sparta remarked that Agamemnon got a good
bargain.)[7] One version of the story of Oidipous has the exposed infant
found and brought up by Sikyonian *hippophorboi*.[8] Some of the names
which appear in the Sikyonian king-lists have a 'hippo-'component (Zeuxippos, Leukippos, Hippolytos, and Zeuxippe daughter of Lamedon),[9] which
may point to a special connection of Sikyon with horses. The tyrants
Myron I and Kleisthenes owned successful chariot-teams.[10] Horse-rearing
was still practised in Sikyonia in the fourth century BC, when Demosthenes
refers to the ownership of a team of white horses from Sikyon as an
example of conspicuous consumption, and in the mid-third century, when
Aratos disguised the purpose of his attack on Sikyon by pretending that
it was a raid on the king's (probably Antigonos Gonatas') horses.[11] The
type of horse known as *samphoras* may have been one from Sikyon branded
with a *san*, the initial letter of the city's name in the archaic local alphabet,
just as the *koppatias* may have come from Korinth.[12]

In the fourth century BC, when various Greek states provided men
and materials for the rebuilding of the temple at Delphi, Sikyon's contribution consisted mainly of timber,[13] which probably came from the
mountains in the southern part of Sikyonia. From the time of Kleisthenes onwards, Sikyon had a substantial fleet, which was probably built
of local timber. Kleisthenes' attempts at westward expansion may have
been partly motivated by the desire to gain control of the well-forested

[6] *Sikya*, Krates Com. fr. 41 K, Plat. *Tim.* 79e, Arist. *Rhet.* 1405b3, Hp. *VM* 22, *Aph.* 5.50, *IG.* ii²,47.8, 11; *sikyone*, Hp. *Steril.* 221, 222. LSJ translate both as 'cupping-instrument', but this seems only correct of *sikya*. Hp. *Nat. Fem.* 61 uses *sikya* in the same way as *sikyone* – again suggesting that the two are identical.
[7] *Il.* xxiii.293 ff.; Plut. *Ages.* 9.7 (also *Mor.*, *passim*).
[8] Schol. Hom. *Od.* xi.271.
[9] Paus. ii.5.7, 6.5, 6.7; Euseb. *Chron.* (ed. Schoene) i.176.
[10] Paus. vi.19.2, x.7.6; Hdt. vi.126.2.
[11] Dem. xxi.158; Plut. *Arat.* 6.2.
[12] Ar. *Eq.* 603, *Nub.* 122, 1298; Eustath. *ad Il.* 783.30. C. A. Böttiger, *Kleine Schriften archäologischen und antiquarischen Inhalts, gesammelt und herausgegeben von Jul. Sillig* (Dresden, 1837), ii,162 suggests that the *samphoras* came from Syra-cuse, but L. H. Jeffery, *Local Scripts of Archaic Greece* (Oxford, 1961), 142 n. 2 associates it with Sikyon.
[13] *FdD* iii, 5, No. 36. A recent reconstruction of this inscription (J. Bousquet, 'Inscriptions de Delphes, notes sur les comptes des naopes', *BCH* Supp. iv (1977), 91 ff.) makes it refer specifically to cypress wood.

mountains of Achaia, in order to supplement the supply from Sikyonia itself.[14]

Various herbs grew in Sikyonia, including the *paideros*, which was said to grow only in the sanctuary of Aphrodite at Sikyon, and the *herpyllos*, which was found wild on the mountains and transplanted into gardens. Garlands of these herbs were used instead of masks by the *phallophoroi* who performed in the theatre at Sikyon. This was perhaps the type of garland known as *iakcha*, which is defined as a 'sweet-smelling garland' made at Sikyon. Floral wreaths are said to have been invented by the Sikyonian Glykera, whose products inspired the flower-paintings of her lover Pausias.[15]

Sikyon appears to have been highly reputed for its fish, especially conger eels, which grew to a remarkable size. They were evidently highly prized by gourmets, and some recipes are preserved, mostly in sources dating from the fourth century BC.[16] Perhaps they were especially sought after at this time.

The principal industry of Sikyon appears to have been the working of metal, especially bronze, and since the products of this belong for the most part to the sphere of fine art they will be discussed elsewhere, along with the question of the Sikyonian pottery industry.[17] Among the minor products of the metal-working industry were strigils, a type of bracelet known as *sikyonion*, and possibly the silver *phialai* which were given as prizes at the Sikyonian Pythia.[18] Copper ore is said to exist in the mountains of the Asopos valley, and clay for pottery similar to that found in neighbouring Korinthia was probably also available, but there is also some evidence that metal was imported; the bronze of which the *thalamoi* dedicated at Olympia were made was said to have come from Tartessos, and the fact that Golgoi in Kypros was supposed to be a colony of Sikyon may indicate that the Sikyonians were interested in the island as a source of metal.[19] Local stone (limestone of varying degrees of fineness) was much used for buildings and sculpture, and was transported to Delphi for the construction of Kleisthenes' buildings and to Olympia for the

---

[14] See p. 51f and n. 13.

[15] *Paideros*, Paus. ii.10.6; *herpyllos*, Theophr. *Hist. Plant.* vi.7.2, Athen. xv. 681e-f, Pliny, *NH* xix.172; *phallophoroi*, Athen. xiv.622c; *iakcha*, Athen. xv.678a, Hesych. s.v. ἰάκχα; Glykera and Pausias, Pliny, *NH* xxi.4, xxv.125.

[16] Athen. i.27d (= Antiphanes, fr. 236 K), vii.288c–289a (= Philemon, fr. 79 K), vii.293f (= Archestratos, fr. 18 Brandt).

[17] See Part III, esp. pp.97–9.

[18] Strigils (exported to Memphis), *P. Cairo Zenon*, 59488; bracelets, Hesych. s.v. σικυώνια; *phialai*, Pindar, *Nem.* ix.51 and Schol., x.43 and Schol. ad loc.

[19] Copper, H. Blümner, *Technologie und Terminologie der Gewerbe und Künste bei Griechen und Römern*, (Leipzig, 1875–7), iv. 63, A. Philippson, *Der Peloponnes* (Berlin, 1892), 414 n. 3; *thalamoi*, Paus. vi.19.2; Golgoi, Steph. Byz. s.v. Γολγοί.

Sikyonian Treasury;[20] it is not, however, known to have been exported for use by non-Sikyonians.

Judging by the number of references to it in literary sources, a major industry at Sikyon was the manufacture of a type of shoe known as *sikyonion*.[21] Lucian gives the price of a pair as two drachmas, and in general they are referred to as a luxury item. Lucian recommends rhetoricians to wear them for display, but normally they were regarded as women's shoes, and Cicero specifically refers to them as *non viriles*. The Macedonian general Polyperchon was accustomed, when drunk, to dress up in a saffron robe and *sikyonia* and dance. He held Sikyon for several years at the end of the fourth century BC, but since these shoes appear to have been quite widely exported his liking for them need not have been acquired at their place of origin. Langlotz identified as *sikyonia* the soft slippers with turned-up toes worn by several of the mirror-supporting *korai* of his 'Sikyonian' school; these certainly appear to conform to Cicero's description of *sikyonia* as *habiles atque apti ad pedem*, and so may indicate that these shoes were being produced well before they become known from literary sources, since the statuettes concerned are of the late sixth and early fifth centuries BC, while the literary references to *sikyonia* do not attest their existence before the late fourth century.[22] Sikyon may also have produced other articles of dress, since some local words for such objects are recorded by the lexicographers, and Athenaios relates an encounter between the kitharode Stratonikos and a Sikyonian *nakodepses*.[23]

Although there is some evidence that Sikyon both imported and exported goods, there is little information about the way in which this trade was conducted. In the absence of colonies (besides Golgoi, we hear only of the migration of the Bronze Age king Phaistos to Krete, and of a settlement of Sikyonians and others on the site of Rome before the Trojan War, neither of which appears to have had much subsequent significance),[24] Sikyon had no such obvious trading links as existed, for

[20] E. Pomtow, 'Die Alte Tholos und das Schatzhaus der Sikyonier zu Delphi', *Zeitschr. f. Gesch. d. Architektur*, iii (1910), 130 ff., La Coste-Messelière, *Au Musée de Delphes* (Paris, 1936), 54 ff. *Olympia*, ii, 41 wrongly identifies the material of the Treasury as sandstone.

[21] Athen. viii.349e–f, Hesych. s.v. σικυώνια, Steph. Byz. s.v. Σικυών, Herodas, vii.56. ff., Pollux, vii.93, Lucil. 1238 (Terzaghi), Virgil, *Ciris*, 169, Festus, p. 337M.

[22] Price, Lucian, *Dial Meretr.* 14.2 (treated as equivalent to two nights with a hetaira); luxury, Clem. Alex. *Paed.* ii, *cap.* x.116.2, Lucr. iv.1121 ff., Lucian, *Rhet. Praec.* 15; effeminacy, Cic. *De Orat.* i.54.231; Polyperchon, Athen. iv.155c, Eustath. *ad Il.* 1302.22 ff. Cf. E. Langlotz, *Frühgriechische Bildhauerschulen* (Nürnberg, 1927), 48.

[23] Hesych. s.v. σειρόν; Pollux, x.131; Athen. viii.352b.

[24] Phaistos, Paus. ii.6.7; Rome, Festus, p. 266M.

example, between Korinth and her colonies, but it is likely on geographical grounds that her principal interest was in the West. The Aegean was only accessible either by sailing out of the Gulf of Korinth and round the southern Peloponnese, which was always dangerous, or by using the Diolkos, which naturally required Korinthian co-operation. Economic motives, especially interest in the western trade route, are often suggested for two major actions of Kleisthenes which we know of, his participation in the First Sacred War and his efforts to find a son-in-law, where several of the candidates came from the West; such motives may have existed, but hardly to the exclusion of the political ones on which the sources tend to concentrate.[25] Sherds with dedicatory inscriptions in the Sikyonian local script, presumably the offerings of Sikyonian sailors on voyages in and out of the Gulf, appear at Perachora from the late sixth century onwards.[26] In the third century BC, the friendship between Aratos and Ptolemy Philadelphos led to the sending of works of art from Sikyon to Egypt as presents for the king, and perhaps stimulated trade in ordinary goods as well, such as the strigils which found their way to Memphis.[27]

[25] e.g. P. N. Ure, *The Origins of Tyranny* Cambridge, 1922, 259 ff.; for further discussion, see pp. 52 f.
[26] *Perachora*, ii, 398, Nos. 99–101, 103. Date, cf. J. Salmon, 'The Heraeum at Perachora and the early history of Corinth and Megara', *BSA* lxvii (1972), 168.
[27] Plut. *Arat.* 12.6.

PART II: THE POLITICAL HISTORY OF SIKYON

1. Sikyon before the Tyranny

The material evidence for the history of Sikyon in the Bronze Age is confined to the discovery of surface sherds at a number of sites, which shows that they were inhabited at this period.[1] Literary evidence is more abundant, but not necessarily of great historical value. The principal sources are the king-lists given by Pausanias and Eusebios,[2] which partially coincide but which differ widely on certain points.

Pausanias claims that his king-list is a record of what the Sikyonians themselves said about their early history. It is not merely a list of names, but gives an account of some of the events which occurred during various reigns. Some of these events were of interest to Pausanias because of their connection with various monuments which he saw at Sikyon, such as Demeter's intervention to secure a live child for Plemnaios, in gratitude for which Plemnaios founded a temple.[3] In other cases he was concerned with questions of genealogy, especially where kings were said to have been brought in from other parts of Greece.

The first of these foreign kings was Epopeus, who came from Thessaly when the king of Sikyon had died childless and took over the throne (it is not clear whether peacefully or by force). Up till this time, says Pausanias, Sikyon had always been at peace, but Epopeus brought about a war with Thebes by abducting Antiope. Her father Nykteus raised an army to recover her, and a battle was fought, in which both leaders were wounded. Nykteus died, leaving the rule of Thebes to his brother, who invaded Sikyonia with an even larger army. Epopeus sought divine help by building a temple to Athena, and was assured of her approval by the appearance of a spring of olive oil in front of the temple; but before he could fight a

[1] Most recently in Hope–Simpson and Dickinson, *A Gazetteer of Aegean Civilization in the Bronze Age, vol. 1: The Mainland and Islands*, A73 (Titane), A75 Krines–Braibey in eastern Sikyonia), A76 (on the plateau), A77 (Moulki), A78 (Lalioti), and A79 (Melissi and Tholeron, both in western Sikyonia).

[2] Paus. ii.5.6–6.7; Euseb. *Chron.* i (ed. Schoene), 173–8.

[3] Paus. ii.11.2.

battle, he died from his wound, and was succeeded by Lamedon, the younger brother of his predecessor, who gave Antiope back without a fight. On the way back to Thebes she gave birth to twin sons, Amphion and Zethos, and some claimed that only one of these was the son of Zeus, the other being the son of Epopeus.[4] Pausanias saw Epopeus' tomb in front of the altar of Athena, but the temple had long since disappeared.[5] Other sources relate that Epopeus died fighting against the gods, a discreditable story which Pausanias does not mention;[6] however, it is remarkable how he is treated as an outsider, if not a usurper, in the king-list, being of foreign origin and leaving no heir.

Lamedon married an Athenian wife, and when in need of allies for a war with the sons of Achaios, he brought Sikyon from Attika and made him his son-in-law.[7] Various genealogies are given for Sikyon; the one favoured by the Sikyonians made him the grandson of Erechtheus. Sikyon's daughter Chthonophyle had a son, Polybos, by Hermes, and was then married to Phlias, the eponymous hero of Phleious; Polybos' daughter became the mother of Adrastos, and when Adrastos was driven out of Argos he took refuge with his grandfather and succeeded him as king of Sikyon. However, Adrastos returned to Argos as soon as he was able, leaving the throne of Sikyon vacant. Ianiskos, a descendant of Lamedon's Athenian father-in-law, was brought in as king, and was succeeded by the Heraklid Phaistos. Phaistos in turn migrated to Krete in obedience to an oracle, and was succeeded by Zeuxippos, son of Apollo and the nymph Hyllis. Phaistos' grandson Hippolytos succeeded Zeuxippos, and in his reign Sikyon came under the rule of Agamemnon. Under Hippolytos' son, Lakestades, Sikyon was conquered by the Dorians, but Lakestades, as a Heraklid, was allowed to go on ruling jointly with Phalkes son of Temenos.

It is in the latter part of the king-list that Eusebios' version differs most markedly from Pausanias' — some names are totally different, and those which are the same appear in a different order. There are also other sources, mostly dealing with Sikyon's participation in the Trojan War, which suggest yet other versions. The chief point of difference concerns the name of the king in whose reign the Trojan War was thought to have taken place. For Pausanias, this was presumably Hippolytos, who became the vassal of Agamemnon; for Eusebios it was Polypheides, the last king but two (a name not in Pausanias); but there was another tradition, going back at least to Ibykos, which took Zeuxippos to Troy.[8] The *Iliad* is

[4] Asios, fr. 1 Kinkel, whom Pausanias quotes.
[5] Paus. ii.11.1.　　　　　　　　　[6] Diod. vi.6.2.
[7] The sons of Achaios were probably thought of as having their base at Argos, cf. Paus. vii.1.6.
[8] Ibykos, *To Polykrates*, 40 f.; cf. J. P. Barron, 'The Son of Hyllis', *CR* n.s. xi (1961), 185–7 and 'Ibycus: to Polycrates', *BICS* xvi (1969), 130 f.

silent on this point, since Sikyon appears in the *Catalogue of Ships* simply as one of the states under Agamemnon, though the fact that Adrastos once ruled there is noted; elsewhere a Sikyonian named Echepolos is mentioned, who bribed Agamemnon to let him stay at home during the campaign, but he seems to be thought of as a wealthy noble rather than a king.[9] Another important difference between Pausanias and Eusebios is that, whereas Pausanias ends his king-list with the Dorian invasion, Eusebios makes no reference to this event, but says that after Zeuxippos Sikyon was ruled by the priests of Apollo Karneios instead of kings. This arrangement lasted until the seventh priest went into exile because he could not bear the expenses of his office, an event which Eusebios dates 352 years before the first Olympiad. There is no trace of this version of Sikyonian history in Pausanias, though he does mention a temple of Apollo Karneios on the ancient akropolis, which suggests that the cult was an old one.[10]

Although the king-lists may not contain much reliable information about Sikyon in the Bronze Age, they are important as showing what was believed by later generations. These beliefs occasionally became important in contemporary politics, as in the celebrated instance when Kleisthenes attempted to eliminate Adrastos from Sikyonian history in order to remove an apparent instance of Argive domination over Sikyon, only to be met by the Delphic Oracle's reassertion of the fact that 'Adrastos was king of the Sikyonians'.[11] The varying datings of the Trojan War in relation to Sikyonian kings may also be, at least partly, the result of Kleisthenic propaganda and attempts to counter it; the placing of Zeuxippos at Troy appears to have been an invention by Ibykos after he had quarrelled with Kleisthenes' successor, being designed to give yet another instance of Argive rule at Sikyon.[12] Another noteworthy feature of the king-list as given by Pausanias, the recurrence of links with Athens, cannot be given an explicit parallel in later Sikyonian history, but may be reflected in Kleisthenes' desire for an Athenian son-in-law.

There is no direct evidence about the history of Sikyon in the Dark Ages, and such information as there is about this period is derived from its supposed effects on later events. It is only with the rise of the Ortha-gorid tyranny that the history proper of Sikyon begins, and it is largely from the policies of the tyrants that deductions can be made about the former condition of Sikyon which they were attempting to change. But a

[9] *Il.* ii.572, xxiii.216 ff.
[10] Paus. ii.11.2. This temple was in ruins, but the cult continued in the Asklepieion (Paus. ii.10.2).　　　　　　　　　　　　　[11] Hdt. vi.67.
[12] For anti-Kleisthenic interpretation, see Barron, *BICS* xvi (1969), 137 f., M. Robertson, 'Ibycus: Polycrates, Troilus, Polyxena', *BICS* xvii (1970), 11 ff., and see below, pp. 57–8.

note of caution is necessary here; the tyrant about whom most is known, Kleisthenes, was not the first of the dynasty and therefore was not dealing directly with Sikyon in its pre-Orthagorid state, but was building upon the work of his predecessors, who may already have carried out extensive reforms of which we know nothing. However, a noticeable feature of his policy which his predecessors are likely to have shared is a deep dislike of Dorians and of Argos, which is often supposed to show that racial tension between Dorians and non-Dorians at Sikyon was one of the factors which brought the Orthagorids (themselves non-Dorians) to power. This tension is supposed to have originated after the Dorian conquest, when the non-Dorian population was reduced to serfdom by its new rulers; certain Sikyonian names for semi-slave populations are supposed to date from this period.[13] However, such information as exists about the rise of Orthagoras suggests that the situation was not quite so simple. The story of Orthagoras begins with a visit to Delphi by a group of Sikyonian nobles, with the *mageiros* Andreas among their attendants. The oracle told them that whichever member of the party first heard that a son had been born to him after his return home would become tyrant. The man to whom this happened was Andreas, but because he was not one of the nobles the fact went unnoticed. So Orthagoras, his son, received an upbringing proper to his station in life, commenced a military career, and was so successful that he was elected polemarch — after which, presumably, he moved on to become tyrant.[14] Although this account makes much of Orthagoras' humble origins, it has been pointed out that on the embassy to Delphi the *mageiros* had important religious functions, and was not a mere cook;[15] and the fact that Orthagoras was able to progress as far as he did in his military career suggests that non-Dorian origin was no barrier to the holding of high office.

In fact the object of Kleisthenes' hostility seems to have been not Dorians but Argives, even non-Dorian ones such as Adrastos. Although

---

[13] *Korynephoroi*, Steph. Byz. s.v. Χίος, Pollux, iii.83 (both list them along with the Helots and other such groups, and Pollux calls them 'between freemen and slaves'); *katonakophoroi*, Athen. 271d, quoting Theopompos and Menaichmos, and calling them 'slaves similar to the *epeunaktoi*'. However, Pollux, vii.68 says that the *katonake* (a woollen garment with a sheepskin border) was worn at Sikyon under the tyrants. Non-Dorians become serfs, e.g. Skalet, *Ancient Sikyon*, 48 ff.; A. Gitti, 'Clistene di Sicione e le sue riforme: studia sulla storia arcaica di Sicione'; *Atti r. accad. Lincei*, vi.2 (1926–9), 553–9 argues that even if there had originally been such an ethnic difference between ruled and ruling classes at Sikyon, this could not have persisted until the time of the tyranny. But this does not exclude that the Sikyonians believed that such a difference existed, and that the belief was politically important.

[14] Diod. viii.24, *P. Oxy.* 1365 (apparently fragments of the same account, presumably derived from Ephoros).

[15] S. I. Oost, 'Two notes on the Orthagorids of Sicyon', *CP* lxix (1974), 118 f.

this hostility was expressed in terms of the heroic past, its root probably lay in more recent relations between Sikyon and Argos. The objection to Adrastos was that he was an Argive hero and yet was supposed to have ruled Sikyon; a similar theme of Argive dominance over Sikyon appears in the story of the conquest of Sikyon for the Dorians by Phalkes son of Temenos.[16] Sikyon thus became part of the 'lot of Temenos', which was 'recovered' for Argos by king Pheidon. Pheidon's date is uncertain,[17] but whenever he ruled he must have threatened Sikyon by his expansionist policies, and perhaps actually conquered it. Orthagoras may therefore have come to power as leader of the Sikyonian resistance to Argive domination, and if justification for this domination was sought in appeals to instances of Argive rule at Sikyon in the Bronze Age, such as that of Adrastos, Kleisthenes' attempts to deny Adrastos a place in Sikyonian history can be seen as logically bound up with the assertion of Sikyon's autonomy. In such a context, Kleisthenes' renaming of the Sikyonian tribes, which at first sight appears to be purely an attack on the Dorians within Sikyon, falls into place as a piece of anti-Argive policy;[18] since the Dorians of Sikyon presumably claimed descent from Phalkes and his fellows, they could be regarded as a potential (or even actual) Argive fifth column, which had to be suppressed for the sake of Sikyon's security against 'Pheidonian' Argos.

However, the military career by which Orthagoras rose to power is said to have taken place in the course of a war not against Argos but against Pellene, Sikyon's western neighbour. This was apparently a long-drawn-out conflict, which had begun before the time of Orthagoras (he became a member, and subsequently commander, of a force of border-guards which was apparently already an established institution), and which perhaps ended only with the capture of Pellene by Kleisthenes.[19] There is also some mention of a boundary-dispute with Kleonai, which is connected with an oracle foretelling the Sikyonian tyranny, and should therefore belong to the early seventh century.[20] Since Kleonai lay between Sikyon

[16] Paus. ii.6.10–7.1.

[17] Ephoros, *FGH* 70, F 115; dated mid-7th century, e.g. A. Andrewes, 'The Corinthian Actaeon and Pheidon of Argos', *CQ* xliii (1949), 70 ff.; T. Kelly, *A History of Argos to 500 BC* (Minneapolis, 1976), esp. 94-111, dates Pheidon *c.* 600 and makes him Kleisthenes' actual enemy, but the earlier date seems preferable.

[18] Hdt. v.68.1; see below, p. 51.

[19] *P. Oxy.* 1241, col. iii, lines 2 ff., cf. Aelian, *VH* vi.1.

[20] Plut. *Mor.* 553a–b; a youth who had won an athletic victory at the Pythian Games was claimed as a citizen by both Sikyon and Kleonai, and torn to pieces in the ensuing riot. However, there is an anachronism here; athletic contests were not introduced at the Pythian Games until after the Sacred War, and it is possible that the incident really belongs in the 6th century.

and Argos and was under Argive domination for much of its history, such a dispute may have involved Argos indirectly. But there is no definite record, as opposed to scholarly reconstruction, of war between Sikyon and Argos until the time of Kleisthenes.

2. The Orthagorid Tyranny

A. Genealogy

Aristotle calls the Sikyonian tyranny 'that of Orthagoras' children and Orthagoras himself', suggesting that Orthagoras was the first tyrant and was succeeded for a period of a hundred years by his descendants, of whom Kleisthenes, named later in the same passage, was one. Other sources which deal with the beginning of the tyranny also make Orthagoras the first tyrant and son of the *mageiros* Andreas, while a later member of the dynasty, Myron, is described as a descendant of Orthagoras and brother of Kleisthenes and Isodamos. It was Kleisthenes who attracted most notice from later historians, at least from surviving sources, and some of these give his genealogy, in which, however, Orthagoras does not appear. The fullest stemma is found in Herodotos, who gives the line, Andreas — Myron — Aristonymos — Kleisthenes; Pausanias gives the shorter version, Myron — Aristonymos — Kleisthenes, and Plutarch, describing not the family relationships of the Orthagorids but the order of succession to the tyranny, refers to Orthagoras' successors as 'Myron and Kleisthenes and their associates'. At the lower end of the dynasty, the last tyrant, deposed by the Spartans, is named as Aischines, while another source states that the Spartans drove out the descendants of Kleisthenes. Kleisthenes is known to have had a daughter, Agariste, the story of whose wooing and eventual marriage to the Athenian Megakles is told at length by Herodotos.[1]

There is therefore a variety of information on the genealogy of the Orthagorids, which, at least at first sight, is internally inconsistent. The worst problem is the fact that the Herodotean stemma leaves out Orthagoras altogether, and thereby appears to contradict Aristotle and Nikolaos of Damascus, who state that the later tyrants were descended from him. Various explanations have been offered — that Herodotos omitted Orthagoras by mistake, or confused him with either Andreas or Myron, or that the Andreas who appears at the head of Herodotos' list was the son of Orthagoras and grandson of the other Andreas, or that Orthagoras and Myron were brothers, sons of one and the same Andreas.[2] It is this last

---

[1] Arist. *Pol.* 1315 b. 13 f.; Plut. *Mor.* 553a–b, 859d; *P. Oxy.* 1365 (+ Diod. viii. 24); Nik. Dam. *FGH* 90, F 61.1–2; Hdt. vi.126–130; Paus. ii.8.1; *P. Ryland* 18, line 22; Schol. Aischin. ii.77.

[2] First view, Grenfell and Hunt, *Oxyrhynchus Papyri*, xi, 108 f. (who prefer confusion to omission); they also discuss but dismiss the second view; second view, re-

explanation which has found most favour with recent historians, since the other two involve adding extra generations to the tyranny, which is considered objectionable on chronological grounds. A plausible refinement of this view is the addition to the stemma of a daughter of Orthagoras married to her first cousin Aristonymos and the mother of Kleisthenes and his brothers — who could thus truthfully claim to be descendants of Orthagoras, but in the female line.[3] There were evidently two Myrons in the family, one the grandfather and the other the brother of Kleisthenes; the younger Myron was named after his paternal grandfather, in accordance with the common Greek practice. The following stemma is thus arrived at:

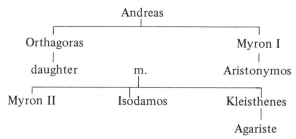

All the known members of the Orthagorid dynasty except Aischines are thus accounted for.

It is not recorded that Myron II had any children, but Isodamos apparently had sons, who risked being excluded from office if he were not purified after his fratricide. The only recorded child of Kleisthenes is Agariste, and it has sometimes been argued that the importance which he attached to her marriage shows that she was his only child and heiress; but there is no suggestion in Herodotos' account of the marriage that the chosen son-in-law was to be groomed for the succession to the tyranny, rather that Kleisthenes was looking for a useful foreign alliance.[4] It is therefore likely that the succession to Kleisthenes was already provided

asserted, M. Lenchantin de Gubernatis, 'Il nuovo storico di Sicione e la dinastia degli Ortagoridi', *Atti r. accad. delle scienze di Torino*, li (1916), 290–305, Gitti, *Atti r. accad. dei Lincei*, vi.2 (1926–9), 586–90; third view, M. Denicolai, 'La genealogia dei tiranni di Sicione secondo un nuovo frammento storico', *Atti r. accad. delle scienze di Torino*, li (1916), 1219–28.

[3] H. T. Wade-Gery, 'The growth of the Dorian States', *CAH* iii, stemma on p. 570. Alternatively, Aristonymos may have been adopted by Orthagoras (Denicolai, 1225).

[4] Isodamos' sons, Nik. Dam. F 61.4; on Agariste's marriage, cf. D. M. Leahy, 'The Dating of the Orthagorid Dynasty', *Historia*, xvii (1968), 11 f.; it has been argued (N. G. L. Hammond, 'The Family of Orthagoras', *CQ* n.s. vi (1956), 51 f.) that Nikolaos' remark about the sons of Isodamos implies that they were already old enough to hold office at the time of their father's fratricide, which suggests that Isodamos was considerably older than Kleisthenes and thus makes it doubtful that they were brothers; but in fact Nikolaos seems to refer to the indefinite future, and the sons may have been mere infants at the time.

for, through sons of his own or of his brothers. Aischines may have been one of these sons, or a more remote descendant; since the date at which the tyranny fell is disputed, so is his chronological relationship to Kleisthenes.

The existence of Isodamos has sometimes been doubted, because he is mentioned only by Nikolaos of Damascus, presumably using Ephoros as his source, and has a politically significant name which looks suspiciously like a later fabrication.[5] However, it is possible to discover a contemporary reference to him in an inscription recorded by Pausanias. This was the dedicatory inscription on a bronze *thalamos* in the Sikyonian Treasury at Olympia, which, according to Pausanias, named the dedicators as 'Myron and the *demos* of the Sikyonians'. This formula is quite unparalleled, the nearest approach to it being an early fifth-century dedication from Olympia which refers to Hieron and the Syracusans, without mentioning the *demos* as such. Seventh-century Sikyonian script would have looked very strange to Pausanias, and the *thalamos* had probably suffered considerable wear and tear by the time he saw it, so it is not surprising that he should have thought he saw the familiar word *demos* instead of the relatively unknown name Isodamos — the loss or misreading of only a few letters is required to bring about the change, thus:

ΜΥΡΟΝΚΑΙΗΟΔΑΜΟΜΜΣϘΥΡΟΝΙΙΟΝΑΝΣ⊕ΣΝ

instead of

ΜΥΡΟΝΚΑΙΝΙΜΡΟΔΑΜΟΜΜΣϘΥΡΟΝΙΙΟΙΑΝΣ⊕ΣΝ

The Myron involved will of course be Myron II, the brother of Isodamos, and not Myron I as Pausanias thought.[6]

The three sons of Aristonymos are all said to have held the tyranny, but Aristonymos himself is not. Myron I is called tyrant by Pausanias, but, as just noted, may have been confused with Myron II. What is believed about the order of succession to the tyranny depends very much on the chronology which is accepted; a 'low' chronology will permit of Myron II's being the immediate successor of Orthagoras, while a 'high' chronology will call for at least one other tyrant in between them. If Myron I and Aristonymos are considered to be eliminated, a favoured candidate is a son of Orthagoras, despite the absence of any ancient authority for the existence of

[5] A. Momigliano, 'La genealogia degli Ortagoridi', *Atene e Roma* n.s. x (1929), 151 suggests that 'Isodamos' was the title of an eponymous magistrate at Sikyon, which later authors took for a personal name; cf. V. Ehrenberg, *RE* xvi *Myron* 2, col. 1117.

[6] Paus. vi.19.1–4; for further discussion of this passage, see Part III.1.B. Hieron's dedication, *LSAG* 275, No. 7, Pl. 51. For description and specimens of early Sikyonian local script, see *LSAG* 138 ff., Pl. 23.

such a person.[7] Similarly, a 'high' chronology will suggest that Aischines was the immediate successor of Kleisthenes, while a 'low' chronology will necessitate the insertion of one or more tyrants in between.

B. Chronology

Discussion of the chronology of the Sikyonian tyranny must begin with Kleisthenes, the only member of the dynasty whose reign is more or less securely dated. The events of his reign which are important for the establishment of the chronology are, firstly, the First Sacred War, in which he took part, and, secondly, his Olympic victory and the marriage of Agariste which followed it.

The dating of the Sacred War is derived from the Parian Marble and the Scholia on Pindar's *Pythian Odes*, both of which refer to the reorganization of the Pythian Games which followed the war. The Pindar Scholia give the fuller account of the two, stating that the Thessalian general Eurylochus re-established the Games after capturing Kirrha, in the archonship of Simon or Simonides at Athens. This contest was *chrematites* — that is, prizes of money and other valuables were given. The surviving Kirrhans held out for another six years in the mountains, and 'later' the Games were held again as an *agon stephanites*, in the archonship of Damasias at Athens. The archonships concerned are dated in 591/0 and 582/1 respectively, so the final defeat of the Kirrhans falls in 586/5, the year in which Pausanias dated the *agon chrematites*, probably due to confusion between the fall of Kirrha and the actual conclusion of the war. Kallisthenes gives the length of the siege of Kirrha as ten years, but he also gives as the *casus belli* the carrying off of various women, which makes his account look suspiciously as though it is modelled on the Trojan War. The figure of ten years may not be so far wrong, however, for the total length of the war, giving a date for its commencement in the mid–590s.[1] The beginning of Kleisthenes' reign must therefore be dated before this.

The date of Agariste's marriage must be sought by working back from what is known of her children. Two of them are important for this purpose, the daughter who married Peisistratos during the brief reconciliation with Megakles which preceded his second exile, and Kleisthenes, the reformer of 508/7. Kleisthenes was archon in 525/4, and should have been born in the early to middle 560s, while Peisistratos' marriage to the

---

[7] E. Cavaignac, 'A propos d'un document nouveau sur les Orthagorides', *REG* xxxii (1919), 64.

[1] *Marm. Par.* 37–8, Schol. vet. Pind. *Hypothesis Pythiorum* b and d, Paus. x.7.4 f., Kallisthenes, *FGH* 124, F 1 and Jacoby's commentary; archon-dates, T. J. Cadoux, 'The Athenian archons from Kreon to Hypsichides', *JHS* lxviii (1948), 99 ff.; W. G. Forrest, 'The First Sacred War', *BCH* lxxx (1956), 34 n. 1 dates the outbreak of the war in 595 'for convenience not from conviction'.

daughter of Megakles and Agariste probably took place *c.* 557, which calls for a birth-date for the girl in 571 at the latest. According to Herodotos, Agariste's marriage took place the year after Kleisthenes' Olympic victory, so it must fall in the second year of an Olympiad — 579, or 575, or 571, and so on.[2] If a child of the marriage was born not later than 571, the latest possible date for the marriage itself is 575. Since another son of Megakles and Agariste, Hippokrates, was probably born in the early 550s, this latest possible date for the marriage is also likely to be the correct one.[3]

Kleisthenes can therefore be supposed to have been tyrant during the twenty years from about 595 to 575. Since Nikolaos of Damascus gives him a reign of thirty-one years, this still leaves some chronological latitude, but certainly fixes his reign in the first third of the sixth century BC. Nikolaos also gives Myron II and Isodamos reigns of seven years and one respectively, immediately preceding Kleisthenes.[4] It seems likely, therefore, that they were in power during the last decade of the seventh century.

The only other piece of solid evidence about the chronology of the Orthagorids is the figure of a hundred years for the duration of the tyranny, given by Aristotle and by the Delphic oracle quoted by Diodoros. Since the oracle, like those about the Kypselid tyranny at Korinth, is under some suspicion of having been fabricated, or at least improved upon, after the event, it seems that the hundred-year duration should be accepted as at least approximately correct.[5] However, in the absence of fixed dates for the beginning or end of the tyranny, it is not at all clear how the fairly precisely dated reigns of Kleisthenes and his brothers are to be fitted into the hundred years.

There is nothing in the available information about Orthagoras' rise to power which throws much light on the date of this event. Because of the problems of the Orthagorid genealogy, it is not even possible to fix Orthagoras approximately by his relationship to the securely dated tyrants — indeed, it is possible for the genealogy to be manipulated to fit

---

[2] Peisistratos' wife, Hdt. i.61 (see F. Jacoby, *Atthis: the local Chronicles of Ancient Athens* (Oxford, 1949), 194 and J. K. Davies, *Athenian Propertied Families* (Oxford, 1971), 375 for date); Kleisthenes' archonship, *Hesp.* viii (1939), 59 ff., No. 21, line 5. His age at the time is uncertain, since other archons of the 520s seem to have been unusually young (Miltiades, the younger Peisistratos). However, Davies, loc. cit., dates his birth not later than 560, on the assumption that he received his name while his maternal grandfather was still alive; in fact this points to a lower limit of *c.* 565. Olympic victory, Hdt. vi.126.2.

[3] Davies, op. cit., 379 argues that he may have been named after Peisistratos' father, and so was probably born during the reconciliation of *c.* 557, and that the ages of his children (Megakles, ostracized 487/6, and Agariste, the mother of Perikles) point to a similar date.

[4] Nik. Dam. F 61.3, and 6.

[5] Arist. *Pol.* 1315b.14, Diod. viii.24; fabrication of oracles, Andrewes, *The Greek Tyrants*, 3rd edn. (London, 1960), 47–8, 57.

a chosen chronology. The first member of the family for whom there is a definite chronological datum is Myron I, who won the chariot-race at Olympia in Ol. 33 (648 BC). Pausanias calls him tyrant, and makes him the dedicator of the bronze *thalamos* which stood in the Sikyonian Treasury; but it seems that Pausanias confused Myron I and II, so it cannot necessarily be assumed that the tyranny was already in existence by 648. However, even if Myron I was not tyrant himself, he would perhaps have been better placed to engage in the expensive sport of chariot-racing after the establishment of the tyranny than before, especially if statements in some of the sources about Orthagoras' lowly origins are to be taken seriously.[6]

As to the date at which the tyranny was overthrown, there is considerable dispute. Ancient historians were interested in the event more from a Spartan than from a Sikyonian point of view, and consequently the Sikyonian tyranny tends to figure in lists of those put down by the Spartans. That given by Plutarch contains many names, ranging from the Kypselids of Korinth and Ambrakia to some Thessalian dynasts who are said to have been overthrown by Latychidas in the early fifth century.[7] A shorter list, comprising the Peisistratids, Lygdamis of Naxos, and the descendants of Kleisthenes, is given by a scholiast on Aischines, in a rather confused note — he appears to have thought that the expelled tyrants were replaced by Spartan harmosts. What should be a more useful account is given by *P. Ryland* 18, where a reference to the anti-tyrant activities of Chilon and Anaxandridas is followed by what appears to be the the beginning of a list: ἐν Σικυῶν[ι] μὲν Αἰ[σχ]ίμην, Ἱππίαν δὲ [- - -] Πεισιστ [- - -]. The obvious reconstruction for the second case in the list is Ἱππίαν δὲ [᾿Αθήνησιν] Πεισιστ[ράτου], giving one of the better-known examples of a tyranny which was put down by the Spartans, but, of course, well after the time of Chilon and Anaxandridas. It is therefore not possible to interpret the passage as a general statement that Chilon and Anaxandridas put down tyrants, followed by a list of their victims.[8] Since the

---

[6] Paus. vi.19.1. cf. p. 42, it was presumably Myron I who won the victory, even if Myron II made the dedication. Orthagoras' origins, *P. Oxy.* 1365, lines 15 ff.; cf. Andrewes, *The Greek Tyrants*, 57 — 'not to be relied on in view of the ingrained Greek habit of attributing low birth to a political opponent', also Oost, *CP* lxix (1974), 118 f.

[7] Plut. *Mor.* 859c–d; the inclusion of the Korinthian Kypselids is startling, and emendation to ἐκ Κηρ ίνθου (in Euboia) has been proposed (G. L. Huxley, *Early Sparta* (London, 1962), 75 f.).

[8] Schol. Aischin. ii.77, *P. Ryland* 18, lines 16 ff.; the author may have intended to produce a list of tyrants expelled by Chilon and Anaxandridas, but if so his error in including Hippias was so gross as to destroy the historical value of the papyrus (Leahy, 'Chilon and Aischines: a further consideration of Rylands Greek Papyrus Fr. 18', *Bull. John Rylands Library*, xxxviii (1956), 424). A desperate attempt to deny that the obvious restoration is correct (Hammond, *CQ* n.s. vi (1956), 50 f.) is unconvincing (M. E. White, 'The Dates of the Orthagorids', *Phoenix*, xii (1958), 7).

papyrus breaks off at this point, it is not certain how the passage continued; the list may have developed into a general one, like Plutarch's, of tyrannies overthrown by the Spartans, with the reference to Chilon and Anaxandridas at the beginning being intended only to give them the credit for initiating the anti-tyrant policy. In that case, the passage would give only a *terminus post quem* for the deposition of Aischines — the ephorate of Chilon, traditionally dated in Ol. 56 (556 to 553 BC).

However, there is an alternative interpretation of the papyrus, which is favourable to a 'low' chronology of the Orthagorid tyranny. According to this, the tyrants listed were all victims of Kleomenes, and the expulsion of Aischines should be dated close to that of Hippias. Similarly, in Plutarch's list of deposed tyrants, which has some claim to be in chronological order, Aischines is placed after the Peisistratids. Finally, Herodotos says that Kleisthenes' new tribe-names remained in use for sixty years after his death, and an obvious occasion for their abolition would have been the overthrow of the tyranny; this calculation again yields a date *c.* 510 for the event.[9]

Such a date for the fall of the tyranny obviously excludes the possibility that it had been established as early as 648, if the hundred-year duration is accepted. This is a positive, but perhaps not very strong, objection to the 'low' chronology; on the negative side, the silence of Herodotos is remarkable, since his account of the tribal reforms of Kleisthenes of Sikyon is a pendant to his account of the similar measures of Kleisthenes of Athens, whom Kleomenes opposed. If the same Kleomenes had put down the Sikyonian tyranny and abolished the Kleisthenic tribe-names, this would have been a striking coincidence which one would have expected Herodotos to remark upon.

A *terminus ante quem* for the overthrow of the tyranny at Sikyon is apparently provided by Kleomenes' abortive expedition to Eleusis in 506, for which his army was drawn 'from all the Peloponnese'.[10] Although the Sikyonians are not specifically mentioned, it seems likely that they were present as allies of Sparta, like their neighbours the Korinthians. Sikyon's co-operation was useful, if not essential, to any Spartan army wishing to operate at the Isthmos or beyond, since, with the most direct route from Sparta to the Isthmos normally blocked by Argos, the army would have to pass through Sikyonian territory.[11] But, of course, Spartan armies

[9] Most recently White, art. cit., 7–13; an alternative is to make the Orthagorid dynasty end with Kleisthenes and a new tyranny ending with Aischines arise in the late 6th century (Lenchantin de Gubernatis, *Atti r. accad. delle scienze di Torino,* li (1916), 290–305, Gitti, *Atti r. accad. dei Lincei,* vi.2 (1926–9), 591–3), but this is inconsistent with the description of those expelled by the Spartans as 'descendants of Kleisthenes'. Tribe-names, Hdt. v.68.

[10] Hdt. v.74.1.

[11] See Gomme–Andrewes on Thuc. v.64.4.

are found north of the Isthmos before 506; not only for Kleomenes' earlier expeditions to Athens, but in the vicinity of Plataia in 519.[12] It is generally assumed that Sikyon did not become an ally of Sparta until after the fall of the tyranny; hence a date for this event before 519 becomes necessary. But in this case two of the items of evidence in favour of the 'low' chronology are removed; Plutarch's list of deposed tyrants cannot be in chronological order, and the overthrow of the Sikyonian tyranny must be dissociated from the abolition of the Kleisthenic tribe-names.

There therefore remains only the question of the interpretation of *P. Ryland* 18, and in the absence of any other evidence in favour of the 'low' chronology it seems preferable to treat this as giving a general list of tyrants overthrown by the Spartans. Aischines may therefore have been deposed as early as Chilon's ephorate in the 550s, and have been Kleisthenes' immediate successor. The tyranny will then have been established in the 650s, and Myron I, whether tyrant himself or not, will have won his Olympic victory as a member of the ruling dynasty at Sikyon.

C. Policy

According to Aristotle, the reason for the long duration of the Orthagorid tyranny was that 'they treated their subjects with moderation and generally obeyed the laws, Kleisthenes in particular was worthy of respect because of his warlike character, and by their diligence in many matters they were demagogues.' There follows an account of how Kleisthenes crowned a judge who had denied him a victory, which is apparently intended to illustrate his law-abidingness, but no details are given of the other aspects of the tyrants' behaviour. More specific information about the policies of Kleisthenes is given by Herodotos, but the other members of the dynasty remain little more than names.[1]

The account of Orthagoras' rise to power by way of a military career, which appears in *P. Oxy.* 1365, is plausible and coherent so far as it goes, but has been suspected of being only a fourth-century rationalization, invented when the true reasons for the establishment of the tyranny had been forgotten.[2] The fact that Aristotle makes warlikeness a reason for the popularity of Kleisthenes in particular rather than the Orthagorids in general may suggest that he did not know of this tradition about Orthagoras. The more or less technical terms *peripolos* and *peripolarchos* used in

---

[12] Hdt. vi.108.2; date from Thuc. iii.68.5.

[1] Ar. *Pol.* 1315b.12 ff.

[2] The papyrus probably goes back to Ephoros or a related historian, since it follows almost without a break from the account of the oracle concerning the tyranny in Diod. viii.24; see e.g. Andrewes, *The Greek Tyrants*, 57.

the papyrus may be genuine archaic Sikyonian survivals, or they may simply have been borrowed from fifth-century Athens. The polemarchy, of course, is a fairly common office, which is also said to have been held by Kypselos on his way to the tyranny at Korinth, though in this case its functions are described as civil rather than military.[3] If the account of Orthagoras' career given in the papyrus is rejected, the means whereby he rose to power must remain totally mysterious; Aristotle's remarks about the Orthagorids do not help to solve this question, since they are concerned with the reasons for the long survival of the tyranny rather than for its establishment.

However, Aristotle's description of the Orthagorids as 'demagogues' may be linked with another passage in the *Politics* in which he remarks of tyrants in general (unfortunately without giving specific examples) that they arise as protectors of the *demos* against the nobles.[4] *P. Oxy.* 1365 refers to some action by the Sikyonian *demos*, but breaks off before stating what it was. The occurrence of the name Isodamos in the family of Orthagoras also suggests that the tyrants considered the *demos* of some importance. However, these scraps of information, while indicating that the *demos* may have played a part in the rise and maintenance of the Orthagorid tyranny, are insufficient to show exactly what that part was. It has been suggested that the tyranny arose out of a conflict between a non-Dorian *demos* and a Dorian nobility, but this view is based on an interpretation of Kleisthenes' policies which is itself questionable, and is open to the objection that Kleisthenes did not necessarily inherit his policies from his predecessors.

The difficulties and dangers of working back from Kleisthenes to his predecessors are emphasized by Aristotle's remark that the replacement of Myron by Kleisthenes constituted a change from one tyranny to another. This was not a change of dynasty, since Myron and Kleisthenes were brothers, but Nikolaos of Damascus' account of Myron's end and Kleisthenes' accession shows that the means by which Kleisthenes came to power were highly irregular, involving the murder of Myron by Isodamos at Kleisthenes' instigation and the removal of Isodamos by a trick.[5] The tradition which lies behind this account was evidently hostile to the tyrants; Myron is shown as a womanizer (it was his seduction of his brother's wife which provided the motive for his murder), Kleisthenes as ambitious and unscrupulous, and only Isodamos, who is represented as the victim of his less virtuous brothers, is regarded with any sympathy. Aristotle's remark may, however, also indicate a change of policy by

[3] *Peripoloi* and *peripolarchoi* in Athens, e.g. Thuc. viii.92.2; Kypselos as polemarch, Nik. Dam. F 57.5 (derived from Ephoros).
[4] Ar. *Pol.* 1310b.12 ff.
[5] Ar. *Pol.* 1316a.29 ff.; Nik. Dam. F 61.

Kleisthenes compared to his predecessors, though it is not possible to be certain about this, since there is no information about Myron's public policy as opposed to his private vices.

Nikolaos' account of the manner in which Kleisthenes' accession was brought about may throw some light on the constitutional basis of the Orthagorid tyranny. After the murder of Myron, Kleisthenes pointed out to Isodamos that since he was polluted by fratricide he could not sacrifice to the gods, and would be in danger of losing his *arche* unless he took Kleisthenes as his colleague. Isodamos did this, and the two ruled jointly for a year. Kleisthenes then disposed of Isodamos altogether by persuading him to leave Sikyon in search of purification, which was necessary, it is again stressed, to enable him to hold the tyranny and leave it to his children. Isodamos handed over the tyranny to Kleisthenes and went to Korinth, whence he never returned, since Kleisthenes accused him of plotting with the Kypselids and raised an army against him. What is interesting about this narrative is its insistence on sacrificing to the gods as an indispensable function of the tyrant, so much so that the legitimacy of his rule became questionable if he could not carry it out. It seems likely that the Orthagorid tyrants held a specific office with religious functions; the title of this may have been 'Basileus', the term under which Nikolaos introduces Myron. There would be obvious parallels with the functions of the Archon Basileus at Athens, though the Sikyonian office seems to have been hereditary and held for life.[6] Isodamos had to allow Kleisthenes to hold this office because he himself was disqualified from it, but Kleisthenes thereby acquired a claim to be the legitimate ruler, and this claim became all the stronger when Isodamos retired to Korinth and handed over to Kleisthenes the other functions of the tyranny as well.

According to Nikolaos, the Sikyonians preferred Kleisthenes to Isodamos because he was 'formidable and energetic', which sounds like an echo of Aristotle's remark that Kleisthenes was popular because of his warlike qualitites. Kleisthenes as tyrant is described by Nikolaos as 'very violent and cruel', a judgement similar to that which he passed on Periander. However, no specific crimes committed by Kleisthenes after becoming tyrant are mentioned in any source, unless we count one of the stratagems by which he is said to have captured Kirrha — poisoning the water-supply.[7] There are no stories of domestic trouble like those about Periander, and in fact all that is known about his family life is the story of

[6] Oost, *CP* lxix (1974), 119 f., citing the Adrastos oracle and Dio Chrys. *Or.* iii.41 as indications that Kleisthenes held the title *basileus*; cf. S. I. Oost, 'Cypselus the Bacchiad', *CP* lxvii (1972), 21 ff. for a similar view about Kypselos.

[7] Frontinus, *Strat.* iii.7.6; perhaps also the treatment of the captured Pellenians, *P. Oxy.* 1241, col. iii, lines 2 ff. and possibly Aelian, *VH* vi.1.

Agariste's marriage, which as told by Herodotos is more comic than tragic. The aspects of his reign which interested later historians are the Sacred War and his attitude to Argos.

According to Herodotos, Kleisthenes was at war with Argos, but the events he relates are not military in nature. What caught the historian's interest was Kleisthenes' campaign of anti-Argive propaganda within Sikyon. The rhapsodic contests, at which epics glorifying Argos and Argive heroes were recited, were abolished, and persistent efforts were made to wipe out the hero-cult of Adrastos, the Argive hero who had also been king of Sikyon.[8] Adrastos had a shrine in the Agora at Sikyon, and various ceremonies were held in his honour, including 'tragic choruses'. Kleisthenes' first intention was to 'throw out' Adrastos, which would presumably have involved removing his bones from the shrine and physically ejecting them from Sikyonian territory; however, when Kleisthenes asked the Delphic Oracle to approve this proposal, he received the insulting reply: 'Adrastos was king of the Sikyonians, but you are a *leuster*'.[9] Faced with this opposition, Kleisthenes abandoned his original plan, and instead sent for the bones of Melanippos from Thebes, installed them in the *prytaneion*, and re-assigned to Melanippos all the ceremonies which had previously been held in honour of Adrastos, except for the tragic choruses, which were given to Dionysos. The point of this transaction was that Melanippos was Adrastos' bitterest enemy, having killed his brother and son-in-law in the battle of the Seven Against Thebes. Kleisthenes evidently hoped that Adrastos would be so outraged by these honours given to his enemy that he would withdraw from Sikyon of his own accord, even if not physically 'thrown out'. This view of a hero's bones as procuring his presence and protection for the place where he was buried has parallels in the Spartan 'Orestes policy' of the mid-sixth century, where the object was to transfer the hero's bones, and with them his help in battle, from Tegea to Sparta. At the same time, an attempt was made to represent Orestes as a Spartan hero; the combination of an attempt to rewrite history with transactions involving heroic bones is strongly reminiscent of Kleisthenes' policy with regard to Adrastos, and may have been directly inspired by it.[10]

---

[8] Hdt. v.67–8.

[9] 'Leuster' literally means 'stone-thrower', and hence perhaps 'light-armed'; the Suda, quoting Ael. fr. 115, makes it passive, 'deserving to be stoned'; or, it may mean 'oppressor', cf. Ael. *NH* 5.15 (LSJ).

[10] Hdt. i.67–8; cf. C. M. Bowra, *Greek Lyric Poetry from Alcman to Simonides*, 2nd edn. (Oxford, 1961), 112 ff. (on Steisichoros' *Oresteia*). Cf. also the acquisition by Sparta of the bones of Teisamenos from Helike in Achaia (Paus. vii.1.8, discussed by Leahy, 'The Bones of Tisamenos', *Historia* iv (1955), 26–38), and, later, the Athenian acquisition of the bones of Theseus from Skyros (Plut. *Kimon*, 8.5 ff.).

The other important anti-Argive measure of Kleisthenes, as recorded by Herodotos, was the alteration of the Sikyonian tribe-names, 'so that they might not be the same for the Sikyonians as for the Argives'. Sikyon had four tribes, the usual Dorian three (Hylleis, Dymanes, and Pamphyloi) and one for the non-Dorians, to which Kleisthenes himself belonged. He changed the name of this tribe to Archelaoi, 'Rulers', and renamed the Dorian tribes Hyatai, Oneatai, and Choireatai — 'Pig-men', 'Ass-men', and 'Swine-men'. These names are obviously insulting, and combined with the honorific name given to Kleisthenes' own tribe indicate that he was concerned to raise the status of that tribe at the expense of the Dorians. It appears, therefore, that in this aspect of his policy Kleisthenes had shifted from an attack on Argos to an attack on the Dorians within Sikyon itself. However, the tribe-names survived the fall of the tyranny, even though this was brought about by the Spartans, who, as Dorians themselves, might have been expected to resent the insulting names; when the names were changed, towards the end of the sixth century, this appears to have taken place in a context of reconciliation between Sikyon and Argos, since not only were the Dorian names restored, but the non-Dorian tribe was renamed Aigialeis, after Aigialeus son of Adrastos.[11] It seems, therefore, that even the Sikyonian Dorians may have accepted the Kleisthenic tribe-names as primarily anti-Argive.

To Kleisthenes' war against Argos may belong a defeat of Sikyon by Orneai, which was celebrated by an offering at Delphi, and the boundary-dispute between Sikyon and Kleonai which forms the background to Plutarch's account of the oracle concerning the rise of the Orthagorids. The foundation of the Nemean Games, which were administered by Kleonai with Argive support, and were closely associated with Adrastos and the Seven Against Thebes, cannot have been pleasing to Kleisthenes, and it has been suggested that they were instituted to celebrate an Argive–Kleonaian victory over Sikyon. The first Nemean Games took place in 573, so the victory in question may have occurred not long before that.[12] It seems likely, therefore, that Kleisthenes' war with Argos was not entirely successful on the military side, whatever the effectiveness of his propaganda campaign.

There is some evidence that Kleisthenes also fought a successful war with Pellene, a continuation or renewal of that in which Orthagoras had distinguished himself. Pellene was apparently destroyed, and the inhabitants

---

[11] See below, pp. 60-1.

[12] Orneai, Plut. *Mor.* 401d, Paus. x.18.5; Kleonai, Plut. *Mor.* 553a-b, and cf. p. 38 n. 20; Nemean Games, Euseb. *Chron. Hieron.* (ed. Helm), 101b, cf. Bury, *Nemean Odes*, 250 ff., H. F. McGregor, 'Cleisthenes of Sicyon and the Panhellenic Festivals', *TAPA* lxxii (1941), 277 f.

savagely treated, though the survivors succeeded in re-founding the city with the support of Delphi. A war with Pellene's western neighbour Aigeira, in which the Sikyonians were defeated by a stratagem, and the destruction by the Sikyonians of Donoussa, a town between Aigeira and Pellene, may also have taken place in the reign of Kleisthenes. Finally, there may have been hostility, if not open warfare, between Sikyon and Korinth at the beginning of Kleisthenes' reign, because of the Kypselids' support for Isodamos.[13]

The most important war in which Kleisthenes was involved, however, was the Sacred War for the control of Delphi. Kleisthenes' main contribution to this was the provision of a fleet, which was of some importance for attacking the coastal state of Kirrha. However, the city eventually fell after a siege by stratagems which are variously described and credited to various commanders of the attacking forces − Kleisthenes himself, Solon, and the Thessalian Eurylochos. It is obvious that accounts of the Sacred War tended to be coloured by the local patriotism of their authors − thus Aischines, addressing an Athenian audience, lays stress on the part played by Solon, while the version which makes Kleisthenes the principal figure may be derived from the Sikyonian historian Menaichmos.[14] Among these conflicting accounts of the events of the war and the personalities involved, it is unlikely that the part played by Kleisthenes can be distinguished precisely. However, the interesting aspect of his participation in the Sacred War is not so much any specific action by him as the fact that he took part in it at all.

The reasons which ancient authors give for the outbreak of the Sacred War are as varied as their accounts of its events, but all agree that the war was undertaken by the Amphiktyons. But the Amphiktyony was essentially a northern Greek organization, with Thessaly as a leading member and its original centre at Anthela near Thermopylai; its membership did not, so far as is known, extend across the Korinthian Gulf to Sikyon. Consequently Kleisthenes took part in the war as an outsider, and whether he was invited to do so by the Amphiktyons or offered his services of his own accord, he must have had some strong reason for doing so. As to what this reason was, there are two main schools of thought. One sees Kleisthenes' motives

[13] Pellene, *P. Oxy.* 1241, col. iii, lines 2 ff., Anaxandridas of Delphi, *FGH* 404, F 1 (the name of the people emended from Ἀπελλαῖοι to Πελλαναῖοι, see U. Von Wilamowitz-Moellendorf, 'Leserfrüchte', *Hermes*, xliv, (1909), 474 and Jacoby ad loc.); probably also Aelian, *VH* vi.1; Aigeira, Paus. vii.26.2–3, Steph. Byz. s.v. Αἴγειρα; Donoussa, Paus. vii.26.13; Korinth, cf. Frontin. iii.9.7, in which Periander's friend Thrasyboulos of Miletos attacks Sikyon and captures the harbour.

[14] Aischin. iii.107–12 is the earliest surviving account of the Sacred War. Kleisthenes figures in Paus. x.37.6, Polyain. iii.5, Frontin. *Strat.* iii.7.6, Schol. vet. Pind. *Nem.* ix, inscr.

as economic, the desire to remove a rival in trade with the western colonies, and the other as politico–religious, to avenge the insulting response Delphi had given his inquiry concerning the removal of Adrastos and to ensure that the oracle would be more co-operative in future. Both views have some ancient evidence in their favour, but derive much of their support from points of chronology and the like which are themselves debatable. Thus there are in favour of the 'economic' view statements that the Kirrhans grew rich by imposing duties on trade with Italy and Sicily, if not by outright piracy, and the fact that several of Agariste's suitors came from the West; but this is not very strong evidence for western interests on Kleisthenes' part, since he chose an Athenian son-in-law.[15] Similarly, in favour of the 'political' view is the fact that there are instances of friendly as well as hostile relations between Kleisthenes and Delphi — his victory in the Pythian chariot-race and the construction of the Tholos and 'Monopteros', These events certainly took place after the Sacred War, so it is tempting to see the oracle concerning Adrastos (and also that which encouraged the Pellenians to re-found their city) as coming before it, so that it was Kleisthenes' participation in the war on the winning side which brought about the change.[16] This view necessitates placing the war with Pellene and the initiation of the anti-Adrastos policy at the beginning of Kleisthenes' reign; there is also a problem concerning the foundation of the Sikyonian Pythia, which certainly took place after the Sacred War, since it was financed from the spoils of Kirrha, but which may be interpreted either as a compliment to the Delphian Apollo or as an insult, since these Games could be regarded as a rival to the Delphic Pythia.

This question is all the more complicated because according to Pindar the Sikyonian Pythia were founded by Adrastos, while the Scholiast ascribes them to Kleisthenes.[17] Pindar's statement probably reflects the rehabilitation of Adrastos at the end of the sixth century, at the expense of his enemy Kleisthenes. The Scholiast quotes as his authority for the foundation of the Pythia by Kleisthenes 'the Halikarnassian', usually taken to be Herodotos, whom he quotes elsewhere on the anti-Adrastos policy. However, there is no reference to the Sikyonian Pythia (or, for that

---

[15] Kirrhan interference with western trade, Strabo, ix.418, Schol. vet. Pind. *Hypoth. Olymp.*; cf. the possibility that the *thalamoi* at Olympia were made of Tartessian bronze (Paus. vi.19.2, who, however, doubted it); suitors, Hdt. vi.127. See e.g. Ure, *Origins of Tyranny*, 259 f., 262 f. and McGregor, *TAPA* lxxii (1941), 276, 282–4.

[16] Pythian victory, Paus. x.7.6; buildings, see Part III.1.C. See e.g. Forrest, *BCH* lxxx (1956), 36–9.

[17] Pind. *Nem.* ix.9 (actually written for a victory at the Sikyonian Pythia) and Schol. inscr., 20, 25b.

matter, to the Sacred War) in Herodotos, nor can any be extracted from his account of the Adrastos cult and those which superseded it, as some scholars have tried to do. The only solution seems to be to regard 'the Halikarnassian' as a different author, and to abandon the attempt to find references to the Pythia in Herodotos.[18] This also has the advantage of freeing the Adrastos policy from a chronological link with events after the Sacred War; its initiation can therefore he dated before the war, and Kleisthenes' participation in the war can be seen as a response to Delphi's rejection of his policy.

This version of Kleisthenes' relations with Delphi has the merit of simplicity (hostility before the Sacred War, friendship afterwards); the version which places the Adrastos oracle after the war has to postulate a more changeable relationship, with a period of friendship represented by his chariot-victory in 582 and the dedication of the Tholos shortly afterwards, followed by hostility shown by the Adrastos oracle and the foundation of the Sikyonian Pythia in rivalry to the Delphian, and finally a reconciliation marked by the building of the 'Monopteros'. There is, however, a more positive reason for placing the Adrastos oracle early in Kleisthenes' reign. The insult which it contains would have particular point if Kleisthenes were being told that 'Adrastos was *basileus* of the Sikyonians' (and therefore, by implication, Kleisthenes himself was not) at a time when Kleisthenes had just acquired this title by dubious means, so that the legitimacy of his claim to it could be challenged. The oracle's response may have been inspired by the Kypselids, who apparently supported Isodamos' claim to the tyranny; it is not known how long their support for Isodamos and consequent hostility to Kleisthenes lasted, but an attempt to restore Isodamos by either force or propaganda would obviously find .an appropriate place at the very beginning of Kleisthenes' reign, before he was firmly established in power.

Further evidence about Kleisthenes' relations with both Korinth and Argos, the significance of which is much disputed, is provided by two of Agariste's suitors — the Athenian Hippokleides, whom Kleisthenes at first favoured because he was related to the Kypselids, and the Argive Lakedes son of Pheidon, identified by Herodotos as 'Pheidon the tyrant who gave the measures to the Peloponnesians and who celebrated the Olympic Games' — that is, the same Pheidon who laid claim to the 'lot of Temenos' and must, of all Argives, have been anathema to Kleisthenes. In fact, the dating of Pheidon's activity in the early to mid-seventh century makes it impossible for Lakedes to have been his son, but it remains probable that he was a member of the Temenid dynasty. The name Lakedes is attested

[18] See my article, 'A new fragment of Dionysius of Halikarnassos ὁ μουσικός', in *Historia* xxviii (1979), 241-6.

as that of the father of the last Temenid king, Meltas, who seems to have been expelled from Argos around 600 BC. This Lakedes is well placed chronologically to have been the son of the famous Pheidon, and Agariste's suitor may have been the son of an otherwise unknown brother of Meltas, also named Pheidon — a pair whom Herodotos could easily have confused with their better-known grandfathers.[19] At any rate, he presumably belongs to a later generation than Meltas, and his wooing of Agariste to a time after the expulsion of the Temenids. He may therefore have been a more attractive ally for Kleisthenes than appears at first sight, since as an exile he would be a potential source of trouble to the existing government at Argos.

Hippokleides is said to have been acceptable to Kleisthenes as a son-in-law not merely in spite of but because of his relationship to the Kypselids. The interpretation of Kleisthenes' attitude depends very much on the chronology of the Kypselid tyranny; if it had already been overthrown by 575, Hippokleides could be viewed in the same light as Lakedes, as the representative of a group of exiles who could be useful to Kleisthenes by opposing an existing government which was hostile to him. However, there is the important difference that Kleisthenes' quarrel over Isodamos was specifically with the Kypselids. Perhaps a more attractive view is that the Kypselids were still in power at the time (which may be indicated by Herodotos' reference to them as 'the Kypselids at Korinth'), and that Kleisthenes desired the marriage as a means of reconciliation with them.[20]

In the event, Kleisthenes rejected Hippokleides and instead gave Agariste to Megakles, whose father Alkmaion had commanded the Athenian contingent in the Sacred War, and who therefore had a personal connection with Kleisthenes.[21] Herodotos' account of the feast at which Kleisthenes announced his decision evidently came from an Alkmaionid source, which related with relish how Hippokleides 'danced away his marriage'.[22] The

[19] Meltas, Andrewes, *CQ* xlv (n.s. i) (1951), 39–45; doubling of Lakedes and Pheidon, Forrest, *BCH* lxxx (1956), 38 f.; McGregor, *TAPA* lxxii (1941), 275 f. suggests that Lakedes' father was the epigraphically attested Pheidon of Kleonai, but surely Herodotos knew the difference between Argos and Kleonai.

[20] The traditional date for Kypselos' accession is 657, which combines with the lengths of reign given by Aristotle (*Pol.* 1315b. 24 ff.) to place the fall of the tyranny in the 580s. However, the Philaid Kypselos was archon in 597/6, and so should have been born in the 630s (Davies, *Athenian Propertied Families*, 295); even if it is assumed that Kypselos had to be tyrant before his daughter would be an acceptable bride for an Athenian aristocrat, this would still allow his accession to be down-dated by as much as 20 years.

[21] Plut. *Solon*, 11.

[22] Hippokleides' reply, 'οὐ φροντὶς Ἱπποκλείδη', became proverbial; a red-figure vase fragment by the Peleus Painter showing a dancing dwarf called ['Ιππο]κλέιδης (Erlangen, 707; Lippold, *RM* lii (1937), 44 ff., Pl. 14; *ARV²*, 1039, No. 6) was probably inspired by Herodotos' popularization of the story.

tale has undoubtedly been improved in the telling, and even its central statement that Hippokleides lost his chance of marrying Agariste because of his foolish behaviour at the banquet may be questioned — would Kleisthenes have thrown away a desirable marriage alliance for purely personal reasons? It is tempting to see political factors, perhaps even the news that the Kypselid tyranny had fallen, influencing Kleisthenes' decision. However, it seems that Kleisthenes was trying to recall epic wooings such as that of Helen in his arrangements for Agariste's marriage; the announcement of her eligibility at Olympia was doubtless intended to bring in suitors from all over the Greek world, and the lavish entertainment of the suitors at Sikyon has a distinctly Homeric flavour. The implied comparison with Homeric kings could only serve to increase Kleisthenes' prestige, and the final banquet at which the name of the successful suitor was to be announced should have been the climax of the 'epic' — but Hippokleides' conduct, if there is any truth in Herodotos' description of it, turned the epic into farce. Perhaps, therefore, Kleisthenes' reaction was one of simple anger at the disruption of a carefully designed scheme of propaganda; but perhaps also, more calculatingly, he saw Hippokleides' failure to appreciate the importance of the occasion as a sign of lack of political acumen, which cast doubt on his likely usefulness as a son-in-law. Such an impression could only have been confirmed by Hippokleides' frivolous reply on being told that he had 'danced away his marriage'; he evidently did not perceive the true magnitude of his loss.

The fact that Megakles was Kleisthenes' second choice seems to indicate that he was determined to have an Athenian son-in-law. Not only had Athens and Sikyon fought on the same side in the Sacred War, but there were far more ancient 'historical' connections between the two states, since the eponymous king Sikyon was of Attic origin, at least in some accounts.[23] Since Sikyon appears before Adrastos in the king-lists, the link with Athens could be said to have priority over that with Argos, and so may have been useful to Kleisthenes as propaganda. However, there is no evidence that an Athenian marriage offered any more material advantages, such as military assistance against Argos. If Megakles was chosen not merely for his personal qualities but for political reasons corresponding to those which existed in the case of Hippokleides, the nature of these reasons must remain obscure. So, indeed, must many of Kleisthenes' aims and policies; although there is a wealth of information about him compared to his predecessors, the total is really very small.

---

[23] Paus. ii.6.5; also the Athenian wife of the Sikyonian king Lamedon, and the Athenian descent of Ianiskos (Paus. ii.6.6).

D. The end of the tyranny

None of the known events of Kleisthenes' reign can certainly be dated after Agariste's marriage, but he probably survived into the 560s. The tyranny then continued for another fifteen years or so, and was overthrown by the Spartans in the late 550s. The last tyrant, Aischines, may have been Kleisthenes' immediate successor, but nothing is known about him beyond the fact of his expulsion. However, it seems likely to have been during his reign that the 'Monopteros' was dedicated at Delphi, even if it had been planned by Kleisthenes; it seems likely, therefore, that Kleisthenes' policies were carried on by his successor.

It was perhaps in this period, after the death of Kleisthenes but before the fall of the tyranny, that three major artists resided at Sikyon; the Kretan sculptors Dipoinos and Skyllis and the Rhegine poet Ibykos. The story of Dipoinos and Skyllis is told by Pliny, and will be discussed elsewhere;[1] that Ibykos went to Sikyon is not stated by any ancient source, but is deduced from the contents of some of his poems, which contain scraps of information about Sikyon, suggesting that he had some interest in the place. The most significant of these as proof that he actually visited Sikyon is a fragment in which he makes the Sikyonian river Asopos flow under the sea from Phrygia; Pausanias quotes the same statement as a local tradition of Sikyonia and Phleiasia. Ibykos' other references to Sikyon are of a historical nature, and are noteworthy because they conflict with statements made by other authors. Thus, he made the eponymous king Sikyon the son of Pelops, and not the son or grandson of Erechtheus as was generally asserted; and in a poem about the Greek heroes at Troy he referred to Zeuxippos as leader of the Sikyonian contingent. Zeuxippos does not appear in Homer, and in Pausanias' king-list it is his successor Hippolytos who appears as the vassal of Agamemnon and therefore, presumably, king at the time of the Trojan War. However, the king-list of Kastor of Rhodes, which may have been derived from Menaichmos and therefore ultimately from Sikyonian local tradition, probably dated the Trojan War in the reign of Zeuxippos. But the interesting point about Zeuxippos is that both Ibykos and Pausanias make him the son of the Argive nymph Hyllis, who was probably a daughter of Hyllos the Heraklid. Because of his Argive and Heraklid origin, the mention of Zeuxippos as king of Sikyon must have been as repugnant to Kleisthenes as the similar description of Adrastos. Furthermore, earlier in the same poem Ibykos referred to Kyanippos, the son or grandson of Adrastos — he and Zeuxippos were apparently said to have been the handsomest of the Greeks at Troy. This poem, therefore, is definitely hostile in tone to Kleisthenes and his anti-Argive policies,

---

[1] See Part III.1.D.

while the affiliation of Sikyon to Pelops implicitly denies the Athenian connection which Kleisthenes may have wished to stress.[2] It is not surprising to learn that the Trojan War poem was not written at Sikyon but at Samos, since it is addressed to Polykrates. This suggests that Ibykos moved to Samos as a result of a quarrel with his Sikyonian patron, and proceeded to attack the latter's policies once he was at a safe distance from Sikyon. The move is dated 564 to 560, and so falls within the reign of Kleisthenes' successor rather than that of Kleisthenes himself;[3] it is possible that Ibykos originally went to Sikyon to work for Kleisthenes, but was unable to secure employment by his successor, and therefore left Sikyon with a grudge against the tyranny. In that case, his career would show a striking parallel with that of Dipoinos and Skyllis, who at much the same date came to work at Sikyon, but left before completing their commission, complaining of undefined ill-treatment. Taken together, these two cases suggest that a policy of attracting foreign artists to Sikyon, which is probably to be attributed to Kleisthenes, was abandoned by his successor, whether as a matter of personal taste or due to economic necessity.

That post-Kleisthenic Sikyon suffered some economic difficulty is suggested by Pliny's statement that the departure of Dipoinos and Skyllis was followed by a famine. Even before this, however, the fortunes of the tyranny may have declined due to lack of success in the war against Argos, which seems to have gone badly in the later years of Kleisthenes' reign.[4] Like all tyrants, the Orthagorids had to justify themselves by success, and once this ceased an opposition could arise. However, in the end the tyranny was overthrown not by internal opponents but by the Spartans.

It is easy to see why the Orthagorid tyranny might have fallen for internal reasons, but less easy to understand what interest the Spartans could have had in putting it down. Assuming that at this time her opposition

---

[2] Asopos, Ibykos, fr. 41 Page, cf. Paus. ii.5.3; Sikyon, Paus. 11.6.5; Zeuxippos, Ibykos, fr. 1 Page, 40 f., cf. Barron, *CR* n.s. xi (1961), 185–7 and *BICS* xvi (1969), 130 ff., Robertson, *BICS* xvii (1970), 11 ff. It is sometimes suggested (e.g. E. Lübbert, *Diatriba in Pindari locum de Adrasti regno Sicyonio* (Bonn, 1884), 4, Gitti, *Atti r. accad. Lincei*, vi.2 (1926–9), 550–3, 599–601) that the king-lists of Kastor and Pausanias go back to rival versions produced by Kleisthenes and his opponents respectively. However, neither seems particularly well fitted to express Kleisthenes' views, since Adrastos and Zeuxippos figure in both.

[3] Suda, s.v. "Ιβυκος; defended by Barron, *CQ* n.s. xiv (1964), 223 ff., cf. M. L. West, 'Melica', *CQ* n.s. xx (1970), 207 ff.; B. M. Mitchell, 'Herodotus and Samos', *JHS* xcv (1975), 80 ff. dates Ibykos' arrival in Samos rather later, and the poem *c.* 540, which makes it harder to see the poem as expressing a grudge against Orthagorid Sikyon acquired some 20 years earlier.

[4] Cf. p. 51 for possible defeat by Argos and Kleonai in the mid-570s; the defeat by Orneai may actually have taken place during Aischines' reign rather than Kleisthenes'.

to tyrants on principle did not yet exist (if it ever did), Sparta had more reason than not to approve of the Orthagorids, since they were enemies of Argos and therefore at least potential allies of Sparta. However, because hostility to Argos was a major feature of Orthagorid policy it was likely that any opposition party within Sikyon would be relatively pro-Argive, and that if this party succeeded in overthrowing the tyranny Sikyon would revert to a policy of friendship and alliance with Argos — a most undesirable situation from the Spartan point of view. It seems possible, therefore, that the Spartan intervention at Sikyon was designed not to assist an internal revolution against the Orthagorids but to forestall it, and to ensure that the new government maintained the anti-Argive policy. If this was the Spartan aim, it can be said to have been successfully accomplished, since the indications are that Sikyon remained hostile to Argos until near the end of the sixth century.

3. Aischines to Euphron: Sikyon as Ally of Sparta

Although the Orthagorid tyranny is no by means well documented in ancient sources, information about it is abundant compared to that which survives for the period following the fall of the tyranny. After the expulsion of Aischines, Sikyon is first mentioned in connection with the Sepeia campaign of *c.* 494; then there are various references to her participation in the Persian Wars, the events of the Pentekontaetia, and the Peloponnesian and Korinthian Wars. These are mostly isolated references, and deal mainly with military affairs (the presence of a Sikyonian contingent at such-and-such a battle, and the like); there is no detailed narrative of Sikyon's internal history until Xenophon's account of the career of Euphron.

As to the nature of the government set up by the Spartans to replace the tyranny at Sikyon there is no evidence at all. If the aim of the Spartan intervention was to prevent a *rapprochement* between Sikyon and Argos, it is obvious that what Sparta chiefly required of the new government was that it be anti-Argive, and in this respect at least carry on the policy of Kleisthenes. That this requirement was fulfilled for a relatively long time is suggested by the survival of the Kleisthenic tribe-names, with their anti-Argive implications. It is also likely, though nowhere actually stated, that Sikyon became an ally of Sparta at the time of the overthrow of the tyranny, or shortly afterwards.[1] It is not recorded that Sikyon took part in any of the Spartan military operations of the second half of the sixth century, but it is probable that she gave at least passive co-operation when a Spartan army had to pass through her territory to reach the Isthmos, on occasions such as the expedition to Athens in 510. Kleomenes' abortive expedition in 506 involved an army 'from all the Peloponnese', so it is highly probable that this included a Sikyonian contingent.[2]

It was perhaps the diminution of Spartan prestige caused by the collapse of this expedition which led to the pro-Argive reaction which appears to have taken place at Sikyon at about this time. If Kleisthenes died *c.* 565, a continued existence of sixty years for his tribe-names gives *c.* 505 as the date of their abolition, and the names which replaced them — the traditional names for the Dorian tribes, and for the non-Dorian tribe

---

[1] Probably before *c.* 550, when Kroisos sought an alliance with Sparta as being the most powerful state in Greece, and in control of most of the Peloponnese (Hdt. i.68.6).   [2] Hdt. v.74.1.

Aigialeis from Aigialeus son of Adrastos — have an 'Argivizing' flavour.
Perhaps at the same time, there was an increase in the respect paid to
Adrastos, probably including a revival of his cult, which colours the
account of the foundation of the Sikyonian Pythia given by Pindar.[3] Thus
the two major items of Kleisthenes' anti-Argive policy were abandoned.
This willingness to acknowledge once again the 'historical' ties between
Sikyon and Argos could only mean that Sikyon's loyalty to Sparta was
somewhat weakened, even if the alliance between them was not actually
broken. It is against this background that Sikyon's participation in the
Sepeia campaign must be seen. According to Herodotos, Kleomenes used
Sikyonian and Aiginetan ships to convey his army to the Argolid, the
Aiginetan ones being 'taken by compulsion'. The Argives fined the
Sikyonians and Aiginetans five hundred talents each, which the Aiginetans
refused to pay, but the Sikyonians, acknowledging that they had done
wrong, settled for a payment of one hundred talents. Obviously there
existed some relationship between Argos on the one hand and Sikyon and
Aigina on the other, such that the participation of these two states in a
campaign against Argos could be held to be an offence meriting heavy
punishment, and possessing sufficient moral force to make the Sikyonians
admit the justice of the Argive claim, even at a time when Argos had no
great military power to back it up. It is likely that the tie was a religious
one, though its exact nature is disputed.[4] In any case, it conflicted with
Sikyon's membership of the Peloponnesian League in so far as this was
directed against Argos, and thus made her a less reliable ally of Sparta —
visibly so for the several years which were doubtless required to pay off
the fine.

During the Persian Wars, however, Sikyon appears to have made a fair
contribution to the Greek forces, providing both ships and men. Herodotos
records the presence of twelve Sikyonian ships at Artemision, fifteen at
Salamis, and three thousand hoplites at Plataia. There was also a contingent of unknown size at Mykale, which suffered heavy losses, including
that of its general Perilaos. Sikyonians also took part in the building of
the wall across the Isthmos. It seems, therefore, that at this time Sikyon
behaved no differently from the rest of Sparta's allies, and she is not
known ever to have showed any sign of joining Argos in medizing. The
part she played in the war was duly acknowledged by the inclusion of her
name in the lists on the Serpent Column at Delphi and on the Zeus dedicated

---

[3] *Nem.* ix.9 ff.
[4] Hdt. vi.92.1–2. K. O. Müller, *Die Dorier* (Breslau, 1824), i², 154, i², 85 f.
suggested that Sikyon belonged to a religious League centred on the sanctuary of
Apollo Pythaieus at Argos; but a centre at Asine is generally preferred, e.g. L. R.
Farnell, *Cults of the Greek States* (Oxford, 1896–1907), iv, 215 note b.

at Olympia.[5] The figure of three thousand for the contingent at Plataia has been considered improbably large by comparison with the apparent size of Sikyonian forces in the later fifth and fourth centuries; it is certainly a very substantial figure, especially as another Sikyonian contingent was operating simultaneously at Mykale, so that it cannot even represent the absolute maximum Sikyonian fighting force.[6]

After thus figuring in the Persian Wars, Sikyon returns to relative obscurity during the Pentekontaetia, being only occasionally noted as a participant in the events of the period. For one of these, the evidence for Sikyon's involvement is archaeological, not literary; a bronze greave recently found at Olympia bears the dedicatory inscription:

ΤΟΙ ΣΕΚΥΩΝΙΟΙ ΑΝΕΘΕΝ ΤΩ ΔΙΙ ΕΞ ΑΛΙΕΙΩΝ
ΑΘΗΝΑΙΩΝ ΕΛΟΝΤΕΣ.

This must refer to the repulse of the Athenian landing at Halieis in 459/8, which Thukydides credits to the Korinthians and Epidaurians.[7] Subsequent encounters with Athens went less well for Sikyon, however. The Athenian admiral Tolmides ended his *periplous* of the Peloponnese with a landing and successful battle in Sikyonia, and in 453 Perikles made a landing there and won a battle. Diodoros gives a detailed description of this campaign, according to which the Sikyonians came out *en masse* to meet the Athenians, but were defeated and besieged in the city. Perikles was unable to take the city by storm, but only withdrew when the Sikyonians received help from Sparta. Since according to Thukydides only a thousand Athenians were involved, this account, if true, does not speak well for the military strength of Sikyon at the time. Plutarch places the battle at Nemea, which is improbably far inland and not even in Sikyonian territory; but perhaps the river Nemea, which formed the boundary between Korinthia and Sikyonia, is meant. It has been suggested that the object of Perikles' attack on Sikyon, and perhaps of Tolmides' too, was to remove Sikyonian pressure on Achaia — Achaia provided forces for the next move in Perikles' campaign, the attack on Oiniadai, and so was evidently on friendly terms with Athens at this time. Under the terms of the Thirty Years' Peace Athens 'gave up' Achaia among other places, and it was perhaps after this that Pellene, the easternmost city of Achaia and Sikyon's immediate neighbour,

---

[5] Hdt. viii.1.2, viii.43, viii.72, ix.28.4 (+ ix.31.3 and Diod. xi.32.1), ix.102.3 ff.; Meiggs and Lewis, No. 27, coil 3, Paus. v.23.1.

[6] J. Beloch, *Die Bevölkerung der griechisch-romischen Welt* (Leipzig, 1886), 118 f., *Klio*, vi (1906), 52–7. Pharaklas, Σικυώνια, 28 ff. considers that a figure of three thousand hoplites and an equal number of *psiloi* (Hdt. ix.29.2) is consistent with his estimate of the total population, but he forgets the contingent at Mykale.

[7] Unpublished, except for a brief mention in ΕΣΤΙΑ 8:5:71. Cf. Thuc. i.105.1, and Gomme, i, 411 f. for data.

joined the Peloponnesian League; in 431 she fought on the Peloponnesian side, while the rest of Achaia remained neutral.[8] Because of her nearness to Sikyon, Pellene could easily be coerced into joining the League, or might do so voluntarily for the sake of security, once Athenian protection was withdrawn. There is, however, no specific evidence of conflict between Sikyon and Pellene during the fifth century.

In 446 Sikyon, along with Korinth and Epidauros, helped Megara to revolt from Athens. This is the same partnership which had repulsed the Athenians from Halieis; perhaps these three states had agreed to act jointly to keep Athenian influence out of the north-east Peloponnese. By this time Sikyon had evidently sufficiently recovered from whatever damage Tolmides and Perikles had inflicted to be able to undertake military activity. Sikyon again had dealings with Korinth, this time of a diplomatic nature, in 435, when Sikyonian and Spartan ambassadors accompanied the Kerkyraians who went to Korinth to complain about Epidamnos.[9] It is not stated what (if anything) these ambassadors did or said, but perhaps they were there to support the proposal that the matter be settled by arbitration by the Peloponnesian League, and to organize the arbitration if it was accepted. Sparta, as head of the Peloponnesian League, was a natural mediator, and Sikyon was perhaps brought in because, having close ties with Korinth, as their joint actions at Halieis and Megara indicate, her ambassadors were more likely to be listened to by the Korinthians.

At the outbreak of the Peloponnesian War, Sikyon was among the allies of Sparta, and supplied a fleet. Hence there was a Sikyonian contingent in the Peloponnesian navy defeated by Phormio in the Gulf of Korinth.[10] Nothing is heard of Sikyonian land forces until 424, when Brasidas was 'around Sikyon and Korinth' recruiting an army for his expedition to Thrace. On hearing that the Athenians had captured the Long Walls of Megara he hastened to attack them with an army which included six hundred Sikyonians, and having frightened the Athenians into abandoning their attempt to capture Megara he disbanded his allies and resumed preparations for the Thracian expedition. The Korinthians, Sikyonians, and Phleiasians whom Brasidas took to Megara seem to be a distinct force from the men he had already collected for the Thracian expedition, who also went to Megara, but are listed separately by Thukydides, and presumably the former are the allies who were disbanded when the Megara campaign was over. Hence it is impossible to be sure that the army which Brasidas took to Thrace included any Sikyonians, though

[8] Thuc. i.108.5, Paus. i.27.5; Thuc. i.111.2-3, Diod. xi.88.1-2, Plut. *Per.* 19.2-3; for date, Gomme, i, 410; cf. J. A. O. Larsen, *Studies presented to D. M. Robinson* (St. Louis, 1953), ii, 800 ff., Anderson, *BSA* xlix (1954), 81 ff., Thuc. ii.9.2.
[9] Thuc. i.114.1; i.28.1.   [10] Thuc. ii.9.3, 80.3.

since he recruited it in the Korinth-Sikyon area this is obviously probable. Some fighting men were left at Sikyon, however, since an attempted landing by the Athenian general Demosthenes, shortly after the battle of Delion, was repulsed with heavy losses.[11]

There were two Sikyonian signatories to the One Year's Truce of 423 — Damotimos son of Naukrates and Onesimos son of Megakles. Neither of these is otherwise known. The Peace of Nikias itself had only Spartan and Athenian signatories, so no Sikyonians are mentioned here. What part, if any, Sikyon played in the diplomatic manœuvrings after the Peace, in which her neighbour Korinth was so prominent, is quite unknown. The Sikyonians next appear in 419 co-operating with the Korinthians to defeat an attempt by Alkibiades to fortify Rhion, which would have given Athens a strong point at the entrance to the Gulf of Korinth — a most undesirable state of affairs for Korinth and Sikyon. In the same year, war broke out between Argos and Epidauros over alleged shortcomings in the Epidaurians' observance of the cult of Apollo Pythaieus, which Argos controlled. Sikyon is not known to have been directly involved in this episode, but it is of some importance as evidence for the existence of a religious organization with Argos at its head, which has been thought to have been the source of the Argive claim that Sikyon ought not to have helped Kleomenes in 494. However, there is no evidence that Sikyon participated in this particular cult, which had its centre at Asine and therefore was more likely to involve states in the Argolid.[12]

A Sikyonian contingent took part in Agis' campaign against Argos in 418, forming part of what Thukydides described as 'the finest Greek army up to that time'. In the abortive three-pronged attack on Argos, the Sikyonians, along with the Boiotians and Megarians, approached by the road from Phleious, through Nemea, but did not find the Argives at Nemea as expected. Instead, the Argives were encircled in the plain, with the Spartan army between them and Argos and the Sikyonians and other allies of Sparta approaching from the north. No battle ensued, however, as Agis and the Argive generals made a four months' truce. For this they suffered considerable odium, as the rank and file on both sides were convinced that they could have won a battle and that their generals had thrown away the opportunity. As Thukydides presents the situation, the optimism of the Argives was mistaken, and that of the Spartans and their allies correspondingly justified. Agis saved himself from a heavy punish-

---

[11] Thuc. iv.70–74, Gomme on iv.70.1; Thuc. iv.101.3–4.

[12] Thuc. iv.119.2; v.52.2; v.53, with Gomme–Andrewes ad loc.; for Asine temple and cult, cf. W. S. Barrett, 'Bacchylides, Asine, and Apollo Pythaieus', *Hermes*, lxxxii (1954), 421–442, O. Frödin and A. W. Persson, *Asine: Results of the Swedish Excavations 1922–1930* (Stockholm, 1938), 149 ff. (where, however, no details of archaic and later finds from the temple site are given).

ment for his failure to fight on this occasion by leading another campaign which ended with the battle of Mantineia. For this he sent for allies from various places, Arkadia, Korinth, and Boiotia (all of which had contributed to the previous campaign against Argos), and Phokis and Lokris (which had not), but, it seems, not including Sikyon, Phleious, Pellene, or Megara. There is no obvious reason why these allies should not have been summoned also; they had been involved in the Argos campaign, but had not suffered heavy losses from which they would have needed time to recover, and being nearer they could have reached Mantineia sooner than the allies from outside the Peloponnese (who in fact arrived too late for the battle, as did the Korinthians). Thukydides remarks that it was difficult for the Korinthians and other allies to reach Mantineia because their route was blocked. This is generally taken to refer to the Athenian capture of Orchomenos, which blocked the route from the Isthmus to the interior of the Peloponnese via Sikyon and Lake Stymphalos, which was normally used by Sparta and her allies since the direct road through Argos was closed to them; but the absence of the Sikyonians and others may indicate that there was trouble elsewhere on this route too. After Mantineia, when the Spartans helped to set up an oligarchy at Argos, they also intervened at Sikyon to make the existing oligarchy more exclusive.[13] Thukydides gives no reason for this action, but the obvious explanation is that the existing government had proved in some way unsatisfactory to Sparta, and so was replaced by one which was expected to be more satisfactory. The nature of the offence committed by the Sikyonians can only be guessed at, but it may have been connected with the absence of the Sikyonians in the Mantineia campaign, and even with their performance in the previous campaign against Argos. This is not known to have been inadequate, but Agis' refusal to fight when apparently in a position to win an overwhelming victory may point to some hidden weakness in his army, such as a suspicion of disaffection among the allies. By the time of the Mantineia campaign, however, an open breach had evidently taken place, with the result that Agis did not even ask the Sikyonians to take part. However, the Mantineia campaign showed that the defection of Sikyon had more serious implications for Sparta than the loss of an allied contingent; a hostile Sikyon could block her main line of communication with her allies north of the Isthmos. Sparta therefore had good reason to intervene at Sikyon to ensure her continued loyalty. The new oligarchy which the Spartans set up continued in power, so far as is known, until Euphron's *coup*.

For the remainder of the Peloponnesian War, Sikyon appears to have functioned as a loyal ally of Sparta. Two hundred Sikyonian hoplites,

[13] Argos campaign, Thuc. v.57-9; topography, Gomme-Andrewes on 59.3; allies at Mantineia, Thuc.v.64.4, 75.2; Spartan intervention at Sikyon, Thuc. v.81.2.

commanded by Sargeus, took part in Gylippos' expedition to Sicily; according to Thukydides, these went 'under compulsion'. Whether this is intended to mean that they were unwilling, or merely to contrast their obligatory service with that of the Arkadian mercenaries mentioned just previously, is not certain.[14] Perhaps the newly established oligarchs took the opportunity to send some of their opponents on an expedition from which, it could he hoped, some of them at least would not return. Later in 413, when the Spartans proposed a shipbuilding programme for themselves and their allies, Sikyon, along with Arkadia and Pellene, was called upon to provide ten ships. There was evidently a Sikyonian contingent in the fleet which won the battle of Aigospotamoi, since the Sikyonian Agasimenes was among the admirals portrayed in the victory-dedication at Delphi, on which several Sikyonian sculptors were also employed.[15]

In the campaigns which took place in Asia Minor after the end of the Peloponnesian War, we hear of a Sikyonian, Soteridas, who took part in the expedition of Kyros. He does not appear in a very creditable light in the incident related by Xenophon, when Soteridas complained of the weight of his shield and Xenophon, although wearing cavalry armour, took it from him until his comrades became indignant and made him take it back. Another Sikyonian, the *lochagos* Athenadas, took part in Derkyllidas' campaign against Pharnabazos, again not very successfully.[16]

There is no information about the activities of Sikyon in the internal affairs of Greece during the period immediately following the Peloponnesian War, but it seems that she did not share the increasing hostility to Sparta shown by some members of the Peloponnesian League, notably Korinth. When the Korinthian War broke out, Sikyon was on the Spartan side, and in fact became its headquarters and a refuge for pro-Spartan exiles from Korinth. One thousand five hundred Sikyonian hoplites fought at the battle of the Nemea, and a Spartan garrison was placed in the city. From here the Spartan polemarch Praxitas set out to capture the Long Walls from Korinth to Lechaion, at the invitation of the pro-Spartan party in Korinth. Members of this party opened the gates and admitted his army in the space between the Long Walls, where a battle was fought. Praxitas' army included a contingent of Sikyonians, who suffered heavy losses at the hands of the Argives and appeared beaten. Some Spartan cavalry under Pasimachos dismounted, took the Sikyonians' shields with their distinctive

---

[14] Thuc. vii.19.4, 58.3, Diod. xiii.8.3; Dover on Thuc. vii.58.3 favours the view that the compulsion referred to was simply the normal obligation on members of the Peloponnesian League to take part in Spartan campaigns.

[15] Shipbuilding, Thuc. viii.3.2; Aigospotamoi, Paus. x.9.7–10.

[16] Soteridas, Xen. *Anab.* iii.4.46 ff.; Athenadas, Xen. *Hell.* iii.1.18 (he made a rash attack on a city's water–supply, in which he lost two men and was wounded himself).

device, and attacked the Argives, hoping to deceive them into not taking these opponents seriously. In fact he and his followers were killed, so the deception was not very successful, but the importance of the incident as it relates to Sikyon is that it shows that the fighting qualities of the Sikyonians were not highly thought of either by their enemies or by their allies. There is no suggestion, however, that their loyalty to Sparta was questioned on this occasion, merely their military competence. This battle as a whole was won by the Spartans, who took the opportunity to place some garrisons in northern Korinthia and in the border-fortress of Epieikia, though Sikyon continued to be their base. Iphikrates and his mercenaries attacked the city, with some success, and inflicted heavy losses on a Spartan *mora* at a point near the coast between Lechaion and Sikyon. As a result of this defeat, all the Spartan garrisons in Korinthia were driven out except that at Lechaion, and the Korinthian exiles at Sikyon were no longer able to make raids on Korinthia by land, though they could still reach Lechaion by sea.[17] After this, there were no more major campaigns in Korinthia, and Sikyon ceases to be mentioned in the sources. However, it seems reasonable to suppose that the Spartan garrison remained there until the Peace of Antalkidas, when the Korinthian exiles returned home and restored their city to the Spartan alliance. In about 380, Sikyon is said to have served as a refuge for a criminal seeking to escape prosecution at Athens.[18]

No more is heard about Sikyon until some years later, when in the expectation of another war with Athens and Thebes the army of the Spartan alliance was reorganized into ten parts. One of these was formed by the Sikyonians, Phleiasians, and inhabitants of the Akte. Diodoros does not give the actual numbers contributed by the various states, so it is not possible to tell how the Sikyonian contingent compared with those supplied on other occasions, such as the battle at the Nemea. This army campaigned in Boiotia, but with no great success. After the Peace of 375 (or possibly that of 371) there were disturbances in a number of Peloponnesian cities, including Sikyon, where some would-be revolutionaries failed and were killed. The identity and precise aims of these people are uncertain, but it is likely that they were hostile to the alliance with Sparta — after Leuktra, Sikyon was among the states which took part in Archidamos' abortive punitive expedition against Thebes, and contributed to the defence

[17] Xen. *Hell.* iv.2.14–16, 4.1 and 7–14, 5.19 (battles at the Nemea and Korinth; the Sikyonians' shield device was probably *san*, which continued to appear as a device on Sikyonian coins for some time after the local script had gone out of use for ordinary purposes, although Xenophon calls it *sigma*); Diod. xiv.91.3, Polyain. iii.9.24 (attack on Sikyon by Iphikrates); Xen. *Hell.* iv.5.11–17 (the *mora*).
[18] Xen. *Hell.* v.1.34 and 36; Isaios vi.20 (delivered 364, but referring to events c. 380).

of Sparta against Epameinondas' first invasion of the Peloponnese.[19]

However, Sikyon was among the cities which surrendered to Epameinondas during his second invasion. How much fighting was involved is not certain; Diodoros' account suggests that the surrender came relatively easily, but Pausanias' narrative shows that there was some fighting (if he was right in placing the incident he relates in this campaign), and Xenophon leaves the matter doubtful. The capture by the Thebans of the harbour-town of Sikyon probably took place on this occasion. The Theban commander is named as Pammenes, who also commanded the force which protected Megalopolis while it was being built. After the withdrawal of the Thebans from the Peloponnese, Dionysios of Syracuse, acting as an ally of Sparta, invaded Sikyonia, won a battle, and captured the fortress of Derai.[20] The Sikyonians were not, however, persuaded to abandon their new alliance with Thebes.

Despite its previous record of loyalty to Sparta, the same oligarchy remained in power at Sikyon after the alliance with Thebes. This was perhaps brought about by Epameinondas, who similarly allowed existing oligarchies to survive when he won over Achaia in 367. On this occasion, however, the Thebans reversed his decision and set up democracies in the Achaian states. The result was that when the oligarchs regained power they became firm allies of Sparta, thereby no doubt confirming the suspicions of the Thebans that oligarchies were naturally pro-Spartan and therefore not to be relied upon.[21] Similarly, Euphron was able to persuade the Arkadians and Argives to support him in establishing a democracy at Sikyon, using the argument that if the oligarchy were allowed to survive it would sooner or later return to the Spartan side, whereas a democracy

[19] Reorganization of army, Diod. xv.31.2 (dated 377/6); its campaigns, Xen. *Hell.* v.4.35–41, Diod. xv.32–34.2 (with no specific reference to Sikyonians); attempted revolution, Diod. xv.40.4 (dated 374, but possibly confusing the Peace of 375 with that of 371, cf. Beloch, *Gr. Gesch.*[2] iii.1, p. 156 n. 1, T.T.B. Ryder, *Koine Eirene: General Peace and Local Independence in Ancient Greece* (London, 1965), 124; the disturbances may in fact belong after Leuktra, e.g. K. J. Beloch, *Griechische Geschichte*, 2nd edn. (Berlin and Leipzig, 1912–27). iii.1, p. 174 n. 2, G. Glotz and R. Cohen, *Histoire grecque* (Paris 1925–38), iii, 151 n. 22, cf. Isokr. *Archid.* 64-9); the revolutionaries are generally held to have been democrats, e.g. P. Meloni, 'La tirannide di Eufrone I in Sicione', *Riv. Fil,* n.s. xxix (1951), 11 f., E. Frolov, in *Hellenische Poleis*, ed. H. Welskopf (Berlin, 1974), 377 (who considers that democratic agitation at Sikyon goes back to the Peloponnesian War, and that the Spartan intervention in 417 was designed to crush this). Campaigns after Leuktra, Xen. *Hell.* vi.4.18, vii.2.2.
[20] Capture of Sikyon, Xen. *Hell.* vii.1.18, Diod. xv.69.1, Paus. vi.3.2-3; harbour-town, Polyain. v.16.3, Aen. Tact. xxix.12, Frontin. *Strat.* iii.2.10, cf. Paus. viii.27.2; Dionysios, Xen. *Hell.* vii.1.22; it is uncertain whether Epameinondas' capture of the Sikyonian town of Phoibia belongs to this campaign or a later one (Paus. ix.15.4, cf. Steph. Byz. s.v. Φοιβία and Βουφία).
[21] Xen. *Hell.* vii.1.42-3.

would be a reliable ally.[22] With their help he set up what rapidly became a tyranny for himself, the progress and downfall of which is relatively fully documented by Xenophon.

The information which we have about Sikyon from the fall of the Orthagorid tyranny to Euphron's *coup*, being concerned chiefly with her external relations, allows few conclusions to be drawn about her internal politics. It is commonly assumed, and there seems to be no reason to doubt, that the government set up by the Spartans after the expulsion of Aischines was an oligarchy, but a sufficiently broadly based one that it could be made narrower in 417. The post–417 oligarchy was apparently based on a property qualification, since Xenophon makes Euphron speak of its members as 'the richest men'. Diodoros says that Euphron exiled the forty richest men in Sikyon and confiscated their property, which may indicate that forty was a significant number in the constitution of 417, perhaps the membership of the *Boule* or some similar body.[23] Since, so far as is known, the Sikyonians continued to be organized in four tribes throughout this period, the number could have been made up of ten from each of these.

---

[22] Xen. *Hell.* vii.1.44. The chronological relationship between this and the events in Achaia just mentioned is doubtful; see p. 71.

[23] Xen. *Hell.* vii.1.44, Diod. xv.70.3.

4. Euphron to Aratos: Tyrants and Macedonians

Both Xenophon and Diodoros pass unfavourable judgements on Euphron; Diodoros says simply that he was 'exceedingly rash and crazy', while Xenophon gives a detailed account of his career and concludes that he was totally unscrupulous in his dealings both with the Sikyonians and with his foreign allies. However, the Sikyonian *demos* supported Euphron in his lifetime and honoured him after his death, and although Xenophon considered their enthusiasm misplaced he had to admit that Euphron had been a benefactor to them.[1]

It is clear that Euphron had been a member of the oligarchy; as a strong supporter of the Spartan alliance, he had had considerable influence until that alliance was broken, and Xenophon makes the motive for his *coup* the desire to acquire similar influence with Sikyon's new allies; hence his offer to make the city's loyalty secure by setting up a democracy, accompanied by the claim that he had long loathed the Spartans and was glad to escape from servitude to them. However, when on a later occasion he was trying to recover the friendship of the Spartans, he claimed that he had really been loyal to them all along, that he had voted against the original proposal to abandon the alliance with Sparta, that he had overthrown the oligarchy in order to punish those of its members who had supported the proposal and thereby betrayed both him and Sparta, and that it was these people whom he had exiled.[2] Xenophon makes it fairly clear that he did not regard this as a true account of Euphron's motives — nor, he suggests, did many people at the time — and perhaps his earlier statements to the Argives and Arkadians are intended to be treated with equal scepticism. What Xenophon makes him say about his actions (voting against the abandonment of the Spartan alliance and so on), as opposed to his motives, may, however, be true.

Euphron's first act in setting up his new government was to call together the *demos* in the Agora, with the Arkadians and Argives standing by. He announced that the constitution was to be 'on fair and equal terms', and called for the election of *strategoi*. Five, including Euphron himself, were chosen, and Euphron's son Adeas was put in command of the mercenary force. Euphron cultivated the support of these mercenaries and brought in more of them, whom he paid for out of public and sacred funds and the

---

[1] Diod. xv.70.3, Xen. *Hell.* vii.1.44–3.12. [2] Xen. *Hell.* vii.1.44, 3.2–3.

property of those he exiled as pro-Spartans. He got rid of his fellow *strategoi* by murdering or exiling them, and openly made himself tyrant, obtaining the acquiescence of his allies by bribery and the use of his mercenaries to fight in their campaigns.[3]

From this description of Euphron's rise to power Xenophon passes to an account of the loyalty of the Phleiasians to Sparta and the attacks which they suffered as a result. This subject eventually brings him back to Euphron, who took part in a campaign against Phleious. He then deals with Euphron's downfall, attempts to return to power, and death.[4] Because the narrative is split up in this way the chronology becomes obscure, and it is difficult to see how the sections of the narrative relate to each other, since one does not necessarily begin where the previous one left off. Even the date of Euphron's original *coup* is doubtful, because Xenophon places this after the Theban conquest of Achaia and the constitutional changes which took place there, ending with the return of the oligarchs and their reversion to friendship with Sparta — 'after' not only in the order of his narrative but, on the most natural reading of his remarks, in the actual order of events. On the other hand, Diodoros places Euphron's *coup* at the end of 369/8, not long after Sikyon's entry into the Theban alliance, and well before Epameinondas' third invasion of the Peloponnese, in which the Achaians were brought over to the Theban side, which he places in 367/6. The campaign against Phleious in which Euphron took part is dated in 367, and since this took place after Euphron became tyrant it seems that Diodoros' date for his *coup* should be accepted in preference to that implied by Xenophon.[5]

If Euphron's *coup* is dated not long after Sikyon abandoned the Spartan alliance, relatively little time is left for certain events which are often placed in the interval, such as the installation of a Theban garrison at Sikyon and, possibly, a change of government from an extreme to a

[3] Xen. *Hell.* vii.1.45–6; a simplified version in Diod. xv.70.3.
[4] Phleiasians, Xen. *Hell.* vii.2.1–23; Euphron on campaign against Phleious, ibid., 2.11–15; further career of Euphron, ibid., 3.1–12.
[5] Xen. *Hell.* vii.1.41–6; Diod. xv.70.3, 75.2. Date of *coup*, Meloni, *Riv. Fil.* n.s. xxix (1951), 18, followed by H. Berve, *Die Tyrannis bei den Griechen* (Munich, 1967), i, 305 and Frolov, *Hellenische Poleis*, 381. In general, Meloni's dating of the events of Euphron's career follows Beloch, *Gr. Gesch.*[2], iii.2, pp. 243 f., and runs as follows:
369 late summer — Epameinondas' second invasion of the Peloponnese. Sikyon goes over to Thebes.
368 spring — Euphron's *coup*.
367 summer — Euphron takes part in the attack on Phleious.
366 — Chares and the Phleiasians capture Thyamia. Aineas expels Euphron. Euphron hands over the harbour-town to the Spartans, but it is captured by the Arkadians. Euphron seeks mercenaries from Athens and (late 366) reoccupies Sikyon with the help of the democrats.
365 early — Euphron goes to Thebes and is assassinated.

more moderate oligarchy.[6] The latter occurrence, although not mentioned in any of the sources, is supposed probable on the grounds that the extreme oligarchs were too deeply committed to the Spartan alliance to survive its abandonment, and evidence for it is derived from the argument attributed to Euphron by Xenophon, that if 'the richest men' gained power in Sikyon the city would return to the Spartan alliance. This is taken as implying that the pro-Spartan oligarchs (identified as 'the richest men') were not in power at the time of speaking, which is obviously true in the sense that they were not in control of Sikyon's foreign policy. However, Xenophon also says that Sikyon retained its existing constitution up to the time of Euphron's *coup*. This suggests that what happened was not a constitutional change, but a struggle between pro-Spartan and pro-Theban elements within the existing oligarchy, in which the pro-Thebans were successful. Euphron may have been speaking something like the truth when he asserted that, having found himself on the losing side in the dispute within the oligarchy, he had turned himself into a democrat in order to recover the position he had lost and to avenge himself on the pro-Thebans.

The installation of the Theban garrison on the akropolis at Sikyon may likewise be removed from the interval between Sikyon's submission and Euphron's *coup*. This garrison is first mentioned by Xenophon in connection with the campaign against Phleious in which Euphron took part, and does not figure in his account of the *coup*; nor is it said to have helped in the resistance to the attack on Sikyon by Dionysios of Syracuse just after the Theban alliance was concluded, as such a garrison might have been expected to do if it had existed at the time. It seems probable, therefore, that the garrison was not sent in until after Euphron came to power, just as Theban harmosts were put into the Achaian cities when democracies were established there. In the self-justifying speech which Xenophon puts into the mouth of one of Euphron's assassins, an exchange of pledges between Euphron and the Thebans is mentioned, and perhaps the placing of a garrison at Sikyon was made a condition for Theban acceptance of Euphron's position. In view of his past record of friendship to Sparta, he could not expect to be accepted at once as a trustworthy ally of Thebes, and the fact that on the Phleious campaign it was the Theban garrison commander who led the Sikyonian citizen army may indicate that Euphron was not trusted to do this, although his presence as commander of the mercenaries was accepted.[7] After this, the Theban garrison seems to disappear as mysteriously as it arrived; when Aineas of Stymphalos, the

---

[6] Suggested by Meloni, 20 f.

[7] Idem, 14 f., 19, Berve, i, 305, Frolov, 378 all assume that the garrison was already there at the time of Euphron's *coup*; but N. G. L. Hammond, *A History of Greece to 322 BC*, 2nd edn. (Oxford, 1967), 504 thinks it was put in afterwards.

Arkadian commander, decided to overthrow Euphron and occupied the Sikyonian akropolis, he apparently found no Theban garrison there. Later, however, a Theban harmost at Sikyon is mentioned once again. It seems, therefore, that the garrison was removed and later put back, but it is uncertain when or why.[8]

There was obvious cause for the Thebans to be suspicious of Euphron if it was true, as he later claimed, that the pro-Theban oligarchs were the principal victims of his campaign of banishment and confiscation. On the other hand, there is some evidence that pro-Spartan oligarchs also suffered, and perhaps the truth is that Euphron attacked them all indiscriminately. Xenophon speaks of 'those exiled without a decree' who were recalled by Aineas of Stymphalos when he decided to overthrow Euphron; these were perhaps the pro-Theban oligarchs, while the group exiled 'with a decree', whose existence seems to be implied by Xenophon's remark, would be the pro-Spartans, whom Aineas had no interest in recalling.[9] The fact that Euphron did not confine himself to exiling those for whom this penalty had been decreed is an indication of his contempt for the democracy which he himself had set up, as is his treatment of his fellow *strategoi*. One of these, Kleandros, may be identical with the Sikyonian of that name who was honoured with a proxeny decree by the Pisatans when they controlled Olympia in 364.[10] Since the Arkadians supported the Pisatan seizure of Olympia, it is likely that anyone honoured there at this time was acceptable to them, as Euphron's fellow *strategoi* presumably were.

Apart from his wholesale elimination of opponents and rivals, and his attempts to build up a private army of mercenaries, little is known about Euphron's internal policy, though it is stated that he freed and enfranchised slaves. As for external policy, he sought to retain the friendship of his newly-acquired allies by offering them the use of his mercenaries on their campaigns, but this offer is known to have been taken up only once, in the campaign against Phleious, and here the mercenaries do not seem to have accomplished much, since most of the fighting was done by the citizen forces from Sikyon and Pellene. The Sikyonians had apparently begun fortifying Thyamia, on the border between Sikyonia and Phleiasia, at

[8] Aineas, Xen. *Hell.* vii.3.1, Theban harmost, ibid., 3.4 and 9. Berve, i, 306 and Frolov, 383 f. assume that the garrison was withdrawn shortly after the Phleious campaign, and put back after Euphron's expulsion and the capture of the harbour by the Arkadians; Meloni, 27 seems to think it was there all the time. On the Phleious campaign the garrison commander is called *archon*, later he is called a harmost, which perhaps implies a change.

[9] Diod. xv.70.3. Xen. *Hell.* vii.1.46, 3.1; cf. Frolov, op. cit., 380 and 384.

[10] *Olympia*, v, 36, in which an otherwise unknown Σωκ[λῆς] is also honoured; similar honours to another Sikyonian at this date in *Olympia*, v, 31. For Pisatan control of Olympia and celebration of the 364 Games, under Arkadian patronage, cf. Xen. *Hell.* vii.4.28 ff.

about the time of Euphron's *coup*, no doubt with a view to using it as a base for invasions of Phleiasia. But in 366 the Phleiasians, helped by the Athenian Chares, captured Thyamia and fortified it for themselves.[11] It was after this defeat, and perhaps partly on account of it, that Aineas of Stymphalos decided to overthrow Euphron, who was failing to justify himself by military success.

Aineas occupied the akropolis of Sikyon and sent for the most powerful men in the city and for some of the exiles. Euphron decided that it was impossible for him to retain control of the city, and so fled to the harbourtown and offered to hand it over to the Spartans. At this point there is a break in Xenophon's narrative, so it is not clear what happened next; there is mention of the capture of the harbour-town by the Sikyonians and Arkadians, and Euphron next appears seeking to recapture Sikyon with a force of mercenaries from Athens. (His own army of mercenaries is not heard of again after the Phleious campaign; it is not known what became of them.) It seems likely that the Spartans refused Euphron's offer, with the result that he was driven out of the harbour-town and had to seek help from Athens.[12] He also found support from the Sikyonian *demos*, and so was able to recapture the city, but could not dislodge the Theban harmost from the akropolis. Thinking that his control of Sikyon could not be complete while the garrison remained, he went to Thebes to try to secure its removal by bribery, and was assassinated there by some of the former exiles. Xenophon puts into the mouth of one of them a speech in selfjustification, which appears to express his own opinion of Euphron, and which is said to have convinced the Thebans that the assassins should be acquitted. In view of Euphron's frequent changes of side, it is not surprising that most of his former allies should have come to regard him as a traitor, so that he was seen equally unfavourably by the Thebans and by the proSpartan Xenophon. Modern authors disagree as to whether his motives were purely selfish (the view of Xenophon) or whether he was acting in what he believed to be the best interests of Sikyon.[13]

The situation at Sikyon at the time of Euphron's death was that the city was held by the democrats, who buried Euphron in the Agora, and the

[11] Phleious campaign, Xen. *Hell.* vii.2.11–15; see Pritchett, *Studies in Ancient Greek Topography*, ii, 96–111, esp. 109 ff.; Thyamia first mentioned, Xen. *Hell.* vii.2.1, immediately after the account of Euphron's *coup*; for suggested identification of site see p. 27; its capture, Xen. *Hell.* vii.2.20–3.

[12] Xen. *Hell.* vii.3.1–3, 4.1; cf. Berve, i, 306, Frolov, 384 f.; Meloni, 29 f. supposes that the Spartans actually sent a force to occupy the harbour-town, and that it was captured while Euphron was at Athens negotiating for the mercenaries.

[13] Xen. *Hell.* vii.3.4–12; Meloni, 23 considers that Euphron was trying to keep Sikyon independent and prevent any one ally from becoming an overlord, Frolov, 387 f. that he was motivated by personal ambition, but that Sikyon benefited incidentally.

akropolis by the Theban harmost, who supported the oligarchs. The pro-
Spartan oligarchs were presumably still in exile. This situation appears
rather unstable, but it is not known how it was resolved. The leadership
of the democrats may have been inherited by Euphron's son Adeas, since
his son Euphron II appears in this position later on. It seems likely, therefore, that a democratic party continued to exist and to look upon Euphron
as a benefactor; on the other hand, the alliance with Thebes also seems to
have continued, since Sikyon fought on the Theban side at Mantineia,
and in 352 joined with the Thebans and other allies to help Megalopolis
resist a Spartan attack.[14] However, after Euphron's death the history of
Sikyon once again becomes the subject of isolated references only, and
cannot be traced in detail. During the second half of the fourth century,
Sikyon and Korinth frequently appear as a pair; apparently both were considered important for the control of the Isthmus, and they tended to form
a unit independent of the rest of the Peloponnese.

The Sikyonian of whom most is known in the period after Mantineia
is Sostratos, a highly successful pankratiast who had victor-statues at
Olympia and Delphi. A figure of an athlete which appears on Sikyonian
coins of the 320s has been identified as a representation of him; if this
identification is correct, he was still famous some thirty years after his
victories. His first Olympic victory is dated in 364, the year when the
sanctuary was occupied by the Arkadians and Pisatans, which places him
alongside Kleandros and other Sikyonians honoured by the Pisatans as a
possible Arkadian sympathizer. His statue at Delphi, the inscription on
which records that he won three Olympic victories, must have been set
up after 356, which associates him with Delphi at about the time when the
sanctuary was occupied by the Phokians, and may indicate that he was
friendly to them too.[15] The story is also told of a Sikyonian youth, the
son of Pythodoros, who, on going to Delphi to dedicate his shorn hair,
received four golden strigils dedicated by the Sybarites as a love-gift from
the Phokian general Onomarchos. However, the Sikyonian Xenotimos,
who was *naopoios* at Delphi at about this time, seems to have had his

[14] Diod. xv.85.2 (not in Xenophon), xvi.39.2. Skalet, *Ancient Sicyon*, 76 ex-
presses doubts about Sikyon's presence at Mantineia, since she should have been
bound to neutrality if she had been a party to the treaty of 366/5 between Phleious
and Thebes (which she apparently was, since she thereby recovered Thyamia, Xen.
Hell. vii.4.6–11); but Meloni, 33 n. 1 considers that this would not necessarily have
excluded her from fighting at Mantineia, and Frolov, 387 accepts that she did so on
the basis of a new alliance with Thebes, perhaps made by Adeas.
[15] Base of Delphi statue, J. Ebert, *Griechische Siegerepigramme auf Sieger au
gymnischen und hippischen Agonen* (Berlin, 1972), 129–32, No. 39, Pl. viii, Fig. 21;
statue at Olympia (apparently with the same inscription as at Delphi), Paus. vi.4.1–2;
coins, L. Lacroix, 'Quelques aspects de la numismatique Sicyonienne', *Rev. Belg.
Numism.* cx (1964), 19–29.

period of office interrupted by the Phokian occupation.[16] As an ally of Thebes, Sikyon would naturally have been hostile to the Phokians, so Xenotimos' interrupted career probably reflects official policy.

References to Sikyon's relations with Macedon are few, but fairly informative. Demosthenes mentions Aristratos and Epichares, who supported Philip and thereby acquired political power, though Aristratos was eventually exiled. Although Demosthenes does not refer to him as such, Aristratos was later classified as a tyrant. He was a patron of the arts, especially of painting, and it was perhaps thanks to him that Sikyonian artists such as Lysippos went to work at the Macedonian court. In the reign of Alexander there is mention of a Sikyonian tyrant known as 'the sports-trainer', who had evidently been expelled and was restored by Alexander, contrary to the provisions of the Peace of 338/7.[17] He may have been identical with Aristratos, though no reason for such a nickname is known.

A Macedonian garrison was kept on the akropolis at Sikyon until 323, when it was driven out by Euphron II. Several literary sources record Sikyon's participation in the Lamian War, but the most detailed account of this is to be found in an Athenian decree in honour of Euphron.[18] This consists of two texts, one of a decree passed in 323/2, honouring Euphron as a friend of Athens because he had brought Sikyon into the war 'first of the cities in the Peloponnese', and the second that of one passed in 318/7, by which time Euphron was dead, reaffirming the grant of Athenian citizenship to him and his descendants and providing for the re-inscription of the original decree, which had been destroyed by the pro-Macedonian oligarchy which had ruled Athens in the interim, after the defeat of the Greeks. The second decree gives a summary of Euphron's career; when the war broke out he returned from exile, expelled the garrison with the support of the Sikyonians, and made an alliance with Athens. He played a full part in the war, and was killed in the course of the Greek defeat. Interestingly, the decree refers to Euphron's ancestors as well as himself as friends of the Athenian *demos* – perhaps a reminiscence of Euphron I's alliance with Athens (though in that case it was Athens which helped Euphron rather than vice versa), or possibly referring to some dealings between Adeas and Athens, of which nothing is known. Euphron II left

---

[16] Son of Pythodoros, Athen. xiii.605a–b; Xenotimos, *FdD* iii.5, 8.ii.10; 19.12, 21, 22, 44, 76, 82; 92A.43, 45.

[17] Aristratos and Epichares, Dem. xviii.48, 294–5; the 'sports-trainer', Dem. xvii.16; Aristratos as patron, Plut. *Arat.* 13.2, Pliny, *NH* xxxv.109; an Epichares, perhaps identical with the tyrant, appears among the Sikyonians who contributed timber for the new temple at Delphi (*BCH* Supp. iv (1977), p. 95, line 7; perhaps Aristratos' name should be restored in line 2.

[18] Diod. xviii.11.2, Paus. i.25.4, Justin, xiii.5.10; *IG* ii², 1.1, No. 448.

a son, about whose well-being the Athenians were somewhat concerned in 318/17, but his name is not recorded and it is not known whether he became a political figure. However, a democratic and anti-Macedonian party continued to exist at Sikyon.

After the Lamian War, Antipater kept the Greek states under control by means of garrisons and pro-Macedonian oligarchies, and this treatment was doubtless applied to Sikyon along with the rest. When Antipater died in 319, and the succession to his position as regent was disputed between his son Kassander and Polyperchon, it became obvious that the garrisons and oligarchies would support Kassander, so Polyperchon decreed their removal and a return to the constitutions which had existed under Philip and Alexander. This may have resulted in the removal of the garrison from Sikyon, and even in the return to power of the democrats.[19] Sikyon appears to have been included in the area of the Peloponnese controlled by Polyperchon during the ensuing war with Kassander. In 315, Polyperchon and his son Alexander allied themselves with Antigonos, and Polyperchon was appointed 'general in the Peloponnese'. Antigonos tried to win the support of the Greeks in the same way as Polyperchon had done, by decreeing that the cities should be autonomous and free from garrisons, and Ptolemy produced a rival decree of the same kind, but these probably had little practical effect at Sikyon, which had to be garrisoned against Kassander. Kassander responded to the new alliance against him with a campaign in the northern Peloponnese which seems to have aimed at the encirclement of Sikyon and Korinth. When Alexander came to the Peloponnese as Antigonos' general, Kassander won him over by offering him the position of 'general in the Peloponnese', and thereby gained control of the whole Peloponnese, either on his own account or through Alexander. However, various cities revolted with help from Antigonos, and in 314 Alexander was assassinated by a group of Sikyonians led by Alexion. Diodoros describes these people as 'pretended friends' of Alexander, and says that their aim was liberation; they appear to have been anti-Macedonian democrats who detested Kassander's policy of controlling Greece by means of oligarchies and garrisons, and who hoped that Antigonos would restore their autonomy. However, the revolt failed, since Alexander's widow Kratesipolis took command of the army, defeated the Sikyonians, and executed their leaders. She and Polyperchon then held Sikyon and Korinth, and resisted attempts by Antigonos to capture these cities.[20]

[19] Diod. xviii.55.2–57.1, 69.3–4.
[20] Diod. xix.35.1, 53.1, 54.3 (Alexander in the Peloponnese); xix.60.1, 61.3–4, 62.1–2 (alliance between Polyperchon and Antigonos and decrees about autonomy); xix.63 (Kassander's campaign); xix.64.2–4 (desertion of Alexander); xix.66–7 (death

The general peace treaty of 311 between the Diadochoi contained a clause giving autonomy to the Greek cities, but this does not seem to have changed the situation at Korinth and Sikyon, which remained in Polyperchon's possession. In 310 he produced a pretender to the Macedonian throne and invaded Macedon, but was won over by Kassander with the title of 'general in the Peloponnese'. However, when he tried to return to the Peloponnese to take up his command he was prevented by the Boiotians and Peloponnesians, with the result that Kratesipolis was left in sole charge of Korinth and Sikyon. In 308 she handed these cities over to Ptolemy, who placed garrisons in them and kept possession of them until 303, when they were captured by Demetrios Poliorketes. During his campaign in Greece in 307, Demetrios had tried to remove the garrisons by bribery, and he also proposed their removal as a condition of peace when fighting Ptolemy around Kypros. In 303 he captured the city of Sikyon relatively easily by means of a surprise attack, after which Ptolemy's garrison on the akropolis surrendered rather than face a siege (or, according to one version, succumbed to bribery).[21]

Demetrios then rebuilt Sikyon on what had formerly been its akropolis. His reason for doing so was that he wished the city to be more secure, so that there could be no repetition of his own relatively easy capture of it. He seems to have taken an interest in other aspects of the new city apart from the purely military, since his mistress Lamia was responsible for the building of the art gallery, and Diodoros says that the new site was pleasant and well watered as well as secure. However, Demetrios also destroyed part of the old city, probably in order to ensure that the inhabitants would not move back into it after his departure; his action was somewhat high-handed, and was probably resented by the Sikyonians. The new city was named Demetrias after its founder, and yearly festivals were decreed in his honour, but these soon fell into disuse and the old name was restored. These changes may have taken place quite soon, perhaps after Ipsos, when it must have seemed that Demetrios' power was permanently broken. It may have been at this time that a treaty was made between Sikyon and Athens, the surviving fragments of which contain references to 'the Sikyonians', but none to the name Demetrias.[22] Demetrios is not known

---

of Alexander and action of Kratesipolis); xix.74.1–2 (Kratesipolis and Polyperchon hold Sikyon and Korinth).

[21] Diod. xix.105.1 (peace treaty); xx.20 (Polyperchon's pretender), 28 (he goes over to Kassander); xx.37.1–2 and Polyain. viii.58 (Ptolemy acquires and garrisons Korinth and Sikyon); Plut. *Dem.* 15.1–3 (Demetrios' early attempts on Sikyon); Diod. xx.102.2, Plut. *Dem.* 25.1, Polyain. iv.7.3 (capture of Sikyon).

[22] Diod. xx.102.2–4, Plut. *Dem.* 25.3, Paus. ii.7.1, Strabo, viii.382; picture-gallery, Athen. xiii.577c; desertion after Ipsos, Plut. *Dem.* 31.2, cf. Newell and Noe, *The Alexander Coinage of Sicyon*, 26 f.; treaty with Athens, *Hesp.* viii (1939), 35 f., No. 9; date, *Hesp.* xvii (1948), 126, No. 39.

to have visited Sikyon again.

There is little or no direct evidence concerning the foreign relations of Sikyon after 303. Korinth continued to be held as a vital strategic point by Demetrios and later by Antigonos Gonatas, but Sikyon seems to have ceased to be paired with it. Rather more is known about the internal history of Sikyon, which was ruled by a succession of tyrants and tyrannicides, including Aratos' father Kleinias, until Aratos' capture of the city in 251. The most detailed account of this period is given in Plutarch's *Life of Aratos*, which used Aratos' own memoirs as a source, and the other sources are in substantial, though not complete, agreement with this.[23] The first known figure in the series of tyrants is Kleon, who, according to Plutarch, was the last of several short-lived tyrants and was replaced by some form of constitutional government led by Timokleidas and Kleinias, the former of whom soon died, while the latter was assassinated by Abantidas. According to Pausanias, however, after Kleon's fall there was a struggle for the tyranny in which Euthydemos and Timokleidas were successful, but were driven out by the *demos*, led by Kleinias, who died soon afterwards. Both sources thereafter agree that Abantidas made himself tyrant, and Aratos became a fugitive. After ruling for an unspecified period Abantidas was assassinated, and his father Paseas took over the tyranny, but he in turn was killed and replaced by Nikokles, who ruled for only a short time before being driven out by Aratos. Aratos is said to have been aged seven at the time of his father's death and twenty when he carried out his own *coup*, so there is some material for constructing a chronology. Since Aratos captured Sikyon in 251, Kleinias must have died in 264, and most of the intervening period was probably occupied by the tyranny of Abantidas, since those of Paseas and Nikokles seem to have been fairly short. Kleinias' period in power before his death was also quite short, so it is likely that the tyranny of Kleon ended not earlier than *c.* 270, and that this tyranny and the others which preceded it covered most of the period back to 303. That the period of tyrannies began this early is suggested by the fact that some of the exiles recalled by Aratos had been away from Sikyon for fifty years.[24] The treaty of *c.* 301 between Sikyon and Athens contains references to the Sikyonian *demos*, indicating that Sikyon was a democracy at this time, but this state of affairs was perhaps short-lived.

Plutarch ascribed the instability of Sikyonian politics in the first half of the third century to the collapse of the 'pure Dorian aristocracy', which

[23] Plut. *Arat.* 2–4, Paus. ii.8.1–3, Polyb. x.22.3, In view of its derivation from Aratos, Plutarch's narrative is generally preferred in cases of disagreement.

[24] Plut. *Arat.* 9.4; cf. Cic. *De Off.* ii.23.81, where the tyrannies are said to have lasted 50 years.

was perhaps a consequence of the removal of the city to its new site — a political and social upheaval corresponding to the physical one. However, not enough is known about the leading families at Sikyon before and after 303 to determine whether it was actually the case that one aristocracy disappeared and a new one replaced it. It seems that at least some of the leading figures in early third-century Sikyonian politics formed a sufficiently homogeneous group to intermarry across party lines; Kleinias' brother was married to Abantidas' sister. A little is known about the foreign relations of the various political leaders; both Antigonos Gonatas and Ptolemy Philadelphos are said to have been ancestral *xenoi* of Aratos, and a Sikyonian named Timokleidas son of Theotimos, perhaps identical with Kleinias' colleague, is the subject of an honorary decree from Delos, which may indicate that he was a friend of Ptolemy. Another Timokleidas, perhaps an ancestor of this man, is named alongside Alexander and Kratesipolis on a base from Delphi. An attempt to overthrow Nikokles was made by the Aitolians, who were friendly to Antigonos at the time, and Kleon is said to have been a pirate, like Antigonos' ally Ameinias of Phokis.[25] These scraps of information about the connections of various Sikyonian politicians with the outside world are not, however, sufficient to determine whether their successes and failures were much influenced by external events, or were due to internal causes only. Aratos appears to have expected at least tacit support from Antigonos for his attempt to overthrow Nikokles, since he made his preparations for this at Argos, which was ruled by the pro-Antigonid tyrant Aristomachos. Nikokles, on the other hand, was expected to receive support from Korinth, which was then held by Alexander son of Krateros, who had revolted against Antigonos. Since the Aitolians also tried to overthrow Nikokles, it seems that Antigonos was anxious to get rid of him, perhaps in order to deprive Alexander of an ally. Aratos himself, however, was hostile to all tyrants on principle; among his associates were the tyrannicides Ekdemos and Demophanes of Megalopolis, whose victim was the pro-Antigonid Aristodemos, and he himself later became bitterly hostile to Aristomachos, despite the debt of gratitude he owed him for having received him as an exile at Argos.[26] For Antigonos, therefore, Aratos was a somewhat doubtful ally, but this was perhaps less obvious at the beginning of his career, when

[25] Intermarriage, Plut. *Arat.* 2.3; Aratos' aunt helped him to escape after his father's assassination. Aratos' relations with the kings, Plut. *Arat.* 4.2; Timokleidas, *IG* xi.4, No. 704 (where, however, it is dated late 3rd century BC), *FdD* iii.4, 464; Nikokles and the Aitolians, Plut. *Arat.* 4.1; Kleon, Aelian, *VH* xii.43.
[26] Nikokles and Korinth, Plut. *Arat.* 9.1; Ekdemos and Demophanes, Polyb. x.22.2–3, Suda, s.v. Φιλοποίμην, Plut. *Philop.* 1.3–4, *Arat.* 5.1; Paus. viii.49.2; Aratos and Aristomachos, Plut. *Arat.* 25.1–3.

his immediate aim of expelling Nikokles was useful to Antigonos, than it became later on.

The story of Aratos' attack on Sikyon, as told by Plutarch, makes exciting reading. Because Aratos was being spied upon by Nikokles' agents, the preparations had to be carried out with the utmost secrecy, and even some of the people who were to participate in the expedition were kept in ignorance of its true purpose. This was the kind of military operation, requiring ingenuity rather than sheer strength, at which Aratos excelled; his capture of Akrokorinth, one of the most famous exploits of his career, was carried out in a very similar manner. Once inside Sikyon, Aratos announced his presence to the inhabitants, and immediately received their support. Nikokles' mercenaries were captured without casualties, and the tyrant himself escaped.[27] The affair thus proved remarkably bloodless.

Aratos' position after his return to Sikyon was somewhat ambiguous. In view of the fact that he had captured the city by force, he could be regarded as yet another tyrant, but it is plain from his subsequent actions — the recall of all exiles, the distribution of the property of the tyrants and the destruction of their monuments, and his later attempts to over-throw tyrants elsewhere in the Peloponnese — that he regarded himself as an opponent of tyranny in general, rather than as a tyrant who had risen to power by putting down another. However, it was certainly the case that he had, or was regarded as having, a position of personal power — actions such as the recall of exiles are attributed by the sources to Aratos, not to the *demos* or the Sikyonians generally. He therefore also had personal responsibility for solving the problems created by his actions. The return of the exiles created a difficult situation at Sikyon, since the former exiles desired the return of their confiscated property, while the new owners, not surprisingly, objected. The dispute was eventually settled with the help of a large subsidy from Ptolemy. However, it was, according to Plutarch, the combination of internal disorder following the return of the exiles and the fear of attack from outside which led Aratos to bring Sikyon into the Achaian League. Polybios, however, suggests that he was already motivated by the desire to liberate the Peloponnese, which could be regarded as the principal aim of the League.[28] Perhaps in fact both motives operated, the League being seen both as a source of security for Sikyon and, at least potentially, as an instrument of liberation for others. In any case, it was the entry of Sikyon into the League which began both the expansion of the League beyond Achaia, and Aratos' career as a politician of more than local importance.

[27] Plut. *Arat.* 5.1–9.2.
[28] Strabo, viii.382 calls Aratos both tyrant and liberator! Recall of exiles, Plut. *Arat.* 9.4–5, 12.1, 13.6, 14, Paus. ii.8.3, Cic. *De Off.* ii.23.81–2; entry into League, Plut. *Arat.* 9.5–6, Polyb. ii.43.3 (cf. 42.2–60, Paus. ii.8.4).

5. Sikyon in the Achaian League

It is not possible to discuss the history of the Achaian League, or even the career of Aratos, in detail here; these subjects need to be considered in the context of the history of Greece as a whole, rather than that of a single state, and the sources provide sufficient material to make separate study of them possible as well as desirable. I shall therefore give an outline of the career of Aratos, with detailed consideration only of events which directly involved Sikyon.

Having brought Sikyon into the Achaian League, Aratos soon became one of its leading figures, despite his youth. He was elected *strategos* of the League in 245 BC, and continued to hold that office in alternate years (the maximum frequency permitted by the League constitution) for most of the rest of his life. Despite Antigonos' efforts to win him over, he remained hostile to the Macedonian presence in Greece, and during his second term of office he captured Akrokorinth, Antigonos' principal stronghold, by a surprise attack rather similar in style to his attack on Sikyon. This success was important not only materially but psychologically, since a number of states promptly decided to join the League. Aratos' next enterprise was an assassination attempt against Aristomachos, the tyrant of Argos, which failed, and then a straightforward military attack on Aristomachos' successor Aristippos. This also failed, due to the Argives' lack of enthusiasm for 'liberation', and Aristippos was awarded thirty minas in damages for having been attacked without provocation. However, Aratos continued the attacks until Aristippos was killed in battle, though Argos was then taken over by the younger Aristomachos and so remained subject to a tyrant.

Aratos then turned his attention to Lydiades, the tyrant of Megalopolis, who decided that the safest course was to resign his tyranny and bring Megalopolis into the League of his own accord. He was promptly elected *strategos*, and thus became Aratos' chief rival for high office; unfortunately, the two men differed not only in their political outlook but also in their temperament, Aratos being cautious to a fault in military matters, while Lydiades was inclined to rashness. Consequently they could seldom agree on matters of policy, and especially about the attitude the League should adopt towards Sparta, which the Arkadian Lydiades regarded as a more serious threat than did the northern Peloponnesian Aratos. Lydiades found support from the Argive tyrant Aristomachos, who imitated him in resigning his tyranny and entering the League (thereby producing another dispute between Aratos and Lydiades over which of them should have the credit for persuading him to do so), and was likewise rewarded with the *strategia*. He too was disturbed by the renewal of Spartan aggressiveness under Kleomenes, and persuaded the League to attack him in spite of Aratos' opposition. Aratos agreed to take part in the war, but with no great enthusiasm, and when Lydiades was killed fighting against a Spartan attack on Megalopolis, Aratos was censured by the League assembly for giving him insufficient support.

As Kleomenes became increasingly ambitious, and demanded the hegemony of the League for himself, he and Aratos became bitter personal enemies. However, Kleomenes was found to have sympathizers in many states of the League, including Sikyon. Aratos was able to crush the opposition in Sikyon, but many states, including Argos and Korinth, went over to Kleomenes. The League elected Aratos general with full powers, and Kleomenes, having failed to buy him off, besieged him in Sikyon. Aratos had become convinced that the only way to defeat Kleomenes was to call in the help of Macedon, now ruled by Antigonos Doson; the price of his help was the return of Akrokorinth to Macedonian control, which was extremely painful to the League and to Aratos personally, but was now accepted as a lesser evil than domination by Kleomenes. Despite his past hostility to Macedon, Aratos was well received by Antigonos, and they became close personal friends. On hearing of Antigonos' approach, Kleomenes abandoned the siege of Sikyon and set himself to defend the Isthmos and Korinth, but was forced to withdraw by the news of a pro-Achaian *coup* at Argos, which, if successful, would have cut off his return to Sparta. Antigonos then took over Akrokorinth, and the cities which had joined Kleomenes returned to the League, and were rather harshly treated; Aratos was blamed for this, and especially for the execution of Aristomachos, who was held responsible for the defection of Argos.[1]

After the final defeat of Kleomenes, Antigonos returned to Macedon, but sent the future king Philip V to the Peloponnese, encouraging him to cultivate the friendship of Aratos and of the Achaians generally. Aratos remained one of Philip's most trusted advisers for some years, surviving a plot against him by envious Macedonian courtiers, and he was given much of the credit for Philip's success in the Social War against the Aitolians. To this period of good relations between Philip and the League doubtless belongs the setting up of a statue of him at Sikyon.[2] However, in the course of time Philip's character changed for the worse (or his true nature

[1] Plut. *Arat.* 11–45; for Kleomenean War, cf. Plut. *Kleomenes*, 3.4–5.1, 6.2–4, 12.1–2, 14–28, Polyb. ii.46–70; capture of Korinth, Polyb. ii.43.3–5.

[2] Plut. *Arat.* 46–8; Macedonian plot, Polyb. iv.76, 82–7, v.102, 4.9–10, 7.1–4, 14.11–16, 25–8; Philip's visit to Sikyon, Polyb. v.27.3; statue, Marcadé, *Signatures*, ii, 129 f.

revealed itself; historians offered both interpretations). He showed an increasing tendency to tyrannize over the Greeks, and turned away from Aratos to other advisers whom he found more congenial, such as Demetrios of Pharos. A famous story, illustrating their differing policies, was told about Philip's conduct at Messene, where he had been called in to settle a civil disturbance; he took Aratos and Demetrios to the top of Mount Ithome, and proposed that, instead of withdrawing from the city when his mission was completed, he should seize the citadel and keep it permanently under his control. Demetrios was strongly in favour of this suggestion, but Aratos said that it would be not only dishonourable but counter-productive, since it would alienate the other Greeks who up till then had supported Philip out of goodwill, and not because they were forced to. On this occasion Philip took Aratos' advice, but reluctantly; besides their political differences, they had an increasingly bitter personal quarrel, since Philip had taken advantage of a stay in Aratos' household at Sikyon to seduce his daughter-in-law (it was even alleged that he had persuaded her to accompany him to Macedon by a promise of marriage). Finally, Philip found Aratos' continued existence intolerable and had him poisoned, at least in the belief of the Achaians and of Aratos himself. Aratos died while *strategos* for the seventeenth time, and the Achaians wanted to bury him at Aigion, the headquarters of the League; however, the Sikyonians succeeded in asserting their claim to have him buried in his native city, where he became the object of a hero-cult.[3]

It is difficult to form a balanced opinion about Aratos, because most of the surviving literature about him is strongly biased in his favour, and even where criticism of him is mentioned it is frequently dismissed as the malice of his enemies. This tendency probably originated with Aratos' own memoirs, which appear to have contained a large amount of self-justification. Plutarch, who used the *Memoirs* as the principal source for his *Life of Aratos*, is particularly guilty in this respect, no doubt partly because he was writing the work for a descendant of Aratos. It was fortunate for Aratos that his principal enemies, Kleomenes and Philip, were both disapproved of by most later historians; had they appeared more respectable, Aratos might have gone down to history with as bad a character as Euphron. Indeed, he seems to have been extensively vilified by Phylarchos, who was a violent partisan of Kleomenes.[4]

[3] Plut. *Arat.* 49–53; Messene story also Polyb. vii.12, and Aratos' death viii.12.2–8; adultery story also in Livy, xxvii.31.7–8; hero-cult, cf. Paus. ii.8.1 and 4; Polyb. v.12.5–8, vii.13–14, and ix.23.9 compares Aratos' good influence on Philip with the evil influence of Demetrios and others.
[4] Dedication of *Aratos*, Plut. *Arat.* 1; Phylarchos, *Arat.* 38.8. Plutarch used the same sources for the *Agis* and *Kleomenes*, but here followed Phylarchos more closely, and so produced a less favourable view of Aratos; see esp. *Kleomenes* 16 on the alliance with Antigonos.

In one important respect, Aratos behaved very similarly to Euphron; in the middle of his career, he made a drastic change of policy, from total opposition to the Macedonians to seeking an alliance with them. He was bitterly attacked for this at the time, especially for agreeing to hand over Akrokorinth, which he himself had taken for the League not so many years before. Aratos could and did plead the necessity of obtaining Macedonian help against Kleomenes, but this necessity was at least partly the result of his inadequacy as a general, which even his warmest supporters had to admit. Those less favourably disposed alleged that he showed acute physical symptoms of fear before a battle, which no doubt affected his performance. It was for the same reason that Philip had to be called in to help the Achaians against the Aitolians, though in fairness to Aratos it must be said that the League does not seem to have had any better generals available at the time.[5] But even if it had, the record of Aratos' relations with Lydiades suggests that he would not have found it easy to co-operate with them; he seems to have been unwilling to tolerate any rival, but to have preferred to see League offices held by his supporters and himself.

Aratos' military inadequacies had particularly unfortunate consequences for Sikyon, because as his home town and, on occasion, headquarters of the League, it was a place his enemies were particularly anxious to attack. The city was besieged for three months by Kleomenes, and its territory was ravaged by the Aitolians and their allies during the Social War. There were also losses in manpower, since Sikyon contributed contingents to League armies and, naturally, shared in their all-too-frequent disasters. The tomb of the Sikyonians who fell in Aratos' campaigns was still to be seen outside the city in Pausanias' time.[6] The opposition to Aratos and support for Kleomenes which existed at Sikyon may have arisen from discontent with these less desirable effects of League membership, though internal causes are also possible, perhaps originating from dissatisfaction with Aratos' settlement with the returned exiles when he first came to power.

The younger Aratos appears to have been intended to be his father's political heir, since he first appears as a hostage sent to Antigonos when the alliance between him and the League was being negotiated, and subsequently became *strategos* of the League in one of the years when his father was not in office. However, he seems to have shared his father's

[5] Polyb. iv.8.1–8, summing up Aratos' qualities and defects, says that he 'filled the Peloponnese with trophies referring to him' (i.e. as loser); physical effects, Plut. *Arat.* 29.5–6; defeat by Aitolians at Kaphyai, Plut. *Arat.* 47.2, Polyb. iv.12; incompetence of other generals, Plut. *Arat.* 48.1–2, Polyb. iv.60.2, v.1.7.

[6] Siege, Plut. *Arat.* 41.4, *Kleomenes* 19.4, Polyb. ii.52.2–5; ravaging, Polyb. iv.13.4–5 (after Kaphyai), 68.1–2 (attempt by Eleians prevented by Philip); tomb, Paus. ii.7.4.

defects as a general, and was not very successful. He bitterly resented Philip's adultery with his wife, and frequently reproached him for this and for his conduct towards the Greeks in general, as in the Messene affair; consequently Philip came to hate him as much as his father and, according to Plutarch, poisoned him too. However, the family continued to exist, with a third Aratos, probably son of the second, playing a part in League affairs in the early second century, and further descendants living at Sikyon and Pellene in Plutarch's time.[7]

Although after Aratos' death Sikyon no longer had the distinction of being the home of the Achaian League's leading figure, it remained a meeting-place and, when the occasion demanded it, military headquarters of the League. For the time being the League remained in alliance with Philip, though relations with him were increasingly strained, and in 209 P. Sulpicius, acting as an ally of the Aitolians, raided the fertile area between Sikyon and Korinth. He was driven off by Philip, who celebrated this as a great victory, but the Romans also claimed that the raid was a success, and the economic consequences for Sikyon may have been quite serious.[8] The Romans later adopted a policy of detaching the League from Philip, and their ambassadors were received at a League meeting at Sikyon in 198. In the ensuing debate, one of the speakers referred to Philip's many crimes against the Greeks, including the murders of Aratos and his son, which obviously had not yet been forgotten. The League decided on alliance with Rome, and since Philip had a major base at Korinth, Sikyon was the obvious site for the League headquarters in the ensuing war against him. However, the Achaian forces were greatly outnumbered and dared not venture out of Sikyon, while Philip's army ravaged the surrounding territory with impunity. Eventually the Macedonian general became over-confident and was driven back to Korinth with heavy losses, but meanwhile Sikyonia had suffered severely. In the winter of 198/7 Flaminius and Attalos of Pergamon held a meeting at Sikyon, and Attalos brought the Sikyonians a gift of money and corn, which was received with the utmost enthusiasm. He was already popular at Sikyon because he had paid off a large debt secured on the sacred land of Apollo, for which he had been honoured with a colossal statue in the Agora; now the Sikyonians set up a golden statue of him and established an annual sacrifice in his honour.[9]

After the Macedonians were driven back to Korinth in 197, Sikyon became less immediately involved in the war against Philip, and appears

---

[7] Plut. *Arat.* 42.2–3, 49.1, 50.1, 54.1; Polyb. ii.51.5, iv.37.1 and 3, 60.2, 70.2, 72.7, v.1.1, 9. Aratos III, see below n. 10; later descendants, Plut. *Arat.* 1 and 54.3.

[8] Livy, xxvii.31.1–3, cf. 33.1–3.

[9] Meeting, Livy, xxxii.19.5, speech, 21.21–24; Macedonian attacks, Livy, xxxiii. 14.6–15.16; Attalos, Polyb. xviii.16.1–4, Livy, xxxii.39.3–4, 40.8–9; cf. *IG* iv, 426 for Sikyonian vote of thanks to a benefactor (name lost, but dated *c.* 200 BC).

correspondingly less often in the sources. Meetings of the Achaian League were held there from time to time, and some individuals became important figures in the League, though none acquired the same dominating position as Aratos had held, and the information about them is extremely scanty. Aratos III was sent on embassies to Ptolemy and to Rome in 181, and he (or another member of the family) appears in the 'great list' of *thearodokoi* from Delphi.[10] Apollonidas also served on a number of embassies, opposed the proposition that the League should ally with Eumenes, and in 188, during the war between Rome and Perseus, opposed those who were eager to bring in the League on the Roman side. In fact, hostility to the pro-Roman party at Sikyon was so bitter that when Kallikrates and Andronidas, its leaders, visited Sikyon for the Antigoneia festival, their opponents refused to use the public baths after them until the water had been changed.[11] Theodoridas and Rhositeles were other Sikyonians who served on embassies, and Theodoridas was also asked to raise a force of mercenaries by Ptolemies VI and VIII when they appealed to Achaia for help against Antiochos. In 168/7 Aemilius Paullus, touring Greece after his defeat of Perseus, visited Sikyon and was impressed by its fortifications. In 156 Oropos appealed to the Roman Senate for protection against Athenian attacks, and Sikyon was appointed to arbitrate. Since the Athenians failed to appear and put their case, the Sikyonians decided on a fine of five hundred talents, which the Senate reduced to one hundred when the Athenians appealed.[12] This is the last occasion on which Sikyon is heard of before the Korinthian War.

[10] Meetings, Livy, xxxv.25.3–10 (192 BC), Polyb. xxiii.17.5 (183 BC), xxviii.13.9 (170 BC), xxix.24.6 (169 BC); Aratos III, Polyb. xxiv.6.3, 8.8; *thearodokoi* list, *BCH* xlv (1921), p. 11, col. ii, line 34 (there dated *c.* 200–175; G. Daux, 'Inscriptions de Delphes inédites ou revues', *BCH* lxii (1949), 21–7 favours raising the date to *c.* 235–221, which makes identification as Aratos II or even I more likely).

[11] Apollonidas, Polyb. xxii.8.1–8, 11.6–12.3, xxviii.6.1–7; treatment of Kallikrates and Andronidas, Polyb. xxx.29.2–3.

[12] Theodoridas and Rhositeles ambassadors, Polyb. xxii.3.6; Theodoridas mercenary commander, ibid., xxix.23.6; Aemilius Paullus, Polyb. xxx.10.4, Livy, xlv.28.3; Oropos, Paus. vii.11.4–5, Plut. *Cato Mai.* 22.1, cf. *Syll.*[3], 675; date, F. W. Walbank, *A Historical Commentary on Polybius* (Oxford, 1959–79), iii, 532.

6. Sikyon in the Roman Period, after 146 BC

Initially, Sikyon seems to have profited from the destruction of Korinth and the imposition of Roman rule on Greece; she took over part of Korinth's territory, and the presidency of the Isthmian Games.[1] However, the next occasion on which we hear of Sikyon is less happy; this was a major dispute among the Artists of Dionysos, which had to be settled by an appeal to Rome.[2] The guild of Artists based at the Isthmos and Nemea, which apparently included members from the whole Peloponnese and from Thebes and Boiotia, had at some date after 146 joined forces with the Athenian guild, the new organization being regulated by a *senatus consultum*, which, among other points, laid down that meetings should be held at Thebes and Argos. However, the new arrangement was not satisfactory, and the Athenians complained to Sisenna, the governor of Macedonia, who ordered the Isthmian Synodos to send ambassadors to explain its side of the case. These ambassadors, instead of putting their case as instructed, made an agreement with the Athenians and proposed a fine of ten talents on the Isthmian Synodos. The Synodos retaliated by bringing charges against them and finding them guilty, but the ambassadors then joined with some of the Artists from Thebes and Boiotia to form a breakaway group which appropriated the archives and valuables of the guild and prevented the carrying out of the proper sacrifices. The Isthmian Synodos then held a meeting at Sikyon,[3] at which it was decided to repudiate the ambassadors' agreement with the Athenians and to expel the Athenians from the guild — which meant, naturally, that they lost their share in the common property. It was at this point that the Athenians appealed to Rome, claiming that the Isthmians had no justification for repudiating their ambassadors' agreement and had acted contrary to the *senatus consultum* which had set up the new amalgamated guild — not only in respect of the decisions taken at the Sikyon meeting, but in holding the meeting where they did. The Isthmians counter-claimed that their Boiotian 'rebels' should be brought back under their authority and that, because of the circumstances under which it was made, the agreement before Sisenna should be declared invalid. The Senate's decision was favourable to

[1] Paus. ii.2.2, Strabo, viii.381, Eustath. *ad Il.* ii.570.290.41.
[2] *FdD* iii.2, 70 (dated June 112).
[3] The place-name is missing on both occasions when it occurs in the inscription, but initial Σ can be distinguished. A Sikyonian figures in a list of names appended to it (fr. e, inv. 966). For Artists of Dionysos at Sikyon, cf. Plut. *Arat.* 53.5–6.

Athens, since it declared that the Sisenna agreement should stand and the expulsion of Athens from the guild be revoked. The language of the decree is highly complimentary to Athens, which was evidently still reaping the benefit of having remained loyal to Rome in 146 — an advantage with which the Isthmians could not compete. Indeed, it may have been a desire to share in Athens' prosperity which caused the Isthmian Artists to seek amalgamation with their Athenian counterparts.[4] How the matter was eventually settled is not known, but presumably the Senate's decision was obeyed.

In the first century BC Sikyon's prosperity appears to have declined. Sulla evidently visited the place while campaigning in Greece, since a base which carried a dedication by him to Mars has been found in the Agora.[5] In 80 Verres visited Sikyon, demanded money from a magistrate, and half-killed him when he refused. Cicero also makes a general reference to the carrying off of works of art from Achaia, but does not go into details.[6] Sikyon, however, was an obvious victim for such treatment. Some time afterwards (the exact date is unknown) the city was obliged to borrow money, and then found difficulty in repaying it; since the lender was Atticus, we hear of this affair several times in Cicero's letters to him between mid-61 and mid-59. At the time when Atticus was trying to recover his money, the Senate passed a decree which, it seems, limited the pressure which could be put on 'free cities' under such circumstances, and the Sikyonians apparently took advantage of this to refuse payment. Atticus hoped for some help from the Senate, perhaps in the form of letters advising the Sikyonians to pay up, but it is not certain whether he obtained this, or indeed whether he ever got his money back.[7] However,

---

[4] The Athenians were also highly favoured at Delphi at this period — their *asylia* and related privileges (originally granted in 279/8) were renewed in *c.* 130 (*IG* ii², 1132), reasserted after their participation in the Pythais of 128/7 (*Syll³*, 698), and again in *c.* 125 and 117/6 (*IG* ii², 1134) — the latter with explicit reference to the quarrel with the Isthmians. The latter had originally been the more favoured group — they had received privileges some time before 279 (*Syll³*, 460), and were probably the only group of Artists involved in the early Soteria (G. Nachtergael, *Les Galates en Grèce et les Sôtéria de Delphes* (Brussels, 1977), 300–4). At some date *c.* 145–125 they took part in the 'Winter Soteria' (Nachtergael, 592 f., No. 80), but there is no record of such extravagant honours for them as for the Athenians.

[5] *PAE* 1938, p. 121 f.   [6] *Verr.* ii.1, 17.44–5.

[7] *Ad Att.* i.13.1 (Jan. 61) — Atticus about to go 'ad Sicyonem oppugnandum'; ibid., i.19.9 (Mar. 60) — Atticus hindered by decree and can only use 'blanditiis'; ibid, i.20.4 (May 60) — no help likely from Senate; ibid., ii.1.10 (June 60) — 'Sicyonii te laedunt' thanks to decree; ibid., ii.13.2 (Apr. 59) — *if* you have letters to Sikyon . . .; ibid., ii.21.6 (July 59) — 'let me know how you get on with the Sikyonians'. Cf. *Ad Fam.* v.5 (late 62), in which Cicero asks C. Antonius, the governor of Macedonia, to help Atticus in some business — perhaps the recovery of the Sikyonian debt (though A. H. Byrne, *Titus Pomponius Atticus: Chapters of a Biography* (Bryn Mawr, 1920), 6 thinks not). The decree may have forbidden provincial governors to help in such matters.

it was in 56 BC that the Sikyonians found it necessary to sell off the contents of their art gallery, which may indicate that they had heavy expenses, such as debt repayments, to meet at this date.[8]

Cicero had Sikyonian friends too. He wrote a letter of recommendation for one Democritus, whom he describes as the leading man in Sikyon and in Achaia generally.[9] He is not otherwise known. Another friend living at Sikyon was M. Aemilius Avianius or Avianianus,[10] who also figures in letters of recommendation, along with his freedmen C. Avianius Hammonius and C. Avianius Evander.[11] Evander is known to have been a sculptor, who had a somewhat chequered career, being taken to Egypt by Antony and brought back as a captive to Rome, where he worked as a restorer of ancient statues, probably in the context of Augustus' restoration of dilapidated temples.[12] Cicero's friend Fabius Gallus bought some statues for him from an Avianius, possibly Evander, though it is not said that they were his work, merely that he was the vendor.[13] Avianianus is described by Cicero as a great friend, Hammonius as a benefactor. Because of Evander's artistic activities it has been suggested that Avianianus himself was an art dealer,[14] but there seem to be insufficient grounds for this. Q. Cicero appears to have had some connection with Sikyon too, perhaps also with Avianianus; in 48, while the brothers were waiting to see what Caesar would do after Pharsalos, they quarrelled, and Quintus went to Sikyon, where he proceeded to slander his brother viciously in public.[15]

Caesar's re-foundation of Korinth in 44 was probably to Sikyon's disadvantage, since the new city naturally became once again the chief city of the area. Antony's wife Fulvia died at Sikyon in 40,[16] but after this distinguished Romans are more likely to be found visiting Korinth. There is little evidence of public building work at this period[17] and few references

---

[8] Pliny, *NH* xxxv.127.
[9] *Ad Fam.* xiii.78 – dated 47/6, or possibly *c.* 62 (see Shackleton Bailey ad loc.).
[10] For the correct form of the name, see Shackleton Bailey on *Ad Fam.* xiii.21.1.
[11] *Ad Fam.* xiii.21 and 27 (Avianianus and Hammonius); xiii.2 (Evander).
[12] Hor. *Sat.* i.3.90 and Porphyrio ad loc.; Pliny, *NH* xxxvi.32.
[13] *Ad Fam.* vii.23.
[14] J. Hatzfeld, *Les Trafiquants italiens dans l'orient hellénique* (Paris, 1919), 74, 76, 123, 228–9, imagines a grand manufacturing enterprise with branches at Athens (run by Evander), Sikyon (run by Hammonius), and Kibyra in Asia Minor (where Avianianus was when Cicero wrote *Ad Fam.* xiii.21).
[15] *Ad Fam.* xi.7.7 and 8.2.
[16] Appian, *BC* v.55.230, 59.249; Plut. *Ant.* xxx.3; Cass. Dio, xlviii.28.2.
[17] Fiechter, 32 assigns the second building period of the theatre to the late 1st century BC or early 1st century AD, and the third to an uncertain date after this (2nd century AD?). The bath-house and its statuary are not very definitely dated, while the statues from the gymnasium are dated to the 1st century AD. (*PAE* 1932, 71–4, Figs. 9–13; 1934, 119, Fig. 5). An inscription, apparently of the early Roman period, records a donation by Sosikrates son of Arkadion of 10,000 *denarii*, the

to native Sikyonians who distinguished themselves — though we should note the successful athlete Aelius Granianos, who lived in the second century A D.[18] Pausanias saw his statue in the Asklepieion at Titane, which was perhaps his home, rather than Sikyon itself.

The next significant event in the history of Sikyon was the great earthquake whose effects Pausanias saw, which appears to have taken place in the mid-second century.[19] Although other cities, such as Rhodes and Kos, which suffered similarly at this time, were restored by the Emperor Antoninus,[20] Sikyon does not seem to have so benefited, and remained in a depressed state at the time of Pausanias' visit — ὀλίγου . . . ἀνδρῶν ἔρημον, he says. The rebuilding of the upper level of the Gymnasium, which is dated to the third century A D, and the conversion of the Bouleuterion into a bath-house, if it took place at this time, may represent belated attempts to make good some of the damage.[21] It seems likely that the centre of population shifted from the city on the plateau to the harbour-town, where a large Christian basilica, dated to the fifth century A D, has been found.[22] The Νέα Σικυών which figures in Hierokles' *Synekdemos*[23] is probably the harbour-town — Νέα, obviously by comparison with the city on the plateau. References to old Sikyon under the names Demetrias and Hellas are also found in later times,[24] so the city evidently continued to exist. It is known to have had two Christian churches, one on the site of the archaic temple in the Agora and the other near the present church of Ay. Triada at Vasiliko. Both are dated to the fourth or fifth century A D.[25]

---

interest from which was to pay for wood for work on the Gymnasium (*ADelt.* x (1926), παραρτ. 21, No. 12; Ἑλληνικά i, 18). There is also a dedication by the Gymnasiarch Menodotos which appears to be later in date (*PAE* 1951, 190 f.).

[18] Paus. ii.11.8; *SEG* xi, 838 (dated *c.* 120–180 AD). Probably identical with the Kranaos of Sikyon who won the stadion at Olympia in Ol. 231 (AD 144) — Euseb. *Chron.* i.217 (Schoene).

[19] Paus. ii.7.1.

[20] Paus. viii.43.4.

[21] *PAE* 1936, pp. 89 f. 1953, p. 188. Further alterations are ascribed to the 4th century AD, and the workmanship is described as 'barbarous'.

[22] *BCH* 1 (1926), 177 ff.; *PAE* 1933, pp. 81–90; 1938, 120 f.; 1954, pp. 219–31.

[23] 646.8.

[24] Demetrias — Nikephoros Gregoras, iv. 9 (i, p. 116.19 ff.). Hellas — Suda, s.v. Σικυών, Malalas, *Chron.* iv.83 (the Sikyonians now called Ἑλλαδικοί).

[25] *ADelt.* x (1926), 47 παραρτ. 23, Nos. 16–17.

PART III: SIKYONIAN ART

1. Archaic Sikyonian Art

A. The problems of ascribing works to a Sikyonian School

Sikyon was highly reputed among ancient art historians as an early home of various arts and crafts,[1] but detailed literary accounts are tantalizingly few, and material evidence remains sparse. Even where the literary sources name individual artists, it is often hard to say whether these were historical characters or not, and even if they were, whether their connection with Sikyon is sufficiently proved.

To the non-historical class certainly belong the Telchines, who are said by one source to have lived at Sikyon and thereby to have given the place its early name of Telchinia. Other sources, however, place them in Rhodes, Krete, and Kypros.[2] The name Telchin appears in the Sikyonian king-list as that of the grandson of Aigialeus, the original founder of the city.[3] The obvious derivation of the name Telchinia, therefore, is from this king, but whether the association of it with the Telchines is simply a mistake arising from the similarity of the names, or the result of a supposed connection between the Telchines and Telchin, it is impossible to say. Since the Telchines were metal-workers,[4] they were particularly appropriate 'ancestors' for the Sikyonian school of sculpture, whose most distinguished members worked in bronze. Hence it might have been tempting for some ancient art-historian to seize upon the name Telchin and explain it as being derived from these 'Kunstdaimonen'. However, Pausanias ascribes the foundation of the temple of Athena Telchinia at Teumessos in Boiotia

---

[1] e.g. Pliny, *NH* xxxvi.9 'Sicyonem . . . quae diu fuit officinarum omnium talium patria'; Strabo, viii.382.

[2] Eustath. *ad Il.* 291.28 f.; cf. Strabo, xiv.653–4, who says that they originated in Krete and migrated first to Kypros and then to Rhodes, which was called Telchinis after them.

[3] Paus. iii.5.6.

[4] Strabo, loc. cit. says that they were the first workers in iron and bronze; Eustath. *ad Il.* 772.1 f. says their names were Chrysos, Argyros, and Chalkos after the metals which they discovered; Diod. v.55.2 says they were the first to make statues of gods.

to some of the Telchines from Kypros,[5] so there may have been other traditions of visits by them to the mainland.

The first known examples of Sikyonian bronze-work are the *thalamoi* which Pausanias records as having been dedicated by Myron at Olympia,[6] and a lost bronze statuette from Sikyon.[7] This appears to have represented a goddess, since she wears a *polos* and held attributes, now lost, in her hands. It has been suggested that she is Aphrodite, a small copy of an early cult-statue which was later replaced by Kanachos' chryselephantine figure, which likewise represented the goddess wearing a *polos* and holding an apple and a poppy.[8] Stylistically, the statuette has been compared to one from Olympia, which is dated in the last quarter of the seventh century.[9] Myron's *thalamoi* have completely disappeared, and are known to us only from Pausanias' description, which, as it stands, raises considerable problems about the nature of these objects and even their authenticity. They will be discussed in a separate section.

A few more products of Sikyonian workshops survive from the sixth century, and in the literary sources some sculptors of this period are mentioned by name. Of these, however, Dipoinos and Skyllis were Kretans who spent only part of their career — and perhaps only a small part — at Sikyon, and since none of their known pupils was Sikyonian it is doubtful if they had any lasting influence on the Sikyonian school. Later in the century Kanachos and Aristokles were Sikyonians by birth, though their activity was not confined to their native city. It is noteworthy that Kanachos was fairly versatile in the materials he used, and Dipoinos and Skyllis even more so; Pliny refers to marble statues by Kanachos, although classifying him as a bronze-worker, and Dipoinos and Skyllis are actually placed among the workers in marble.[10] Surviving specimens of sixth-century Sikyonian sculpture likewise show that stone was in use at this time — from Sikyon itself, the *kore* head in Boston and some items in the Sikyon Museum, and from Delphi, the metopes of the 'Monopteros'.[11]

[5] Paus. ix.19.1 — but the derivation of the epithet from the Telchines is his own conjecture (ἐστιν εἰκάξειν).　　[6] Paus. vi.19.1.-4.
[7] E. Gerhard, *Antike Bildwerke zum ersten Male bekannt* (Munich, 1828-44), Pl. 309.6, p. 33 n. 85, p. 398 (reported by Sir W. Gell); *VS* 142 f., Fig. 108; Langlotz, *Frühgriechische Bildhauerschulen*, 30, No. 1. Now lost, and known only from Gerhard's drawing (reproduced in *VS*).　　[8] Paus. ii.10.5.
[9] E. Kunze, 'Kleinplastik aus Bronze', *VII Olympiabericht* (1956-8), 166 ff., Fig. 98, Pl. 69; G. M. A. Richter, *Korai: Archaic Greek Maidens* (London, 1968), 34, No. 28, Figs. 104-7.　　[10] *NH* xxxvi. 41 and 9-10.
[11] *Kore* head, Boston 04.10, Caskey, *Cat.* 8 f., No. 5; Burlington Fine Arts Club, *Exhibition of Greek Art* 1904, p. 80, No. 49; Langlotz, *Frühgriechische Bildhauer-schulen*, 32, No. 37, Pl. 22a; Chase, *Guide* (1950), 29 f., 32, Fig. 35; Richter, *Korai*, 60, No. 99, Figs. 301-3; G. M. Chase and C. C. Vermeule, *Greek Etruscan and Roman Art: The Classical Collections of the Museum of Fine Arts, Boston* (Boston, 1963), 48, 62, Fig. 48; M. Comstock and C. C. Vermeule, *Sculpture in Stone: The*

Some bronzes also survive, notably the statuette of a bull-calf with dedicatory inscription in Sikyonian script found in the sanctuary of Hera Limenia at Perachora.[12] A fragmentary relief plaque, now in Boston, was bought at Xylokastro, and so may have originated from Sikyon.[13] A fragment of an inscription in the Sikyonian alphabet on a bronze strip from Olympia dates from the first half of the sixth century. The strip was evidently cut from a bronze plaque and reused for some other purpose; attempts have been made to identify it as part of the dedicatory inscription from Myron's *thalamoi*, but such words as can be made out on the fragment do not bear any obvious relation to the contents of the inscription on the *thalamoi* as paraphrased by Pausanias.[14] Perhaps it formed part of some other early sixth-century Sikyonian dedication, but it is impossible to say what this may have been.[15]

From the early fifth century there are finds of small bronzes from Sikyon itself, namely a statuette of a *kriophoros*, now in Basel, and two mirrors.[16] These take us beyond the end of the archaic period, the mirrors being dated towards the middle of the century. No sculpture in stone survives from this period, though several inscriptions on stone are preserved, from funerary or other monuments, some of which may have had sculpture associated with them.[17] In the generation after Kanachos

Greek, Roman and Etrustan Collections of the Museum of Fine Arts, Boston (Boston, 1976), 8, No. 14. Items at Sikyon, unpublished, include a relief head which bears some resemblance to that of Kastor in the 'Cattle-raid' metope. Delphi metopes, see § C.

[12] Athens 16156, *Perachora*, i, 136, Pl. 43.5-7 — dated in the last quarter of the 6th century.

[13] Boston 98.652, Robinson, *Ann. Rep.* (1898), 24 f.; *AA* (1899), 136; Addison, *Boston Museum of Fine Arts*, 295; Comstock and Vermeule, *Bronzes in Boston*, 450 f., No. 660.

[14] Purgold, *AZ* xxxix (1881), 179; *LSAG* 139 f. 143, No. 3, Pl. 23.

[15] One made by Kleisthenes after his victory in the chariot-race?

[16] *Kriophoros*, Basel BS 06/123, *Nuove Memorie del' Ist.* ii (1865), Pl. 12 (= W. Vischer, *Kleine Schriften* (Leipzig, 1877-8), ii, Pl. 17.3); Langlotz, *Frühgriechische Bildhauerschulen*, 32, No. 35; K. Schefold, *Basler Antiken in Bild*, 21, Pl. 11a; id., *Klassische Kunst in Basel* (Basel, 1956), 35; *Führer durch das Antikenmuseum Basel*, 80. Mirrors: one lost, from a grave at Tragana, near Sikyon, *PAE* 1936, p. 92 f., 91, Fig. 5; *AJA* xli (1937), 336 f., Fig. 3; *AA* (1937), p. 14 f., Fig. 14; *AA* (1942), p. 471 f.; *JdI* lxi/lxii (1946/7), 101 n. 2; L. O. K. Congdon, 'Greek Caryatid Mirrors', unpublished thesis, Harvard, 1963, No. 69. The other, Paris, Musée des Arts Decoratifs, Fröhner, *Coll. Rhousopoulos, vente 1895*, No. 68, Pl. 8; E. Franck, *Griechische Standspiegel mit menschlicher Stützfigur* (Berlin, 1925), No. 17; Langlotz, *Frühgriechische Bildhauerschulen*, 31, No. 16, Pl. 15d; *JdI* lxi/lxii (1946/7), 101 n. 2; Congdon, *Greek Caryatid Mirrors*, No. 66.

[17] Base, Sikyon Museum, *PAE* 1951, p. 189 f., No. 3, Fig. 4; *SEG* xiv, No. 309; *LSAG* 143, No. 9. Grave-stele (?), Sikyon Museum, Ἑλληνικά, x (1937-8), 12 f., No. 2; *REA* xlv (1943), 189, 191; *SEG* xi, No. 259; *LSAG* 143, No. 11, Pl. 23. Fragment of stele, Sikyon Museum 915, *PAE* 1932, p. 70, No. 1, Fig. 8; *REA* xlv (1943), 183, 191; *SEG* xi, No. 257, xiv, No. 310; Moretti, *Iscrizioni agonistiche*

and Aristokles, no names of Sikyonian sculptors are known; the next major figure to appear was Polykleitos, who although a native of Sikyon, seems to have been associated with Argos for most of his working life. It is possible, therefore, that the Sikyonian school of sculpture was in decline during the first half of the fifth century, at least so far as the production of major works was concerned.

The identification of surviving objects as products of a Sikyonian school of sculpture is difficult, in view of the small number involved; clearly, objects actually found at Sikyon must provide the starting-point, but the possibility of both import and export must be taken into account. The Boston *kore* head is a striking example; both style and material appear un-Peloponnesian, and it is now considered to be Kypriot. If the alleged provenance is correct, therefore, it must be an import. This is interesting in view of the other references to connections between Sikyon and Kypros, but offers no help in determining what the native Sikyonian style of the time was like.[18] The most important attempt to put together a Sikyonian group of archaic sculpture is that of Langlotz, whose list in fact contains only four objects found at Sikyon, including the Boston *kore* head.[19] The rest of the objects which Langlotz links with these are supposedly connected by features of style, some of which are more obvious than others. The most interesting group is that of the mirror-supports, which has been added to by the subsequent finding of a mirror at Sikyon itself,[20] which has several of the characteristics described by Langlotz as Sikyonian — notably the curious gesture of holding up the skirt with two fingers and thumb, and the conspicuous group of vertical folds at the centre front of the skirt. However, some mirror-caryatids which have these features are considered non-Sikyonian by Langlotz, and other attempts to classify these objects by local schools have produced different results.[21] Korinth and Aigina are likely alternative sources for at least some mirrors of this type, and since Sikyon and Aigina are known to

---

greche, 29 f., No. 12; *LSAG* 143, No. 13a-b, Pl. 23. Traces of cutting on top for bronze statue (*LSAG* 141). Stele, now lost, from Moulki, *AJA* iv (1888), 427 f.; *IG* iv, No. 425; Roehl³, 50, No. 6; *REA* xlv (1943), 183, 191; *SEG* xi, No. 245; *LSAG* 143, No. 16, Pl. 23.

[18] Comstock and Vermeule, *Sculpture in Stone*, p. 8, No. 14 — dated *c.* 520 BC, rather than *c.* 530 as in Richter. Cf. V. Karageorghis and C. C. Vermeule, *Sculptures from Salamis* (Nicosia, 1964-6), i, 7-8 — a torso from Salamis to which the head might belong (but does not appear to join).

[19] *Frühgriechische Bildhauerschulen*, 30 ff.; the objects from Sikyon are Nos. 1, 16, 35, and 37 in his list.   [20] The lost specimen from Tragana.

[21] e.g. Congdon, *Greek Caryatid Mirrors*; H. G. G. Payne, 'A bronze Herakles in the Benaki Museum, Athens', *JHS* liv (1934), 173 f. Payne's view appears to have been that several apparently distinct classes of objects were in fact all made in one place, probably Korinth; he consistently declined to discuss the possibility of attributing objects to Sikyon, on the grounds that there were not enough specimens from the site to provide a starting-point.

have been artistically connected during the late archaic period through the school of Aristokles it is quite credible that they should have produced small bronzes of similar types. Sikyon's ancient reputation as a major centre of the arts suggests that some such objects should have been made there, and on present evidence Langlotz's classification of 'Sikyonian' objects appears correct in principle, if not in detail.

Because excavations at Sikyon have been concentrated on the Hellenistic city-site, our knowledge of the buildings and other features of the archaic city is literary rather than archaeological. The only archaic building of which remains have been found is a temple, which had been extensively reconstructed in the Hellenistic period. A few architectural terracottas, apparently dating from the third quarter of the sixth century, survive.[22] Pausanias records the existence of other early temples at Sikyon, in particular that of Athena, which he describes as unusually large and richly decorated; however, it had already disappeared by the time he visited Sikyon, so his account of it was presumably derived from local tradition. He ascribes its foundation to the Bronze Age king Epopeus.[23] Pausanias gives other temples at Sikyon an equally early origin — in particular, that of Apollo, which was said to have been founded by Proitos. In this case again, however, Pausanias did not see the original temple, which had been burnt down and rebuilt at an uncertain date. It had contained a number of objects for which mythological associations were claimed, such as Marsyas' flutes; most of these had no obvious connection with Sikyon, and their preservation there was probably regarded as a matter of pure chance.[24] In the same temple stood a statue made of χαλκὸς κολυμβήτης from Demonesos, an island at the entrance to the Bosporos.[25] There is no evidence whether this, or any of the other objects recorded as being in the temple, was of Sikyonian manufacture. The other ancient sanctuaries seen by Pausanias at Sikyon were mostly in a semi-ruined condition, and he recorded little about them but the names of their supposed founders.[26]

Evidence from a number of sources suggests that the tyrant Kleisthenes was responsible for a considerable amount of building at Sikyon. Pausanias

---

[22] *PAE* 1937, p. 95, 96, Fig. 4. The shape appears transitional between the early types from Korinth (e.g. *Corinth*, iv, 1. A3) and the Megarian Treasury type (*NC*, Fig. 112B).

[23] Paus. ii.11.1.

[24] Paus. ii.7.8–9; Ampelius, *Lib. Mem.* 8.5. According to Pausanias, Marsyas' flutes fell into the River Maiander and reappeared in the Sikyonian Asopos (there was believed to be a subterranean link between the two rivers, Paus. ii.5.3).

[25] Aristotle, *Mirab. Auscult.* fr. 58 Giannini.

[26] Paus. ii.11.1–2.

ascribes to him a stoa in the Agora of the Hellenistic city, which had been paid for from the booty of the Sacred War.[27] Although no trace of this stoa has been found, it is by no means improbable that it should have stood on the site later occupied by the Hellenistic Agora, since it would then have been near the ancient temple of Apollo — the god on whose behalf the Sacred War had allegedly been fought. Evidence of other building activity by Kleisthenes is given by Herodotos in his accounts of the tyrant's exploits. When Kleisthenes brought the bones of Melanippos to Sikyon, he gave the newly-imported hero a *temenos* in the *prytaneion*, which may have involved some additions or alterations to the existing building.[28] When he entertained Agariste's suitors at Sikyon for a year, he built a running-track and a *palaistra* where they could show off their athletic prowess.[29] If the construction of the Tholos and 'Monopteros' at Delphi is correctly associated with Kleisthenes,[30] this would give further evidence for his interest in building, and also in sculpture, which played a prominent part in the decoration of the 'Monopteros'. Aristotle mentions the existence of a seated statue in the Agora at Sikyon, which was supposed to be the portrait of a judge who had denied Kleisthenes an athletic victory and had been crowned by him;[31] the implication is that this statue dated from the time of Kleisthenes. If Kleisthenes was a patron of the arts, one would expect Sikyon's reputation in this field to have been particularly high in the early part of the sixth century, and this is precisely the period to which Pliny refers when describing the situation there at the time of the arrival of Dipoinos and Skyllis.[32] One may surmise, indeed, that it was the existence at Sikyon of an artistically minded tyrant as a possible source of patronage which prompted the Kretan sculptors to go there rather than to any other mainland city — though it is not certain whether their activity at Sikyon took place during Kleisthenes' reign or after his death.

Turning to the minor arts, we are faced with the problem of Sikyonian pottery — whether there is such a thing. The pottery now known as Proto-corinthian was once ascribed to Sikyon, but now that this is considered to have been made at Korinth there is no class of archaic pottery which can be called 'Sikyonian'.[33] Investigation of this question too is hampered by the lack of archaic remains at Sikyon — no trace of a Kerameikos has been found, and even individual vases from the site are relatively few. Those which are known are mostly imported, being Korinthian, Lakonian, or

---

[27] Paus. ii.9.6.   [28] Hdt. v.67.3.
[29] Hdt. vi.126.3.
[30] e.g. La Coste-Messelière, *Au Musée de Delphes*, 78 ff.
[31] *Pol.* 1315b.18 ff.   [32] *NH* xxxvi.9.
[33] See Payne, *Necrocorinthia: a Study of Corinthian Art in the Archaic Period* (Oxford, 1931), Ch. iv.

Attic.[34] The exceptions are a number of red-figure squat lekythoi of fourth-century date, which their excavator thought might be local imitations of Attic work.[35] Athenaios refers to a type of one-handled cup called a *kotylos* which was common at Sikyon and Taras,[36] but without actually stating that it was made in these places. On present showing, therefore, archaic Sikyonian pottery-production, if it existed at all, must either have been confined to coarse wares or have imitated imported wares — especially, one would suppose, Korinthian.

Several inscriptions on vases in the Sikyonian alphabet are known, but none provides sufficient proof that the vase which bears it was made in Sikyon. In one case at least, that of the *dinos* by Exekias,[37] it certainly was not; since the inscription is a graffito, added after firing, it was not necessarily put on the vase at the time of its manufacture, and even if it was, it can be explained as a special commission, for which Exekias copied a text supplied by the customer.[38] There are several sherds from Perachora which bear inscriptions in the Sikyonian alphabet, but all of these are graffiti, and those of which enough survives to make sense are dedicatory; hence it is probable that they were added at the time of dedication, and so indicate only that the dedicator was Sikyonian. The fifth-century sherds have been identified as Attic, and there is no reason why the sixth-century ones should not be of non-Sikyonian origin too.[39] Another sherd with a graffito in Sikyonian script, probably of sixth-century date, comes from the Kerameikos at Korinth.[40] In view of its provenance, it is to be assumed that the vase was made at Korinth, but the inscription is interesting as showing that Sikyonians frequented the Korinthian Kerameikos, whether as workers or as customers. The remaining

---

[34] The pottery in the Sikyon Museum is largely unpublished, and includes Corinthian and Attic black- and red-figure. Some is from Pitsa, not from Sikyon itself. There are several pieces of Protocorinthian and Corinthian in Leiden and Bologna which are said to come from Sikyon (recorded in the catalogues of Brants and Pellegrini respectively), but the provenance appears unreliable in some cases. The only vase from Sikyon which has attracted a substantial bibliography is the Lakonian kylix, London B3 (*AZ* xxxix (1881), Pl. 13, 1; *BMCat.* ii, 50; E. A. Lane, 'Lakonian vase-painting', *BSA* xxxiv (1933–4), 150, No. 3, 160, Pl. 46a; B. B. Shefton, 'Three Laconian vase-painters', *BSA* xlix (1954), 302, No. 23, Pl. 51d; C. M. Stibbe, *Lakonischen Vasenmaler des Sechsten Jahrhunderts Vor Chr.* (Amsterdam, 1972), No. 308).

[35] *PAE* 1936, p. 91 f.

[36] Athen. xi.478b, quoting Diodoros, ἐν τῷ πρὸς Λυκόφρονα.

[37] *LSAG* 143, No. 5 and bibliography. The donor's inscription is in Sikyonian script, the signature of Exekias in his normal Attic, but so far as comparison is possible the same hand could have written both.

[38] See T. B. L. Webster, *Potter and Patron in Classical Athens*, 45.

[39] 6th-century sherds, *Perachora*, ii, 398, Nos. 99–101, 103 (all kotyle fragments); 5th-century sherds, ibid., 398, Nos. 113–15.

[40] KP 1400.

two known vase-inscriptions in the Sikyonian alphabet[41] are rather more important, since they are painted, and therefore suggest that Sikyonians were engaged in the pottery industry. On the Late Corinthian krater, at least (the aryballos is too fragmentary to be certain), the inscriptions give the names of the figures in the main scene, a quite common practice on Corinthian vases, so there is no reason to believe that this is another case of a special commission like the Exekias *dinos*. The obvious explanation for the existence of these two inscriptions is that the vases were painted by Sikyonians who used their native alphabet as a matter of course; but this is not to say that they were working at Sikyon rather than at Korinth.

Literary evidence for a Sikyonian pottery industry hardly exists, being confined to the story of Boutades, the supposed inventor of clay-modelling.[42] Although described by Pliny as a Sikyonian, Boutades is closely associated with Korinth by Pliny's statement that he worked there, by the fact that his original clay model was supposed to have been pre-served there until the destruction of the city by Mummius, and by his alleged invention of human-head antefixes, which are found among the architectural terracottas from Thermon, Kalydon, and Korkyra, being apparently either actual imports from Korinth or local imitations of Korinthian work.[43] An alternative version of the invention of this craft is given by Athenagoras,[44] who tells a similar story to Pliny's, but makes its chief characters a Korinthian maiden and her (nameless) father. If Boutades is to be regarded as a historical character at all, therefore, Korinth has a better claim than Sikyon to have been his place of work; and if, as is perhaps more likely, he was a fictitious 'inventor', the fact that he was said to have been Sikyonian proves only that Sikyon claimed to have been the original home of the art of modelling — a claim which was evidently dis-puted by Korinth. Pliny's statement that he was a Sikyonian working at Korinth may simply represent an attempt to reconcile the rival claims of the two cities.

Many archaic and later architectural terracottas have been found at Sikyon,[45] and are for the most part closely paralleled by specimens from Korinth, so there is no reason to believe that they were made on the spot rather than imported from the neighbouring city. The only terracotta figurines so far reported from the site are from a grave dated in the fourth or third century BC.[46] Among the figurines from the Kerameikos at

---

[41] LPC aryballos fragment, *LSAG* 143, No. 1; LC krater, *LSAG* 143, No. 4.
[42] Pliny, *NH* xxxv.151-2.
[43] *NC* 253 ff.   [44] *Leg. pro Christ*, 17.3.
[45] e.g. those from the archaic temple mentioned above, and a number of light-on-dark simas (*ADelt* x (1926) 48–50, *BCH* 1 (1926), 180 f., and several unpublished), also a number of other antefixes and ridge-palmettes (unpublished).
[46] *PAE* 1932, p. 75 f., Fig. 15 – from a grave near Moulki.

Korinth, however, there are several specimens of *korai* with 'Sikyonian' vertical folds in the skirt. One type which particularly resembles the mirror-caryatids in its pose is dated to the third quarter of the fifth century — slightly later than the latest 'Sikyonian' mirrors.[47] Terracottas of this and similar types have also been found at Pitsa, Tiryns, and Olynthos, and at a small sanctuary near Thermon in Aitolia, where some were apparently Korinthian imports and others local imitations, judging by the colour of the clay, and where there was also found a fragmentary inscription in which the distinctive Sikyonian *epsilon* occurs.[48] It can hardly be doubted that the terracottas found in the Korinthian Kerameikos were made there, so again we must either postulate immigrant Sikyonian craftsmen or accept that objects of 'Sikyonian' style were in fact Korinthian products.

I have already mentioned a number of Sikyonian inscriptions on sherds and other objects. The Sikyonian alphabet is easily recognized by its distinctive X form of *epsilon*, which appears to have continued in use until about the middle of the fifth century.[49] Inscriptions from Sikyonia itself are relatively few in number, the most important being a bronze plaque bearing the rules of an association and a list of seventy-three members, dated *c*. 500 BC.[50] Fifth-century inscriptions show the gradual disappearance of the local alphabet, with the sibilant *san* (M) being replaced by *sigma* and X by E. Several of these inscriptions have lozenge-shaped *theta* and *omikron*, which appears to be a Sikyonian peculiarity.

The distinctive alphabet enables us to recognize as Sikyonian inscriptions found in other areas of Greece, such as those already mentioned from Perachora. One of the earliest, judging by its appearance, is a graffito from Delphi, which reads MXየYFONIIOM. It may have been made by a mason working on the site or by a casual visitor, and if it is as old as it looks it may be evidence of Sikyonian activity at Delphi before the time of Kleisthenes.[51] From Olympia, besides the fragmentary plaque already

---

[47] *Corinth*, xv.2, 84 ff. Class X — esp. No. 4.

[48] *EAA* vi, 203, Fig. 223 right; *Tiryns*, i, Pl. viii, 1–3; *Olynthus*, vii, Pl. 19, No. 157; *ADelt* vi (1920–1), 69 ff., Figs. 4–6. Inscription, *ADelt* vi (1920–1), 65 ff., Fig. 2, *LSAG* 144, No. 19; but M. Lejeune, 'En marge d'inscriptions grecques dialectales', *REA* xlvii (1945), 111 ff. considers the alphabet of the inscription Aitolian, in which case the form of *epsilon* might be due to independent development. *LSAG* suggests a 6th-century date for the inscription — earlier than the terracottas, therefore.

[49] See *LSAG* 138 ff. for a description of the Sikyonian alphabet and catalogue of inscriptions.

[50] Athens 16355, from Tzami in Sikyonia. Ἑλληνικά, x (1937–8), 5 ff., Fig. 1; *AM* lxvi (1941), 200 ff.; *REA* xlv (1943), 185 ff.; *SEG* xi, No. 244; Buck, *Greek Dialects*, No. 96; *LSAG* 143, No. 8, Pl. 23.

[51] *LSAG* 143, No. 2, Pl. 23, date and origin discussed, 140. The block which bears it does not belong to either the 'Monopteros' or the Tholos. It has been suggested that it comes from the temple burnt down in 548 (Daux, *BCH* lxi (1937), 60 n. 1).

mentioned, come masons' marks and other inscriptions on the Sikyonian Treasury, and a number of dedications.[52]

The exact date at which Sikyon began to issue coins is uncertain, but it seems likely to have been around or before 500 BC, since the earliest types have *san* as the initial letter of the city's name. Some coins, which perhaps date from the middle of the fifth century, have *san* on the reverse, but on the obverse a dove and the initial letters ΣΕ of the city's name (*sigma* and ordinary *epsilon*).[53] By the time these coins were issued, therefore, the local alphabet had gone out of normal use, though *san* could still be used as an emblem.

B. Myron's Thalamoi

Pausanias thus describes two bronze *thalamoi* dedicated by Myron, tyrant of Sikyon, at Olympia:[1]

There is a treasury at Olympia called 'the Sikyonians'', a dedication of Myron when he was tyrant of the Sikyonians. Myron built this after winning the chariot-race at the thirty-third Olympiad. In the treasury he also made two *thalamoi*, one Doric, the other of the Ionic order. I saw them, made of bronze; but whether it is Tartessian bronze as the Eleians say, I do not know . . . [here follows a digression on Tartessos] . . . At Olympia there are inscriptions on the smaller of the *thalamoi*, about the weight of the bronze, that it is five hundred talents, and about the dedicators, that they were Myron and the *demos* of the Sikyonians.

It is not, perhaps, entirely clear from Pausanias' account what kind of objects these *thalamoi* were; the excavations at Olympia have revealed no recognizable trace of them, and have shown that Pausanias made at least one major error of fact — in ascribing the building of the treasury to Myron. The date arrived at for the treasury is in the second quarter of the fifth century BC, if not later,[2] over a century and a half after Myron's victory, which Pausanias dates in 648 BC. Pausanias apparently took the dedicatory inscription as referring not only to the *thalamoi* but to the treasury as well — a type of misinterpretation which has been detected elewhere in his work.[3] However, remains of an earlier building have been detected beneath the existing Sikyonian treasury, which could belong

---

[52] *LSAG* 143, No. 12, 15a-b, n.1; 144, No. 21; Pl. 23.

[53] *LSAG* 142 and 143, No. 17. The coinage of Sikyon is being studied in detail by Mrs J. Cargill-Thompson (brief summary in *Num. Chron.* 1968, *Proc.* x; also in C. M. Kraay, *Archaic and Classical Greek Coins* (London, 1976), 96 ff.)

[1] Paus. vi.19.1-4.

[2] *Olympia*, ii, 43.

[3] e.g. x.11.6, where the building of the Athenian Stoa at Delphi is dated some time after 429 BC, because spoils from Phormio's naval victories of that year were dedicated in it.

to 'Myron's treasury'.[4] An important negative conclusion about the *thalamoi* can be drawn from the archaeological evidence — that, since they were of earlier date than the building which eventually housed them and have left no visible traces upon its members, they cannot have formed an integral part of its structure. This conclusion is of some significance in determining the likely nature of these objects.

In Homer, the fundamental notion of a *thalamos* appears to be that it is a room of a particularly private and secure kind — either a bedroom, whether of a married couple or of a single person, or a storeroom.[5] On the few occasions, apart from the passage under discussion, when Pausanias uses the term, it is a Homeric sense — thus, a priestess and her lover 'used the temple as a *thalamos*', obviously in the sense 'bridal chamber'; near Tiryns, Pausanias saw the *thalamoi* of the daughters of Proitos, and at Argos, the foundation of the bronze *thalamos* which Akrisios built for Danae, the structure itself having long since disappeared.[6] This latter building is particularly interesting for comparison with Myron's *thalamoi*, since it was of the same material, and because of its mythological importance it is mentioned by several other authors. What Pausanias saw was an underground chamber, on top of which, according to him, the bronze *thalamos* had stood. This scheme is more in accordance with Horace's description of Danae's prison as a brazen tower than with that given by other authors, who make it an underground chamber.[7] Obviously, in the latter case the *thalamos* could only be thought of as having the interior of its walls lined with bronze, whereas if it stood above ground it could have been regarded either as a structure entirely of bronze, or as having the walls faced with bronze inside or outside or both.

There is a certain amount of literary and archaeological evidence for the existence in archaic Greece of buildings wholly or partly decorated with bronze. The most famous of these was the sanctuary of Athena Chalkioikos at Sparta, which was decorated with bronze reliefs of mythological subjects, described by Pausanias — unfortunately leaving their location so vague that it has been argued that the decoration was on the cult-statue

---

[4] *Olympia*, ii, 41 (a roof-tile); C. Weickert, *Typen der archaischen Architektur in Griechenland und Kleinasien* (Augsburg, 1929), 88 n. 1 (remains of foundations, dated contemporary with the Heraion); H. V. Herrmann, *Olympia: Heiligtum und Wettkampfstätte* (Munich, 1972), 99 f. (dated later than the mid-7th century, hence considered too late to have been built by Myron).

[5] e.g. *Il.* vi.243–50 (of Priam's children and their wives and husbands), *Od.* i.425 (of Telemachos), *Il.* xxiv.191 (storeroom).

[6] Paus. vii.19.3, ii.25.9, ii.23.7.

[7] Hor. *Odes* iii.16.1; Soph. *Ant.* 944 f. . . . . ἐν χαλκοδέτοις αὐλαῖς . . . ἐν τυμβήρει θαλάμῳ; Apollod. ii.4.1 ὑπὸ γῆν; Pherekydes, *FGH* 3, F 10, κατὰ γῆς.

rather than the building.[8] Pausanias also mentions the tradition that the third temple of Apollo at Delphi was built of bronze, adducing as evidence for the probability of this the existence of Danae's *thalamos*, the Chalkioikos, and the bronze roof of the Forum at Rome.[9] Elsewhere he refers to this bronze roof as a particularly noteworthy feature of Trajan's Forum, but does not explain how it was constructed.[10] Bronze plates, with nails for attachment, have been found on the Chalkioikos site, and evidently come from the walls of the building, though there is no trace of relief decoration such as Pausanias describes;[11] some bronze reliefs recently found at Kyrene may come from a similar structure.[12] At Sparta again, a gorgoneion and a lion *protome* found in the portico between the Chalkioikos and the theatre may have been hung on the wall, but as individual decorative plaques rather than as parts of a complete bronze facing.[13] From Olympia itself come a number of bronze reliefs which may have been used to decorate buildings, though some, on account of their size, are more likely to have been attached to pieces of furniture.[14] A fragmentary bronze relief in Boston, bought at Xylokastro and so possibly from Sikyon itself, may also come from a piece of furniture.[15]

It should be noted that in all these cases bronze is used only in the form of plaques to decorate buildings constructed of other materials, and that there is no question of an all-bronze structure. It seems reasonable, therefore, to suppose that Danae's *thalamos* and the third temple at Delphi were similarly merely faced with bronze. But any attempt to reduce Myron's *thalamoi* to structures of this kind runs into difficulties. One might imagine that what Myron did was to build a treasury of stone or wood, with two rooms inside, and to cover the walls of these with bronze reliefs of an architectural nature. However, this interpretation is excluded by the surviving remains of the Sikyonian treasury; not only do its wall-

---

. [8] Imhoof-Blumer and Gardner, *NCP* 58; however, both the archaeological evidence and Pausanias' reference at x.5.11 show that it was in fact the building which was so decorated.

[9] Paus. x.5.11.

[10] Paus. v.12.6; see Hitzig-Blümner, ad loc.

[11] *BSA* xiii (1906-7), 139 f.

[12] *Libya Antiqua*, iii–iv (1966-7), 196 f., Pl. lxxii.

[13] *BSA* xxvi (1923-5), 266 f., Pl. xxi.

[14] *Olympiabericht*, i, 93 f., Fig. 43 (bronze strip with double-volute pattern, possibly from a sima). The she-griffin (ibid., 90 f., Pls. 34-5) is considered to be from a chest or similar object; however, P. Verzone, 'Il bronzo nella genesi dei tempio greco', *Studies presented to D. M. Robinson*, i, 290, suggests that with the addition of a fairly wide border it could have formed a metope of the Heraion.

[15] Boston 98.652. Robinson, *Ann. Rep.* 1898, 24 f.; *AA* 1899, 136; J. Addison, *Boston Museum of Fine Arts* (Boston, 1910), 295; Comstock and Vermeule, *Bronzes in Boston*, 450 f., No. 660. The preserved width, about half the total if the composition was symmetrical, is 0.172 m.

blocks bear no trace of nail-holes or other marks such as the attachment of bronze plaques would leave, but the presence of a Doric cornice running round the top of the *cella* walls on the inside excludes the possibility that the interior was divided into two compartments, one Doric and one Ionic.[16] Furthermore, it would have been extremely difficult to transfer such a decoration from the old treasury to the new without causing considerable loss and damage.

We must therefore assume that Myron's *thalamoi* were free-standing structures, which could survive removal from one building to another. One unusual feature of the Sikyonian Treasury which gives colour to this suggestion is the presence of an unusually substantial floor-foundation in the rear half of the *cella* — plainly intended to support some heavy object.[17] Pausanias records that the inscription on the smaller *thalamos* gave the weight of the bronze as five hundred talents; this has been assessed as anything from thirteen to twenty-five tons, and it is disputed whether the weight given is that of both *thalamoi* or only the smaller,[18] but even on the lowest estimate it is clear that a considerable weight was involved. This raises a further question concerning the method of construction — whether so much bronze (whatever the exact amount) could have been used up in covering a wooden structure, or whether the *thalamoi* were made entirely of bronze. In this case, the technical difficulties of construction would have been considerable.

From Pausanias' description, it must be assumed that the *thalamoi* were given a sufficiently architectural form to be identifiable as belonging to certain orders — in fact, that they were something like temple-models, perhaps with two columns *in antis* with Doric and Ionic capitals respectively. In view of the fact that Homer and Pausanias use *thalamos* to mean a room of some kind, Myron's *thalamoi* should perhaps have conformed to this description to the extent of being large enough for a man to stand inside. The strengthened area of the treasury floor is large enough to have accommodated two such objects.

Once the likely nature of the *thalamoi* has been established, the question arises whether it is credible that such objects were dedicated at the date which Pausanias assigns to them. The *terminus post quem* is 648, the year of Myron's victory, and the dedication should have been made well before the end of the seventh century to come within Myron's lifetime. An alternative, which would call for a date *c.* 600 for the dedication, is that it was made by Myron II, who was probably the grandson of the Olympic victor. This view

---

[16] *Olympia*, ii, 42.　　　　　　　　　　[17] *Olympia*, ii, 43 f.
[18] Levi on Paus. vi.19.1 ff. suggests 25 tons; *Olympia*, ii, 43, f. suggests 13. Both take the inscription as referring to the smaller *thalamos* only. Weights found at Olympia suggest that the smaller figure is more nearly correct.

is particularly attractive because of the possibility that the second dedicator was not the Sikyonian *demos*, as Pausanias says, but Isodamos, Myron II's brother.[19] A later date does not seem possible, however, unless Pausanias was totally wrong about the dedicator's name.

If the *thalamoi* were constructed by hammering bronze sheets over a wooden core, there is no particular difficulty in dating them to the late seventh century — such a method of construction would only be a large-scale application of the *sphyrelaton* technique of statuary which was already in use in Greece at this time. It is less likely that an all–bronze structure, which would have involved some fairly complicated casting operations, could have been produced at this time. However, the real difficulty arises from the architectural form of the *thalamoi*. In the second half of the seventh century BC the Greek orders were still in a relatively early stage of development, and the design of the *thalamoi* is unlikely to have been more advanced than that of contemporary buildings; hence it is likely that they did not exemplify what later came to be the canonical forms of the orders, but had sufficient distinguishing features to justify Pausanias in assigning them to their respective orders — perhaps the triglyph frieze in the case of the Doric *thalamos*, and the volute capital in the case of the Ionic. Recognizably Doric buildings begin to appear in Greece towards the end of the seventh century, for instance at Thermon, and the Heraion at Olympia itself comes a little later; the construction of the Doric *thalamos* at this date therefore appears quite possible. However, there is more difficulty about the Ionic one, since the distinctive features of the Ionic order, including the volute capital, did not certainly begin to appear until about 600, and were not transmitted from East Greece to the mainland until some time after that.[20] This difficulty may be overcome by taking the Doric *thalamos* alone as Myron's dedication, identifying it as the one which bore the inscription, and making this refer only to the one *thalamos*. (Since Pausanias does not quote the inscription verbatim, it is impossible to tell how much information he derived from it and how much he merely assumed.) The Ionic *thalamos* could then be taken as a dedication of later date, and perhaps not of Sikyonian origin — Pausanias records that other non-Sikyonian objects were kept in the Treasury.[21] A possible Sikyonian dedicator is Kleisthenes, who won the Olympic chariot-race, and might have chosen to recall Myron's victory by making a similar dedication. The most probable date for Kleisthenes' victory is 576, and he is unlikely to have lived more than ten years longer;[22] a victory-dedication

[19] See p. 42.

[20] The 'proto-Ionic' capitals from Larissa and Neandria are dated *c.* 600 BC (A. W. Lawrence, *Greek Architecture*, 3rd edn. (Harmondsworth, 1973), 130 f.)

[21] e.g. Paus. vi.19.6 — the ivory horn of Amaltheia dedicated by Miltiades.

[22] See p. 57.

by him would therefore have to date from the late 570s or early 560s. Even this date is a little early for the appearance of Ionic forms on the mainland, as seen in such works as the Naxian Sphinx, but it is possible that Kleisthenes saw some very early Ionic structure at Delphi, a sanctuary with which he had close connections, and chose to imitate it in a *thalamos*. In any case, the Ionic *thalamos* must pre-date the construction of the present Sikyonian Treasury, since this was designed to contain the two.

C. The Sikyonian buildings at Delphi

When Pausanias visited Delphi, the first treasury which he came to on his ascent of the Sacred Way was that of Sikyon. On the basis of this information, the Sikyonian Treasury can confidently be located on the foundation III, which is precisely the first treasury-foundation now visible. Very little remains of the superstructure of the Treasury which Pausanias saw,[1] and the chief interest of the building lies in the foundation, which contains reused material from two other buildings — one rectangular and one round. Various attempts have been made to reconstruct these buildings and to establish whether they too were erected by the Sikyonians.[2] It is desirable that the latter question should be settled, because both buildings are of some artistic significance — the round one as being an early specimen of its kind, the rectangular one for its sculptured metopes. Their likely date is such that, if of Sikyonian origin, they should be associated with Kleisthenes.

Pomtow believed that the round building (Tholos) had originally stood on the site now occupied by the Sikyonian Treasury, and that almost all its masonry could be found reused in the Treasury foundations. The reconstruction which he eventually arrived at was that of a small *cella* with a peristyle of thirteen Doric columns and, above, a frieze of twenty triglyphs and metopes, which were necessarily arranged irregularly in relation to the columns. This reconstruction is still generally accepted, and the curious (and, one would imagine, unattractive) arrangement of the triglyphs is taken as evidence that at the time of its construction a round building was something new, posing problems of design which were not altogether successfully solved in this instance.[3] Stylistically, the Tholos belongs in the early sixth century; the tall, slender columns, relatively widely spaced, with their wide flatly curving capitals, the absence of guttae

---

[1] Paus. x.11.1. The remains of the later Treasury discussed by Pomtow, *Zeitschr. f. Gesch. d. Architektur*, iii (1910), 127–40.

[2] Pomtow, ibid., 97–127; iv (1911), 171–214 (cf. *Delphica*, ii, 67, = *Berl. Phil. Woch.* 1909, p. 350); *BCH* xlvi (1922), 510; La Coste-Messelière, *Au Musée de Delphes*, 42 ff.

[3] For architectural oddity in early round buildings, cf. the funerary building in the Athenian Kerameikos (*AA* 1969, 31 ff.) with its mixture of Doric and Ionic forms.

from the mutules and regulae, and the unequal width of the mutules, those over the metopes being narrower than those over the triglyphs, all place the building at an early stage in the development of Greek architecture in stone.

The exact nature of the rectangular building has been the subject of rather more dispute; relatively few pieces of it have been identified, and Pomtow originally thought that it might have been a small entrance-hall attached to the Tholos. He later abandoned this view, and acknowledged the existence of a separate 'Rechteckbau' which he reconstructed as having four Doric columns prostyle. The material reused in the Sikyonian Treasury foundation was, he believed, derived only from the *pronaos* of this, since he found stylobate blocks, column-shafts and capitals, and pieces from the entablature above the columns (including, of course, the sculptured metopes), but no wall-blocks or other pieces which could be identified as coming from the *cella*. The latter, he supposed, had either been reused in the superstructure of the new Treasury, or had not been used by the Sikyonians at all. There are still no wall-blocks which are certainly known to belong to this building, though more pieces of the architrave have been found, and for this reason an alternative reconstruction has been put forward which would make it a 'Monopteros', that is, a rectangular structure of fourteen columns supporting a roof, with no *cella*. Such a structure would be unparalleled in Greek architecture, and the correctness of the reconstruction has therefore been questioned.[4] The 'Monopteros' appears to be of slightly later date than the Tholos, but still belongs to the first half of the sixth century BC. Pomtow found it impossible to distinguish the columns and capitals of the two buildings, and other early features of the 'Monopteros' are the absence of triglyphs over the intercolumniations, as a result of which the metopes are unusually broad in proportion to their height, and the unequal length of the mutules over triglyph and metope. There are, however, guttae on the mutules and regulae, so in this respect the 'Monopteros' represents a more advanced stage of development than the Tholos towards the canonical Doric order. On stylistic grounds, the metopes are commonly dated in the second rather than the first quarter of the sixth century BC;[5] hence we arrive at a date *c.* 560 for the 'Monopteros' and, allowing twenty years as a reasonable interval

---

[4] The word 'Monopteros' is in fact a modern coinage to describe this building. La Coste–Messelière, 42 ff. claims that the architrave blocks all have smooth lower surfaces, showing that they rested on columns, not on a wall. In that case, reconstruction as a prostyle building is excluded, and a *cella* within a peristyle of the required dimensions would be hopelessly small, so the 'Monopteros' form is arrived at by elimination. But W. B. Dinsmoor, *Architecture of Ancient Greece*, 3rd edn. (London, 1950), 116 f. retains the reconstruction as a tetrastyle prostyle building.

[5] Pomtow, *Zeitschr.* iii (1910), 115 f.; La Coste–Messelière, 54.

for the requisite architectural developments to take place, one *c.* 580 for the Tholos.

Obviously these dates bring the buildings, if they are of Sikyonian origin, into close association with Kleisthenes; the construction of the Tholos falls in the aftermath of the Sacred War and, in particular, about the time of Kleisthenes' chariot-victory at the Pythian Games of 582. Since he died *c.* 565, the 'Monopteros' may have been built during the reign of his successor, but planned by Kleisthenes. Discussions of the possible connections of the buildings with Kleisthenes are, however, in some danger of becoming circular; the dating of them, in particular, may be unduly influenced by the desire to place their construction during Kleisthenes' reign.[6] In view of Kleisthenes' interest in Delphi, it is quite likely that he engaged in building at the sanctuary, but in the absence of dedicatory inscriptions or other direct evidence it cannot simply be assumed that he was responsible for the Tholos and 'Monopteros'.

In fact, it cannot be shown conclusively that the Tholos and 'Monopteros' were Sikyonian buildings at all. Since neither dedicatory inscriptions nor literary descriptions of them exist, the only evidence for their origin is indirect. The most obvious argument for their being Sikyonian is the fact that material from them was reused in the later Sikyonian Treasury. To make this possible, the Sikyonians must either have owned the material already or have been given it by some other state or states to which it belonged. A complicating factor is the question which, if either, of the buildings stood on the later Treasury site.[7] One view is that both stood in the area later occupied by the Alkmaionid temple, in which case they must have had a relatively short life, and have been demolished in the latter part of the sixth century when the Alkmaionid temple was built. The absence of weathering on the metopes of the 'Monopteros' suggests that these were not long above ground, either in position on the building or, still less, lying loose in its ruins.[8] Their re-use and burial must therefore have

---

[6] A particularly blatant case occurs in Pomtow, *Zeitschr.* iv (1911), 213 f., where the 'Rechteckbau', regarded as Kleisthenes' Treasury, is dated *c.* 580–572, and the Tholos *c.* 600 – this despite his previous acceptance of a rather later date for the metopes.

[7] Pomtow, *Zeitschr.* iii (1910), 122 argued that the Tholos stood here but not the 'Rechteckbau'; however, he also (ibid., 125 f., *Zeitschr.* iv (1911), 213) took the view that the Tholos was built not by the Sikyonians but by the Amphiktyons or Delphians, and that the 'Rechteckbau' was Kleisthenes' Treasury. La Coste-Messelière, 63 ff. quotes Daux on the absence of earlier foundations under the existing Treasury, and places both building in the Alkmaionid temple area.

[8] E. Bourguet, *Les Ruines de Delphes* (Paris, 1914), 61 remarks that at the time of excavation the metopes retained much of their original paint. La Coste-Messelière, 61 ff. compares their condition with that of the poros sculptures from the west pediment of the Alkmaionid temple, which remained *in situ* from the late 6th century to 373, and are badly weathered.

taken place not long after the destruction of the 'Monopteros', so if the latter was demolished to make way for the Alkmaionid temple the new Sikyonian Treasury must have been built *c.* 500. Unfortunately the date of the later Treasury is very doubtful, and has been placed well down in the fourth century BC.[9] Hence neither the original location of the Tholos and 'Monopteros' nor the date of their destruction can be considered at all certain, and no proof of their Sikyonian origin can be derived from such doubtful evidence.

The principal rival suggestion about the origins of the 'Monopteros' is that of Dinsmoor, who restored it as a prostyle tetrastyle building and regarded it as an archaic Syracusan treasury. The Syracusan Treasury which Pausanias saw was built after the defeat of the Athenian expedition in 413; Dinsmoor placed both it and its predecessor on the foundation V, on the other side of the Sacred Way from the Siphnian Treasury and hence quite close to the Sikyonian site, and suggested that when the Syracusans demolished their old treasury to make way for the new one they gave the materials to the Sikyonians, perhaps out of gratitude for Sikyonian help in the defence of Syracuse.[10] However, both the placing of the Syracusan Treasury on the foundation V and the suggestion that an archaic Syracusan Treasury existed at all have been disputed.[11] Dinsmoor also argued for the Syracusan origin of the 'Monopteros' on technical and stylistic grounds — thus the L-shaped section of the architrave blocks and the frieze with triglyphs above the columns only are both said to be paralleled in the temple of Apollo at Syracuse, and the closest parallels to the metopes in subject-matter and style are found at Selinous.[12] These arguments too have been disputed; the reconstruction of the temple at Syracuse is highly debatable, and the comparison of the metopes with those from Selinous reveals as many differences as similarities.[13] If the attribution of the 'Monopteros' to Syracuse is rejected, Sikyon is left as the most likely

[9] In the absence of remains from the superstructure of the Treasury, its date has to be determined from technical details of the foundations, such as the thickness of the orthostates. On these grounds Pomtow, *Zeitschr.*, iii (1910), 135–8 dates the new Treasury in the 4th century, and follows T. Homolle, *FdD* iv *Monuments figurés: Sculpture* 1 (Paris, 1909), p. 22 in attributing the destruction of the Tholos and 'Monopteros' to the earthquake of 373. W. B. Dinsmoor, 'Studies of the Delphian treasuries', *BCH* xxxvi (1912), dates it *c.* 400, and La Coste–Messelière, 57 ff. defends a date *c.* 500.

[10] Dinsmoor, *BCH* xxxvi (1912), 460 ff.; Sikyonians at Syracuse, Thuc. vii.19.4. There seems no reason why the Syracusans should have been especially grateful to them.

[11] La Coste–Messelière, 21 ff.

[12] *BCH* xxxvi (1912), 472 f.; cf. Homolle, *FdD* iv.1, pp. 36 f. for comparison with the metopes of Selinous Temple C.

[13] La Coste–Messelière, 31 ff. and 210 ff.; a different reconstruction of the Syracuse temple, *Mon. Ant.* xli (1951), col. 824, Figs. 93 and 101.

place of origin, since there is no positive evidence to associate the building with any other state.

The ascription of the Tholos to Sikyon has not given rise to so much argument either for or against, perhaps because despite its architectural oddities it lacks features of such outstanding artistic significance as the 'Monopteros' metopes, which it is considered important to assign to a local school. There is no particular reason against the Tholos being a Sikyonian building, though the only positive evidence that it was is the re-use of its materials in the later Treasury.

The material of both buildings is consistent with their being of Sikyonian origin, since it is poros of a type common in the Peloponnese, including the area around Korinth and Sikyon. The later Treasury at Delphi and the Sikyonian Treasury at Olympia were built of similar stone, which is rather different from the material of other poros buildings at Olympia, and therefore is generally considered to have been imported from Sikyonia. The 'Monopteros' metopes are made of a finer type of poros, which is also found in the Korinth-Sikyon area.[14]

The dating of the 'Monopteros' is based principally on the style of the metopes and the comparison of them with other reliefs of the same period, especially the metopes of Temple C at Selinous.[15] Despite their relative freedom from weathering, the 'Monopteros' metopes have suffered much breakage (in particular, the faces of the figures are almost entirely lost), so comparison has to be that of over-all composition rather than of details. Here the uniqueness of some of the subjects is a disadvantage; the 'Cattle-raid', for instance, has no close parallels in sculpture or any other art. The Argo is likewise an unusual subject, and appears to have been treated in an unusual manner, as a single composition covering two metopes, one showing each end of the ship, with the central part thought of as being covered by the intervening triglyph.[16] Here, however, it is possible to compare the frontal horses of the Dioskouroi with those of the *quadriga* on one of the Selinous

[14] Pomtow, *Zeitschr. f. Gesch. d. Architektur*, iii (1910), 130 ff., La Coste-Messelière, 54 ff. (cf. *Olympia*, ii, 41, where it is wrongly identified as sandstone). Poros of metopes, *Au Musée de Delphes*, 97 ff.

[15] e.g. Homolle, *FdD* iv.1, pp. 34 ff. However, G. M. A. Richter, *Sculpture and Sculptors of the Greeks*, 4th edn. (New Haven, 1970), 250 dates the Selinous metopes c. 540, chiefly on the style of the drapery, while leaving the Sikyonian ones c. 575–560 − in contrast to Homolle's opinion that the latter are slightly more advanced in style than the former. E. Langlotz, *The Art of Magna Graecia* (London, 1965), 255 dates the Selinous metopes c. 530.

[16] This is the simplest explanation for the existence of a fragment (La Coste-Messelière's F) showing part of a ship of similar appearance to the Argo, but which will not fit into the Argo metope. This treatment is reminiscent of the 'porthole' composition used by the Spartan Hunt Painter for tondi − similarly, the 'Cattle-raid' metope (where the hindquarters of the rearmost animals were apparently cut off by

metopes, and with those in various vase-paintings. The Kalydonian Boar is another subject which may have formed part of a scene extending over several metopes; the surviving piece shows only the Boar itself, so the hunters may have appeared in the metopes on either side.[17] Parallels for this subject are to be found in vase-painting rather than sculpture. Europa and the Bull also appear on a metope from Selinous (not from Temple C, but from an earlier series); given that the basic scheme of the girl sitting on the bull's back is the same, the differences between the two are more striking than the similarities. The Ram metope is very fragmentary, so that it is not even certain whether the rider was male (Phrixos) or female (Helle). In either case, it is a rare subject.

The choice of subjects for the metopes of a building which may have been commissioned by Kleisthenes of Sikyon is interesting, because Kleisthenes is known to have conducted a form of cultural warfare in which he banned the recitation of epics which in his opinion excessively glorified Argos,[18] and may therefore have attempted to suppress the representation of 'Argive' subjects in sculpture too. Certainly the Trojan and Theban Cycles, which were contained in the offending epics, are absent from the surviving metopes. Two of these, the Ram and the Argo, represent episodes in the story of the Golden Fleece; the Dioskouroi appear in the Argo metope and again in the 'Cattle-raid', and were perhaps also shown among the hunters of the Boar, while the Apharidai, who survive only in the 'Cattle-raid', also figure in lists of the Argonauts and the Boar-hunters,[19] and perhaps appeared in lost parts of the appropriate metopes. Thus some unity of subject-matter can be seen or postulated between four of the metopes, but Europa appears to have no connection with the other figures. Nor do any of the subjects appear especially 'Sikyonian', though all of them can be shown to have at least a remote connection with the place.[20] It is not, therefore, legitimate to interpret the metopes as embodying an attempt by Kleisthenes to promote 'Sikyonian' mythological subjects in opposition to the 'Argive' ones which he found so objectionable.

---

the edge of the metope) is closely paralleled by his treatment of a processional scene in a tondo, Berlin 3404 (Stibbe, *Lakonische Vasenmaler*, Pl. 74.1, dated *c.* 560–550); the similarities and differences noted by La Coste–Messelière, 205.

[17] Idem, 115 ff.

[18] Hdt. v.67.1.

[19] Apollod. *Bibl.* i.8.2 (Boar-hunt), i.9.16 (Argonauts). His lists have several other names in common – e.g. Meleager, Atalanta, Theseus, Admetos, Jason, Peleus, Telamon, Amphiaraos. But the Apharidai do not appear among the hunters on the François Vase, which La Coste–Messelière (130 ff.) considered a close parallel to his reconstruction of the hunt scene on the metopes.

[20] The Dioskouroi were worshipped at Sikyon (Paus. ii.7.5), and the 5th-century Sikyonian poetess Praxilla made Europa the mother of Karneus (fr. 7 Page, = Paus. iii.13.5), perhaps on the basis of some local tradition about her.

D. Dipoinos and Skyllis

Dipoinos and Skyllis stand rather awkwardly on the borderline between myth and history — works and pupils of theirs are named, they are given at least an approximate date and some biographical details, in the face of which we can hardly doubt that they really existed, but they are made into the pupils or sons of Daidalos, and much of the information about them proves to be anything but solid. Pliny puts them among the marble-sculptors, calling them the first to distinguish themselves in the use of this material[1] (though this claim is rivalled by that of the Chiot school, which immediately follows in Pliny's account). The source for his section on Dipoinos and Skyllis may have been Xenokrates, and in any case was favourable to Sikyon's claims to have been a major artistic centre from a very early date — 'quae diu fuit officinarum omnium talium patria'. The suggestion seems to be that the Kretan sculptors migrated to Sikyon of their own accord, attracted by the artistic reputation of the place, rather than that the Sikyonians sent for them because they were already established as important artists. Once there, Pliny's narrative continues, they were employed to produce a number of statues of gods, but became dissatisfied and moved to Aitolia, leaving their work at Sikyon unfinished. The Sikyonians were then afflicted by famine, and on consulting Delphi about a remedy for this were told that Dipoinos and Skyllis must finish the statues they had begun, which, with some difficulty, they were persuaded to do. Pliny names the statues as an Apollo, an Artemis, a Herakles, and an Athena, the last of which was later struck by lightning.

These four statues are the only works of Dipoinos and Skyllis which Pliny mentions by name, but elsewhere he says that Ambrakia, Argos, and Kleonai were crammed ('refertae') with the works of Dipoinos ('and Skyllis' presumably to be understood, since they seem always to have worked as a team).[2] Works by them at Argos and Kleonai are mentioned by Pausanias, one at each place; in view of Pliny's choice of words, perhaps there were originally more. No details are known of their works in Ambrakia, which were presumably produced during their stay in north-west Greece after leaving Sikyon. In addition, Clement of Alexandria mentions a *xoanon* of Artemis Mounychia at Sikyon, which may or may not be identical with Pliny's Artemis, and a Herakles at Tiryns; another Herakles by them found its way to Armenia; and among the celebrated statues in the Palace of Lausos at Constantinople was an Athena Lindia by them, carved out of an emerald four cubits tall (!), which had been given by Sesostris of Egypt to Kleoboulos of Lindos.[3] Since Kleoboulos was a

---

[1] *NH* xxxvi.9–10. [2] *NH* xxxvi.14.
[3] Paus. ii.15.1 and 22.5; Clement, *Protrept.* iv.47.8; Moses of Chorene, *Hist. Armen.* ii.11, p. 103 (ed. Whiston); Kedrenos, *Comp. Hist.* 322b.

sixth-century figure, while Sesostris is variously identified as Rameses II
or the even earlier Pharaoh Senosret III, the description of this last work
appears improbable on grounds both of material and of chronology, but
perhaps the bare fact that Dipoinos and Skyllis made an Athena Lindia
can still be accepted.

Leaving aside this doubtful piece and the Athena at Kleonai, the
material of which is not stated, it can be seen that Dipoinos and Skyllis
worked in a variety of materials — wood (the *xoanon* of Artemis Mounychia and the Dioskouroi group at Argos), ivory (parts of the horses in the
Dioskouroi group), gilded bronze (the Armenian Herakles). None of their
works, in fact, is explicitly said to have been of marble, though it seems
reasonable to suppose that this was the material of the four statues at
Sikyon which Pliny mentions.

The majority of their known works appear to have been cult-statues —
the Athena at Kleonai, Herakles at Tiryns, Artemis Mounychia, Dioskouroi
group, and possibly Athena Lindia all fall into this catecory. The nature of
the four statues at Sikyon is debatable, since it is possible either that they
were individual cult-statues or that they formed a group. It happens that
the four figures (Apollo, Artemis, Herakles, and Athena) were those which
commonly appear in sixth-century representations of the Struggle for the
Tripod, so it is possible that they formed such a group. They could appropriately have been erected at Sikyon in the aftermath of the First Sacred
War, when this story of violent conflict over the Delphic Oracle would
have had a topical flavour. Since the surviving representations of the subject date from fairly late in the sixth century, a group set up at Sikyon
earlier in the century could even have been the protype from which these
were derived.[4] In favour of the view that the statues did not form a group
is Pliny's statement that the Athena was struck by lightning, which has
led to its being identified with the cult-statue of Athena at Titane, which
suffered a similar fate. (Alternatively, it may have stood in the temple of
Athena at Sikyon, which was also struck by lightning.)[5] This same theory
identifies the remaining statues as the Armenian Herakles and the Apollo
and Artemis which went with it, though the latter were not of marble, as
the Sikyonian statues probably were, but of gilded bronze.

The view that Dipoinos and Skyllis were commissioned by the Sikyonians

---

[4] First suggested by K. O. Müller, *Kleine Schriften* (Breslau, 1847-8), ii, 634-8;
elaborated by H. W. Parke and J. Boardman, 'The Struggle for the Tripod and the
First Sacred War', *JHS* lxxvii (1957), 276-82. Müller also suggested that after the
destruction of the Athena the surviving statues were disposed of to Kroisos, although
only the Herakles is explicitly said to have been by Dipoinos and Skyllis, and the
Apollo and Artemis are not. For arguments against this suggestion, see H. Von Rohden,
'Die Götterbilder des Dipoinos und Skyllis in Sikyon', *AZ* xxxiv (1876/7), 122 f.

[5] Paus. ii.11.1, 12.1.

to make a group commemorating the Sacred War naturally requires that they were active in the first half of the sixth century. Pliny says that they were born around Ol. 50 (580 to 577 BC), and the Armenian Herakles is said to have been looted by the Persians from Lydia, and should therefore have been made before the middle of the century. Pliny's birth-date, which incorporates a reference to Persian history ('etiamnum Medis imperantibus priusque quam Cyrus in Persis regnare inciperet'), may simply have been intended to bring the start of their career sufficiently long before the fall of Sardis. If it is accurate, they cannot have come to work at Sikyon very soon after the Sacred War, and their stay there should probably be placed in the reign of Kleisthenes' successor rather than that of Kleisthenes himself.

Apart from the Armenian Herakles, none of the works of Dipoinos and Skyllis is definitely dated, so the only remaining source of evidence on this subject is what we know of their pupils and other associates. Endoios, who was also known as a pupil of Daidalos, worked in the second half of the sixth century, and several of the pupils of Dipoinos and Skyllis seem to have done so too.[6] The case of Medon–Dontas is particularly interesting; Pausanias saw some statues by him in the Megarian Treasury at Olympia, which he believed were much older than the Treasury itself, apparently simply because they were by a pupil of Dipoinos and Skyllis. From his own account, however, it seems likely that the statues were in fact made for dedication in the Treasury at the time when it was built, in the second half of the sixth century. A date for Dipoinos and Skyllis earlier in the century therefore appears likely.

The only work of theirs of whose appearance there is any record is the Athena at Kleonai, representations of which have been identified on coins of the city.[7] The figure is in the typical pose of a Palladion, with helmet, shield, and raised spear, but is less rigid than most representations of such statues; folds are shown in the skirt, and the feet appear to be in a walking rather than a standing position. The upper part of the body is covered by an aegis with a large gorgoneion, which seems to be a mid- to late sixth-century feature, found also in Endoios' Athena and in the slightly later figure 142 from the Athenian Akropolis.[8] The statue therefore appears to

---

[6] For a possible sketch of Endoios' career, see *DAA*, 491 ff., where the Athena is dated shortly after 528. His signature on the monument of Lampito (*LSAG* 78, No. 40) is dated in the last quarter of the century. Pupils of Dipoinos and Skyllis, Paus. vi.19.12 ff. (Medon–Dontas), ii.32.5 (Tektaios and Angelion, teachers of Kallon, whose surviving signature (*DAA*, 91 f. No. 85) is dated *c.* 500).

[7] Imhoof-Blumer and Gardner, *NCP* 32, No. 1, Pl. H i.

[8] The walking position also seems to be a mid-century innovation, which first appears in *korai* late in Richter's Group III, dated *c.* 575-555. See esp. *Korai*, 50, No. 69, Figs. 225-7.

date from the middle of the century or later, and may have been a late work of Dipoinos and Skyllis.

The representations of the Kleonai Athena are not sufficiently detailed to permit close comparison with sixth-century Sikyonian sculptures such as the 'Monopteros' metopes, so it is not possible to tell whether Dipoinos and Skyllis brought a Kretan influence into Sikyonian art or rather were themselves influenced by the native Sikyonian style. The latter is perhaps more probable, if they came to Sikyon when quite young and still relatively inexperienced in their craft. It has been suggested that the reason for their discontent and departure from Sikyon was rivalry with local sculptors, but there is no evidence of this. It is noteworthy, however, that no Sikyonian pupils of theirs are recorded; in fact, the next important figures in Sikyonian sculpture, Kanachos and Aristokles, belong to the generation after the pupils of Dipoinos and Skyllis. It may be, therefore, that artistic activity at Sikyon decreased in the mid-sixth century, and this in turn may have been connected with the decline of the tyranny and the ending of the fairly generous patronage of Kleisthenes, which was perhaps what attracted Dipoinos and Skyllis to Sikyon in the first place.

The connection of Dipoinos and Skyllis with Sparta is also interesting — they are not known to have actually worked there, but they had several Spartan pupils. It is possible, too, that the Armenian Herakles was commissioned by the Spartans for presentation to Kroisos, like the bronze bowl which the Samians seized.[8] The sculptors' contact with Sparta may have come about through Sikyon, after the overthrow of the tyranny by the Spartans; their second period of activity at Sikyon perhaps took place after this event. Their work at Argos, like that at nearby Kleonai, perhaps belongs after this, towards the end of their joint career. Whatever the exact chronology, it is plain that some of the cities in which Dipoinos and Skyllis worked were hostile to others, but it does not follow that they chose their places of work for political reasons. When they quarrelled with the Sikyonians they did not go to Argos, which would have been an obvious insult to Orthagorid Sikyon; nor did they, so far as is known, produce explicitly anti-Sikyonian (or anti-Kleisthenic) works, as Ibykos did.[10] It seems likely, therefore, that their reasons for choosing or refusing to work in a certain place were purely professional or financial.

E. Kanachos and Aristokles

Kanachos and Aristokles are the first named Sikyonian sculptors who were natives of the city. They were brothers, but their artistic ancestry is unknown, and they themselves are somewhat shadowy figures. Pausanias

---

[9] Hdt. i.70.　　　　　[10] Cf. pp. 57–8.

records of Aristokles that he was scarcely less famous than his brother, but no works of his are mentioned in the passage in question, which only introduces him as the founder of a school. The only known work of Aristokles is one of a group of three Muses which he made jointly with Kanachos and the Argive Hageladas. For Kanachos, rather more works are known, both from literary sources and from copies, but in his case too the information is scanty — surprisingly so, since he was reputed one of the most important sculptors of his time.[1]

Even the date at which Kanachos and Aristokles worked is not entirely clear, since most of the information about this comes in the form that they were contemporaries of certain other artists, whose own dates are equally doubtful. Thus, Pausanias makes Kanachos a contemporary of Kallon of Aigina and slightly older than Menaichmos and Soidas of Naupaktos; this is of some help, since there exists a signature of Kallon which is dated *c.* 500 BC, and Menaichmos and Soidas, although not securely dated, are said to have made a cult-statue for the sanctuary at Kalydon, probably at the time of the building of the late archaic temple there, again around 500 BC.[2] Some of the information about Hageladas suggests that he too was active around 500, since he made a number of Olympic victor-statues relating to victories in the late sixth century, and had a son who was working as a sculptor in the early fifth century. On the other hand, some statues by him are dated later in the fifth century, and Pliny gives him the *floruit* Ol. 87 (432 to 429 BC). Not all these dates can be correct, since they would give Hageladas an impossibly long career; one solution is to postulate two sculptors with the same name, in which case it was undoubtedly the elder who was the collaborator of Kanachos and Aristokles.[3]

The only dated work of Kanachos is the Apollo Philesios at Branchidai, which was carried off by the Persians after the sack of Miletos in 494. In fact Pausanias says that the statue was removed by Xerxes as a punishment

---

[1] Cic. *Brut.* 18.70 puts Kanachos in a standard list of great sculptors as representing the late archaic period. (But Quint. xii.10.7 has Kallon and Hegesias in a corresponding position.) Aristokles, Paus. vi.9.1. Muses, *Anth. Gr.* xvi (*Planud.* iv), 220 (Antipater of Sidon).

[2] Paus. vii.18.10; Kallon's signature, *DAA*, 91 f., No. 85; Kalydon temple, *DAA*, 508 f., F. Poulsen and K. Rhomaios, *Erster Vorläufiger Bericht über die Ausgrabungen von Kalydon* (Copenhagen, 1927), 19.

[3] Victor-statues, Paus. vi.8.6, 10.6, 14.11; signature of Argeiadas, *LSAG*, 160 ff., 169, No. 19, pl. 28 (dated *c.* 480–475); late works, Paus. iv.33.2 (Zeus Ithomatas, said to have been made for the Messenians at Naupaktos), Schol. Tzetz. Ar. *Ran.* 501a (Herakles Alexikakos at Melite in Attika, said to have been set up after the Great Plague). The latter ascription may have given rise to Pliny's *floruit* (*NH* xxxiv.49), but the association with the Plague may only have been deduced from the epithet (cf. Paus. i.3.4).

for the poor performance of the Milesian fleet at Salamis, so strictly speaking the *terminus ante quem* is 480, but since the sanctuary, like Miletos itself, was plundered and destroyed in 494, it is unlikely that the statue was dedicated after this.[4] It may, of course, have been dedicated a good deal earlier.

In the absence of known works, Aristokles' date has to be sought by working back from what is known of his school. Ptolichos of Aigina, who is said to have been a second-generation pupil of Aristokles, made an Olympic victor-statue for Theognotos of Aigina, whose victory may have taken place in 476. Pantias of Chios, who is described as 'seventh from Aristokles', made a victor-statue for Aristeus of Argos, who seems to have won no earlier than 420.[5] This 'genealogy' points to a date for Aristokles' activity around 500 or rather earlier.

Although it is not known by whom Kanachos and Aristokles were taught, their contemporary Kallon was a pupil of Tektaios and Angelion, who in turn were pupils of Dipoinos and Skyllis; it is tempting to associate Kanachos and Aristokles with their most celebrated predecessors at Sikyon, but it does not seem chronologically possible to do so. However, a connection with Tektaios and Angelion is possible, since their statue of Apollo at Delos had as an attribute a group of three Charites playing musical instruments, which is closely paralleled by the three Muses of Kanachos, Aristokles, and Hageladas.[6] Perhaps Kanachos and Aristokles were fellow pupils of Kallon.

The Apollo Philesios appears to have been a famous work in its time, and representations of it have been identified on coins and elsewhere. The coins suffer from the usual disadvantages of small size and lack of detail, but a more useful picture of the statue is given by a relief from the theatre at Miletos, which shows the god in front view, standing with the left leg advanced and holding a bow in his left hand and a stag in his right. According to Pliny's description of the statue, the stag was attached to the hand by an ingenious mechanism which allowed a thread to be passed under its feet. It is hard to know what to make of Pliny's description; even the translation of the passage is disputed, let alone its interpretation in practical terms.[7] No

---

[4] Paus. i.16.3, viii.46.3; but cf. Hdt. vi.19.3. The statue was restored to Branchidai by Seleukos.

[5] Theognetos, Paus. vi.9.1, *P. Oxy.* 222, col. i, line 15 (but the restoration is doubtful); Aristeus, Paus. vi.3.11 and 9.3, *P. Oxy.* 222, col. ii, line 28 (victory in 448 of a Kimon, probably identical with Aristeus' father Cheimon).

[6] Paus. ix.35.3, [Plut.] *De Mus.* 1136a; on coins, Imhoof–Blumer and Gardner, *NCP*, Pl. CC, xi–xiv; on a gem, *Charites*, Pl. xxxiv 1.

[7] R. Kekule von Stradonowitz, 'Über den Apoll des Kanachos', *Sitzungsber. Preuss. Akad. Wiss.* (1904), 786–801; Pliny, *NH* xxxiv.75. A reconstruction of the mechanism is suggested by E. Petersen, 'Kunstgeschichtliche Miscellen: 1. Der Apollon mit dem Hirsch von Kanachos', *AZ* xxxviii (1880), 22 ff. and 192 ff., but it is not very satisfactory.

indication of it appears in the Miletos relief, where the stag simply stands on the hand. In fact, the whole notion of such a mechanism appears odd in connection with a cult-statue, and perhaps arose from a misunderstanding of some arrangement whereby the stag could be detached from the hand for cleaning or safe keeping. This would at least have served some useful purpose, whereas the kind of device which Pliny describes would simply have been an ingenious but pointless show-piece.[8]

Pausanias mentions the Philesios several times, but does not describe it, since it was situated outside the geographical limits of his work. He does, however, describe the Apollo Ismenios at Thebes, which was supposed to be an exact replica of the Philesios, also by Kanachos, but made of cedarwood instead of bronze.[9] Unfortunately, Pausanias obviously expected his readers to be acquainted with the Philesios, and therefore does not describe the Ismenios in detail. He does not even state whether this Apollo also held a stag, though this can safely be assumed in view of the exact resemblance to the Philesios, much less whether there was any peculiarity in the method of attaching it to the hand. If whatever mechanism there was in the Philesios was concealed inside the hand, it could have been omitted from the Ismenios without making any change in the external appearance.

One possible explanation for the exact likeness between the Philesios and the Ismenios is that the wooden statue was the original from which the mould for casting the bronze was made, but it may equally have been the case that Kanachos repeated a composition which he had found satisfactory on a previous occasion — even, perhaps, that he was requested to do so by those who commissioned whichever' statue was made second, if the first had already become famous. Other instances of replicas in Greek sculpture are known, though not necessarily by the same sculptor; thus Pausanias mentions Strongylion's Artemis Soteira at Megara, and its 'double' by an unknown sculptor at Pagai. Even more striking is the case of the 'Penelope' type, where there is concrete evidence for the existence of two specimens of the same type, which appear to have resembled each other very closely.[10]

---

[8] E. Simon, 'Beobachtungen zum Apollon Philesios des Kanachos', *Charites* (Bonn, 1957), 42 considers such a piece comparable with works ascribed to Hephaistos and Daidalos, and describes it as 'archaisch-naiv'. But the stag mechanism seems hardly on a par with walking statues and similar marvels, and the individual works ascribed to Daidalos by Pausanias are perfectly ordinary statues with no mechanical additions. Fronto, *Ad M. Ant. de Eloq.* i.1 (Van den Hout, p. 131) speaks of the improbability of Pheidias' making *ludicra* or Kanachos' making statues of gods, the suggestion apparently being that each sculptor might work in a genre normally associated with the other; this may suggest that the stag mechanism was regarded as a *ludicrum* which detracted from Kanachos' reputation as a serious sculptor of divine statues.   [9] Paus. ix.10.2.

[10] Paus. i.40.3, 44.4; B. S. Ridgway, *The Severe Style in Greek Sculpture* (Princeton, 1970), 101 ff.

The third cult-statue by Kanachos, the Aphrodite at Sikyon, was a chryselephantine work, so it can be seen that he was versatile in his use of materials. Pliny also puts him among the sculptors in marble, though without mentioning any individual work in this material, and admitting that he was primarily thought of as a bronze–worker, under which heading he gives his main account of Kanachos. Here, besides the Philesios, he mentions *celetizontes pueri*, which were presumably of bronze. These may have been victor-statues which stood at Olympia or some other site of major Games, even, possibly, at Sikyon itself. Both the material and the location of the group of Muses are unknown, though here again Sikyon is a likely place for them, since three was the number of Muses recognized there.[11] It is possible, therefore, that Kanachos worked extensively at Sikyon, but he may also have travelled to Miletos and Thebes to work on his statues there.

Since the only known work of Aristokles is his contribution to the group of Muses, there is no evidence as to the scene of his activity. He may, however, have specialized in athletic sculpture, since all the known products of his school were victor-statues. In this case, he is likely to have worked mainly at Olympia and other such sites. The known members of his school came from Aigina and Chios, which may indicate that he worked in the islands. Since only one case of collaboration between him and Kanachos is known, and then with the addition of a third party, it does not seem that the two brothers regularly worked together as a team as did Dipoinos and Skyllis or Tektaios and Angelion.

Pausanias gives little information about the school of Aristokles, mentioning only the victor-statues by Ptolichos and Pantias. He states that these sculptors were taught by their respective fathers, Synoon and Sostratos, so these names can be added to the list, but nothing further is known about them. Pausanias also mentions Askaros of Thebes, who may have been a pupil of Kanachos;[12] no other pupils of his are known. It is especially noteworthy that neither Kanachos nor Aristokles is said to have had any Sikyonian pupils, nor indeed is there any mention of Sikyonian sculptors in the generation after theirs. It appears that Sikyonian sculpture was in decline in the early fifth century, and only became famous again with the appearance of Polykleitos and his Sikyonian pupils.

[11] Aphrodite, Paus. ii.10.5; marble sculpture, Pliny, *NH* xxxvi.41; 'celetizontes pueri', *NH* xxxiv.75; Sikyonian Muses, Plut. *Mor.* 746e.
[12] Paus. v.24.1, where the text is corrupt and only the teacher's ethnic is given.

2. Polykleitos and his School

A. Polykleitos the Sikyonian?

The only literary evidence for the existence of a Sikyonian Polykleitos is found in Pliny's long account of the great fifth-century sculptor.[1] Here 'Polykleitos the Sikyonian' is said to have been the pupil of Hageladas, sculptor of the Doryphoros and other celebrated athlete-statues, and inventor of a new system of proportions for representations of the human body. However, this account must be treated with some caution, not least because the wide chronological span of the works associated with the name of Polykleitos makes it plain that this name was borne by more than one sculptor.

Pausanias knew of the existence of a second sculptor named Polykleitos, and went to some pains to distinguish him from his predecessor,[2] but it must be suspected that Pliny knew of only one, since he dismisses the suggestion that a Polykleitos made a portrait of Alexander's friend Hephaistion on the grounds that 'he lived a century earlier', and does not admit the possibility that this was a later artist with the same name. The existence of a Polykleitos who worked for Alexander is attested by Apuleius as well as by the negative evidence of Pliny, so he may have been a real person. If so, he was probably the third bearer of the name, since Pausanias' second Polykleitos apparently worked in the early fourth century. A fourth Polykleitos left his signature at Kameiros in the mid-third century. A Polykleitos was also the architect of the theatre and Tholos at Epidauros; he may have been identical with the sculptor who worked for Alexander.[3] Given such a large number of homonymous artists, confusion between them is almost inevitable, and it is to be feared that Pliny, who recognized only one Polykleitos, has included in his list works by several different hands.

For Pausanias, 'Polykleitos I' was the sculptor of the chryselephantine cult-statue in the Argive Heraion, and 'Polykleitos II' the pupil of Naukydes and maker of a victor-statue at Olympia. Only on one occasion does he state the distinction between the two, and on other occasions when the name is mentioned he does not say which is meant, perhaps because he himself did not always know. However, it seems clear on chronological

[1] *NH* xxxiv.55-6.
[2] Paus. vi.6.2, where the second Polykleitos is called 'not the maker of the statue of Hera, but the pupil of Naukydes'.
[3] Pliny, *NH* xxxiv.64; Apuleius, *Florida*, 7; C. Blinkenberg, *Lindos*, ii (Berlin, 1941), 52, No. 23; Paus. ii.27.5.

grounds that the various pupils of Polykleitos to whom he refers were taught by his Polykleitos I. It is significant, therefore, that he calls both Polykleitos II and the founder of the school 'Argive'.[4]

The founder of the school should also be identical with Pliny's Polykleitos, since it was his Kanon which was followed by members of the school. However, apart from this there is no positive evidence that Pliny and Pausanias were talking about the same man, since their lists of his works do not coincide. The problem is particularly acute in the case of the Argive Hera, to which Pausanias and other authors devote sufficient attention to make it clear that this was a famous work (though considered inferior to the chryselephantine statues of Pheidias), whose absence from Pliny's list is therefore rather surprising.[5] However, the two authors show a similar divergence in their treatment of other sculptors, apparently because Pausanias, by the nature of his work, described statues which were still in Greece in his time, while Pliny tended to concentrate on those which had already been brought to Italy and therefore were most likely to be familiar to himself and his readers. Even the famous chryselephantine statues of Pheidias are passed over by him in a very summary manner, so it is not altogether surprising that he should have made no mention at all of a less famous statue of this type.

It is possible, however, that Pliny makes an indirect reference to the Argive Hera in the *floruit* (01. 90 = 420 to 417 BC) which he gives for Polykleitos. The statue was set up in the new Argive Heraion built to replace the one burnt down in 423, so 420 is about the earliest date at which it could have been made. In fact, this date may be too early; the style of the metopes and pediment-sculptures and certain architectural details suggest that the building of the temple was not finished until about 400 or later, and such attempts as have been made to identify copies of the statue also favour such a date for it.[6] A date around 400 for the Hera creates a chronological difficulty for its ascription to Polykleitos I, whose career is normally supposed to have lasted *c.* 460 to 420. It is therefore tempting to assign the Hera to a second Polykleitos, almost certainly an Argive, and to leave Polykleitos I as a sculptor solely of athlete-statues,

---

[4] Polykleitos II, Paus. vi.6.2; founder of school, Paus. v.17.4, vi.13.7.

[5] Strabo, viii.372, says that the workmanship of the Hera was very fine, but in richness and size it was inferior to the works of Pheidias. The latter, especially the Zeus, received vastly more attention from authors, although the Hera was by no means neglected.

[6] Pliny's *floruit*, *NH* xxxiv.49; Heraion fire, Thuc. iv.133. On the date of the new building, P. Amandry, 'Observations sur les monuments de l'Héraion d'Argos', *Hesp.* xxi (1952), 272 ff. suggests 420–380, but in *Charites*, 80 ff., decides that 420 is too early. A. Linfert, *Von Polyklet zu Lysipp*, (Freiburg, 1966), 2 ff., follows Amandry's *Charites* dating. G. Roux, *L'Architecture de l'Argolide* (Paris, 1961), 58, dates the main building to the end of the 5th century or even the 390s. Copies, Linfert, 8 ff.

and probably a Sikyonian.[7] In this case, of course, Pausanias' second Polykleitos will become Polykleitos III.

The separation of the sculptor of the Hera from the sculptor of the Doryphoros is based not only on chronology but on the supposition that Greek sculptors specialized fairly narrowly in the types of statues they made and the materials in which they worked, so that a maker of cult-statues (*agalmatopoios*) could be distinguished from a maker of human figures (*andriantopoios*). It is true that Greek sculptors often became celebrated for works of a particular type or material, as Pheidias for his chryselephantine cult-statues, but this does not mean that they confined themselves to producing such works.[8] There can hardly have been a strict division between athlete-statues and statues of gods and heroes, since many of the latter were represented in athletic poses. Members of the school of Polykleitos made works of both kinds, so there seems no reason why their master should not have done the same. It may, however, have been true that he was most successful at athletic sculpture, and less happy when representing gods, as some criticisms of his work suggest.[9]

References to Polykleitos in fourth-century BC authors suggest that at that time the name was sufficiently famous to be used quite commonly when a sculptor's name was required to illustrate a philosophical argument.[10] He is generally referred to as an *andriantopoios*, but one passage in the *Protagoras* calls him an Argive and places him alongside Pheidias as an *agalmatopoios*, and is therefore generally taken as referring to the sculptor of the Hera. Another passage in the same dialogue speaks of Polykleitos' sons, who were also sculptors but failed to match their father's eminence; they are said to have been contemporaries of the sons of Perikles. Although these are only passing references and not intended as systematic art history, there seems no reason to doubt that the same Polykleitos is meant in both these passages, and that this man was famous both as a maker of athlete-statues and as the sculptor of the Argive Hera.

[7] Amandry, *Charites*, 79 ff., followed by Linfert, 60 n. 2. The sculptor of the Hera is called an Argive in the epigram *Anth. Gr.* xvi (*Planud.* iv), 216 (Parmenion). The architect of the temple was the Argive Eupolemos (Paus. ii.17.3).

[8] Pheidias was also famous for bronze statues, esp. the Athena Lemnia (Pliny, *NH* xxxiv.54, Paus. i.28.2), and worked in marble and wood besides (Pliny, *NH* xxxvi.15, Paus. i.14.7, ix.4.1, 10.2). The school of Polykleitos made mostly athlete-statues, but also cult-statues such as Naukydes' Hebe (Paus. ii.17.5) and Kleon's Aphrodite (Paus. v.17.3).

[9] Quint. *Inst. Orat.* xii.10.8 says of Polykleitos: 'nam ut humanae formae decorem addidit super verum, ita non explevisse deorum auctoritate videtur'.

[10] Plato, *Prot.* 311c (*agalmatopoios*), 328c (sons); Arist. *EN* 1141a 10 f. (Polykleitos *andriantopoios* and Pheidias *lithourgos*); Xen. *Mem.* i.4.3 (Polykleitos *andriantopoios* and Zeuxis painter). Cf. a passage in the *Dissoi Logoi* (Diels *VS*[6], 90, vi.8) where Polykleitos is said to have taught his son *andriantopoiia*.

The earliest literary evidence is therefore in favour of ascribing the Hera to Polykleitos I.

The chronological difficulties of this ascription must therefore be considered. There is some evidence that Polykleitos I's career began before 450 BC; not least the second passage in the *Protagoras* mentioned above, which implies that he was a contemporary of Perikles. Pliny's story of the contest of the Amazon statues at Ephesos, though it does not definitely date this event, similarly associates Polykleitos with the 'Periklean' sculptors Pheidias and Kresilas. Archaeological evidence for his activity in the mid-fifth century is provided by the base of the victor-statue of Kyniskos at Olympia, which is generally dated in the 450s, and which Pausanias ascribes to Polykleitos. However, the ascription has been doubted, since there is no signature on the base to support it.[11] The question then arises whether a sculptor who was already active in the 450s could still have been working around 400. Such a long career does seem possible by comparison with those of other artists — notably Lysippos, who seems to have remained active for rather more than fifty years.

In the present state of the evidence, therefore, it still appears more likely than not that the same Polykleitos made both the Doryphoros and the Hera. This makes the problem of his origin more difficult, since the sculptor of the Hera is frequently called an Argive, as against the solitary statement of Pliny that Polykleitos was a Sikyonian. If there is a mistake, it was almost certainly made by Pliny, since he was writing a considerable time after the event, and used one source (Xenokrates) who seems to have been particularly concerned to praise Sikyonian artistic achievements, and might have gone so far as to appropriate Polykleitos for Sikyon because of his importance in the history of Peloponnesian sculpture. The fact that Polykleitos' school included both Argives and Sikyonians no doubt helped to promote confusion about the origins of the master.

Some light may be thrown on Polykleitos' origins by the known bases bearing his signature. The Kyniskos base is not actually signed, and the inscription is in Arkadian local script, which no doubt reflects the Mantinean origin of Kyniskos, so it gives no help with regard to Polykleitos. The bases of the victor-statues of Xenokles and Aristion both bear signatures, but without ethnic and in Ionic script. The Aristion base at least appears to date from the second quarter of the fourth century, so the sculptor was probably Pausanias' Polykleitos II. The remaining signed base, that of the

[11] Pliny, *NH* xxxiv.53; Paus. vi.4.11, *LSAG* 216, No. 30. The dating of the inscription tends to be influenced by opinions about Polykleitos' career; Amandry, *Charites*, 75 places it in the 460s, on epigraphical grounds. G. Donnay, 'Faut-il rajeunir Polyclète l'Ancien?', *L'Ant. Class.* xxxiv (1965), 448–63 down-dates Polykleitos' career to *c.* 435–395, which makes easier the ascription to him of the Argive Hera but necessitates the dropping of the Kyniskos.

victor-statue of Pythokles, is more promising, since despite much later recutting the name of Polykleitos in Argive local script is preserved. The date of this must be later than Pythokles' victory in 452, and the inscription is usually dated well down in the fifth century, about 410, which gives rise to doubt as to which Polykleitos made the statue. However, if it is accepted that Polykleitos I was still active around 400 there seems no objection to regarding this signature as his. The script is shown to be Argive by the distinctive form of *lambda* (ⱶ), but another feature, the rhomboid *omikron* (◊), is characteristic of the fifth-century script of Sikyon.[12] It is interesting that the signature of a sculptor who was claimed by both Argos and Sikyon should contain elements from the local scripts of both states.

Although Polykleitos I's patronymic is not known, it may be possible to identify some members of his family, in the light of the knowledge that his sons also became sculptors. The sculptor Naukydes is described by Pausanias as brother of Polykleitos and son of Mothon, but also as the teacher of Polykleitos II. While it is not impossible that the elder brother should have taught the younger, the manner in which Pausanias speaks of the two brothers suggests that Polykleitos was the more famous, and Naukydes is associated with Polykleitos I by his chryselephantine statue of Hebe, which stood beside the Argive Hera. Naukydes may therefore have been the brother of Polykleitos I. However, he seems to have been a good deal younger, since his career extended well into the fourth century. One of the surviving signatures of Naukydes calls him the son of Patrokles, and this brings him into association with Daidalos of Sikyon, who had the same patronymic. Daidalos was active *c.* 400 to 365, and his father was probably the Patrokles named by Pausanias as one of the sculptors of the Aigospotamoi dedication at Delphi, and to whom Pliny gives the *floruit* Ol. 95 (400 to 397 BC), no doubt derived from the date of this work.[13] This Patrokles can hardly have been the father of Polykleitos I, but could have been the father of Polykleitos II. Thus two genealogies are possible, one of which makes Naukydes, Polykleitos II, and Daidalos brothers, while the other makes Naukydes and Polykleitos I the sons of a Patrokles who must be distinct from the father of Daidalos. The second genealogy offers the intriguing possibility that the second Patrokles

[12] Xenokles, Paus. vi.9.2, *IGB* 70, No. 90; Aristion, Paus. vi.13.6, *IGB* 71 f., No. 92; Pythokles, Paus. vi.7.10, *IGB* 71, No. 91, *LSAG* 170, No. 45, Pl. 30, *P. Oxy.* 222, col. ii, line 14. Sikyonian letter-forms, *LSAG* 138 ff.; ibid., 167 calls the rhomboid *omikron* 'a device not usual in Argive',

[13] Naukydes brother of Polykleitos, Paus. ii.22.7; his Hebe, Paus. ii.17.5; his signatures, *IGB* 67 f., Nos. 86–7. Copies of his Diskobolos (Pliny, *NH* xxxiv.80) have been identified, and the original is dated in the early 4th century (Linfert, *Von Polyklet zu Lysipp*, 20, D. Arnold, *Die Polykletnachfolge* (Berlin, 1969), 122 f.). Patrokles, Paus. x.9.10, Pliny, *NH* xxxiv.50 (where the same *floruit* is given to Naukydes). Daidalos, see pp. 127–30.

was the grandson of the first, and one of the undistinguished sons of Polykleitos I.

Whichever genealogy is accepted, both Argives and Sikyonians figure in it, as in the school of Polykleitos generally. Naukydes and Polykleitos II are known as Argives, while Daidalos is normally called Sikyonian, but appears in a fragmentary signature as (probably) Phleiasian.[14] His father's ethnic is unknown, but Patrokles is generally supposed to have been Sikyonian because of his relationship to Daidalos and his association with the Sikyonian Kanachos. It seems, therefore, that the family had branches at both Argos and Sikyon, and it is not possible to tell from which city it originated or, specifically, to which Polykleitos I belonged. Like the script of his signature, Polykleitos' genealogy makes him appear both Sikyonian and Argive.

An attractive explanation for the mixed origins of Polykleitos is that he was born at Sikyon but migrated to Argos, perhaps quite early in his life when he became Hageladas' pupil. Since Kanachos and Aristokles did not leave any Sikyonian pupils, so far as is known, such a move may have been necessary for any aspiring Sikyonian sculptor in search of a teacher. Later, Polykleitos' association with Argos was confirmed by the making of the Hera, for which he was perhaps rewarded with Argive citizenship, and so could be called 'Argive' with strict propriety. However, it is gratifying to think that Pliny may have preserved a true but otherwise forgotten piece of information when he called Polykleitos 'Sikyonian'.

B. The School of Polykleitos

The school of Polykleitos can be traced for three generations, and had a large number of Sikyonian members. Several of the first generation worked on the monument set up at Delphi to celebrate the Spartan victory at Aigospotamoi; this consisted of a group of gods and heroes, among whom was the victorious admiral Lysander being crowned by Poseidon, and, as subsidiary figures, the admirals of the various states which fought on the Peloponnesian side. The exact arrangement of the figures, and even the position of the monument along the Sacred Way, are disputed, but the surviving bases suggest that the admirals stood in a row, and that each of the sculptors concerned was responsible for a section of it.[1] It was on

---

[14] Marcadé, *Signatures*, i, 23 f.

[1] Paus. x.9.7–10. *FdD* iii.1, pp. 24 ff. and Figs. 6–7 places the group in the large rectangular niche on the north side of the Sacred Way, and suggests that the gods stood in a row along the centre back, while the admirals were in two groups in the back corners. This, however, conflicts both with Pausanias' statement that the monument stood opposite the Arkadian dedication (which stood in front of the rectangular niche) and wth his description of the internal arrangement of the group, which places the admirals behind the gods. Consequently J. Pouilloux and G. Roux, *Énigmes*

this part of the monument that some Sikyonian sculptors worked —
Alypos, a pupil of Naukydes, and Kanachos and Patrokles, who are named
together by Pausanias and appear to have worked in partnership, though
no signatures of theirs are preserved to confirm that this was so.

Pliny gives both Kanachos and Patrokles the *floruit* 01.95 (400 to 397
BC), which was probably derived from the date of their work on the
Aigospotamoi monument. He also ascribes to Patrokles a variety of subjects — *athletas autem et armatos et venatores sacrificantesque.*[2] The
Aigospotamoi admirals would presumably be classified as *armatos*, but
there is no literary record of any statues of the other three types by
Patrokles. He is, in fact, the least well documented of the three sculptors
under discussion, since no other work of his is described by Pausanias,
though it is highly probable that he should be identified with the Patrokles
named by Pausanias as the father and teacher of Daidalos.[3] In fact, no
ancient source states that he was either Sikyonian or a pupil of Polykleitos,
but these facts are inferred from his association with Kanachos and Daidalos.
A fragmentary base from Olympia bears the signatures of Daidalos and of
another Sikyonian sculptor whose name is lost. Since the latter's ethnic is
spelt 'Sekyonios' in the old-fashioned way which Daidalos and other
fourth-century sculptors abandoned, it is tempting to see this work as a
collaboration between father and son, and the fragmentary signature as
that of Patrokles. The remains of the patronymic, ending '-itou', call to
mind the possibility that Patrokles was the son of Polykleitos.[4]

Kanachos should properly be known as Kanachos II, in order to distinguish him from his late-archaic namesake. Pausanias states that he was
a Sikyonian and a pupil of Polykleitos, and that he made the victor-
statue of Bykelos, the first Sikyonian to win the boys' boxing event at

---

à Delphes (Paris, 1963), 16 ff. and 57, Fig. 18 place the monument on the south
side of the Sacred Way and reconstruct the statues in two rows, with the admirals
raised on a step to compensate for their smaller size. Arnold, *Die Polykletnachfolge*,
ch. iv discusses only the internal arrangement, taking the view that the admirals
stood in a single row, and accepting Pausanias' list of figures as more or less in order.
She suggests that the potentially dull row of figures was diversified by arranging
them in groups of two or three, varying their armour and other equipment, and
introducing pieces of 'furniture', perhaps including a whole ship (pp. 101 ff. and
Fig. 40a). This 'interesting' composition is seen as typical of the Sikyonian branch of
the Polykleitan school. On the other hand, Roux, 57, Fig. 18, arranges the surviving
bases in a different order, apparently seeking to take all the marks of attachment
as 'footprints'.
   [2] The *floruit*, *NH* xxxiv.50; Patrokles' subjects, *NH* xxxiv.91.
   [3] Paus. vi.3.4.
   [4] Daidalos' signature, Marcadé, *Signatures*, i, 23; fragmentary signature, ibid.,
i, 61, where it is restored as a signature of Kleon (cf. Purgold, *AZ* xl (1882), 192 ff.,
No. 437). This seems improbable in view of the old-fashioned spelling of the ethnic.

Olympia.[5] This victory is not dated, and the statue-base has not been dicovered. It seems, however, that on this occasion he worked alone, not in partnership with Patrokles.

Alypos, the pupil of Naukydes, was probably somewhat younger than Patrokles and Kanachos, and may have been only just beginning his career when he received the Aigospotamoi commission. Several bases from his section of the group have been found, including one which bears his signature. He signs himself without patronymic or ethnic. Pausanias also mentions a number of victor-statues by him at Olympia, but none of the bases has been found, and the victories to which they related are undated.[6]

These three sculptors must therefore remain rather shadowy figures, little known through either literary or archaeological evidence. They are, however, better known than the other first-generation members of the school of Polykleitos, most of whom are mere names. The surviving copies of statues which may be attributed to this generation of pupils suggest that their chief characteristic was a fairly rigid adherence to their master's Kanon, producing works barely distinguishable in style from Polykleitos' own. There is therefore little hope of success in ascribing statues of which copies are known to individuals, especially in the absence of detailed descriptions of any of their works. However, there does exist a late fifth-century bronze statuette, of distinctly Polykleitan appearance, from Sikyon, which because of its date, style, and provenance it is natural to associate with Kanachos and Patrokles.[7]

Daidalos, the son and pupil of Patrokles, is far better known than his predecessors, both through literary evidence and from surviving signatures. His career can be approximately dated *c.* 400 to 365 BC. He is not known to have worked on any of the Spartan victory-dedications which occupied so many members of the Polykleitan school around 400, but one of his earliest works appears to have been a trophy set up by the Eleians at Olympia to celebrate a victory over Sparta at about this time.[8] The lower

---

[5] Paus. vi.13.7.

[6] Signature, Marcadé, *Signatures*, i, 3; other bases, *FdD* iii.1, Nos. 61-2, 64-5; the fragmentary base, ibid., No. 63 belonged to one of the two Korinthian admirals, and therefore may be assigned to either Alypos or Kanachos and Patrokles; the base of the herald (ibid., No. 67), not mentioned by Pausanias, is placed by Arnold (op. cit., Fig. 25) in Alypos' section of the row. Victor-statues, Paus. vi.1.3 and 8.5.

[7] Athens, NM 7474; A. Furtwängler, *Meisterwerke der griechischen Plastik* (Leipzig, 1893), 475; W. Lamb, *Greek and Roman Bronzes* (London, 1929), 168, Pl. 62a; Charbonneaux, *La Sculpture grecque classique*, i, Pl. 27; J. Charbonneaux, *Les Bronzes grecques* (Paris, 1958), 92, Pl. xxiii.1; Arnold, *Die Polykletnachfolge*, 85 f., 135, 227.

[8] Pausanias' account of the battle, iii.8.3 ff. + v.4.8 + v.20.4 + v.27.11 + vi.2.3 + vi.2.8; possibly identical with a battle near Elis in 402, Diod. xiv.17.9-10. Other suggested dates are 418, when Elis was allied with Argos against Sparta (Thuc.

limit of his career is fixed by his contribution to the Arkadian dedication at Delphi, consisting of a group of Arkadian national heroes with Apollo and Nike, of which Daidalos made the Nike and the Arkas. The inscriptions on this monument show that it celebrated a successful Arkadian invasion of Lakonia, which must be the one led by Epameinondas in 369, in which the Arkadians took part.[9] Two of Daidalos' Olympic victor-statues can be given *termini post quem* – those of the Eleians Eupolemos and Aristodemos, who won in 396 and 388 respectively.[10]

Besides these works, Pausanias records others to which no definite date can be assigned, and others still are known from surviving bases. The monument at Olympia on which Daidalos collaborated with another Sikyonian sculptor, possibly Patrokles, has already been discussed; this was presumably an early work. Another Olympic victory-monument, that of Timon and Aisypos of Elis, was a substantial group in which Aisypos was shown on horseback, he having won the horse-race and Timon the chariot-race. Pausanias also describes a second dedication of Timon, consisting, apparently, of a *quadriga* driven by Nike, but the sculptor of this is not named.[11] The fragmentary base of the victor-statue of Tharykidas of Phigaleia gives some hint of an important event in Daidalos' life, since his ethnic here ended ΊΟΣ, and should probably be restored [Φλειά]σιος – at any rate, the reading Σικυώνιος is excluded. There is no mention of such a change of citizenship in Pausanias, who in fact calls Daidalos Sikyonian even in his description of this very statue, and other signatures which give his ethnic also make him Sikyonian, so the change probably took place late in his career. He may have become a political exile under the tyranny of Euphron in the 360s, when Phleious, as one of Sparta's few remaining allies, was an obvious place of refuge for the victims of an anti-Spartan tyrant. There is no record of any major work by Daidalos at Phleious or for Phleiasians which might have earned him honorary citizenship.[12] In this respect he had far closer links with Elis, but the remains of the Tharykidas signature exclude the reading Ἠλεῖος.

v.58.1, 61–2), and 364, when there was a battle in the Altis between Eleians and Arkadians (Xen. *Hell.* vii.4.28–32). In the latter case, Pausanias must be supposed to have wrongly identified one side in the battle.
   [9] Paus. x.9.5–6; he appears to be under the impression that the monument celebrated the Battle of the Fetters (Hdt. i.66.3–4). Epameinondas' invasion, Xen. *Hell.* vi.5.22–32; inscriptions, *FdD* iii.1, Nos. 3 and 6.
   [10] Eupolemos, Paus. vi.3.7, viii.45.4. Euseb. *Chron.* (ed. Schoene) i.204; Aristodemos, Paus. vi.3.4, Euseb. *Chron.* (ed. Schoene) i.206. The epigram on Aristodemos' statue is preserved in Hephaistion (ed. Consbr.), 60.6 ff., 65.7 ff.
   [11] Timon and Aisypos, Paus. vi.2.8; Timon's *quadriga*, vi.12.6 (a lacuna makes the exact description of this monument doubtful).
   [12] The monument, Paus. vi.6.1; the form of the name (which Pausanias gives as 'Narykidas'), F. Hiller von Gaertringen and H. Lattermann, *Hira und Andania* (Berlin, 1911), 10, Wade-Gery, 'The Rhianos – Hypothesis', in *Ancient Society and*

Pausanias does not describe any athlete-statues at Delphi, but the base of one by Daidalos has survived. This was the victor-statue of an Athenian, Glaukon son of Taureas. Taureas (a rather uncommon name) may be identical with the relative of Andokides who was accused of being involved in the mutilation of the Herms but was later released, and who was assaulted by Alkibiades when they were rival *choregoi*, and was perhaps also the man after whom the 'palaistra of Taureas' was named. Nisaios, son of Taureas, was also accused and released in 415, but a Glaukon is not otherwise known. If his victory was won *c.* 400 or later, which would fit with the fact that Daidalos made the statue, he may have been too young to be implicated in the Herms affair.[13] Another base bearing the signature of Daidalos was found at Ephesos but subsequently lost again. The statue to which it belonged was that of Euthenos son of Eupeithes, who is otherwise unknown. It has been suggested, however, that the 'Ephesos Athlete' is a copy of this work. Since this statue is an *apoxyomenos*, it could be one of the 'pueros duos destringentes se' ascribed to Daidalos by Pliny, but Pliny does not say where these statues stood, so the identification of the 'Ephesos Athlete' as a copy of one of them depends mainly on the fact that both it and a base signed by Daidalos were found at Ephesos, which could be pure coincidence. The Athlete is not, strictly speaking, an *apoxyomenos*, but is shown cleaning his strigil after use, as other copies make clear; furthermore, it is not universally agreed that the statue should be associated with Daidalos at all.[14] Daidalos' signature also appears on a base from Halikarnassos, but, judging by the letter-forms, cannot be original; it may have been attached to a copy of one of his works, or have been a recutting of a genuine signature.[15]

Institutions: Studies presented to Victor Ehrenberg on his 75th birthday (Oxford, 1966), 293; the base, Marcadé, *Signatures*, i, 23 f.; Sikyonian exiles under Euphron, Xen. *Hell.* vii.1.46, Diod. xv.70.3.

[13] The base, Marcadé, i, 22; Taureas and Nisaios, Andok. i.47 and 68; Taureas and Alkibiades, Dem. xxi.147, Plut. *Alk.* xvi.5, [Andok.] iv.20-1; palaistra of Taureas, Plato, *Charm.* 153a.

[14] The base, Marcadé, i, 24; *apoxyomenoi*, Pliny, *NH* xxxiv.76. F. Hauser, 'Eine Vermuthung über die Bronzestatue aus Ephesos', *ÖJh.* v (1902), 214 ff. identified the Athlete as one of these, believing that it was a 4th–century original and that the copy in Boston was from another work by the same hand, thus making a pair. Arnold, *Die Polykletnachfolge*, points out the objections to the identification, but continues to accept the Athlete as a copy of a work by Daidalos. Linfert, *Von Polyklet zu Lysipp*, 44 sees the work as influenced by Skopas, and tentatively identifies the original as the victor-statue of Tharykidas, in which case the association of the statue wih the Ephesos base must be abandoned. S. Lattimore, 'The bronze Apoxyomenos from Ephesos', *AJA* lxxvi (1972), 13–16 suggests that the Athlete, whether original or copy, is an early Hellenistic work, possibly from the school of Lysippos, and not connected with Daidalos or the Polykleitan school. A. F. Stewart, 'Lysippan studies 3: not by Daidalos?', *AJA* lxxxii (1978), 473–82 makes a similar suggestion.

[15] Marcadé, i, 24.

However, unlike the other known signatures of Daidalos, this one gives neither patronymic nor ethnic, and so may not refer to the same man.

There are also some literary references to statues by a Daidalos where it is not certain that the fourth-century Sikyonian sculptor is the one in question. Pliny, in a corrupt passage, speaks of a marble statue of Aphrodite bathing, and may give the sculptor's name as Daidalos, but this statue has been identified from copies as a Hellenistic work, and is generally ascribed to Doidalsas of Bithynia.[16] Another work by a Daidalos in Asia Minor was an Artemis at Monogissa in Karia,[17] which goes geographically with the Halikarnassos base and may have been by the same sculptor.

Little can be discovered about Daidalos' style, unless the 'Ephesos Athlete' is rightly connected with him. This work has the square proportions of the body associated with Polykleitos, and the pose with one leg bearing the weight and the other free, but the arrangement of the arms is new, not balancing that of the legs with one performing an action and the other hanging free, but both active and forming a circular pattern. Where the 'footprints' of statues by Daidalos are preserved on their bases, they show that the stance was Polykleitan, but, of course, give no evidence about body proportions or the position of the arms.

Kleon is the sole known third-generation member of the school of Polykleitos, being the pupil of Antiphanes who in turn was the pupil of Periklytos, and he of Polykleitos.[18] His career, however, overlapped considerably with that of Daidalos, just as Antiphanes' career overlapped with Patrokles'. Two firmly dated works of Kleon are known, both probably belonging to a fairly early stage in his career. He made at least two of the Zanes set up at Olympia after the Games of Ol. 98 (388 BC), the first time such statues were paid for out of fines imposed for cheating;[19] assuming that fairly prompt payment of the fine was insisted on, this puts the start of Kleon's career in the early 380s, if not before. As a slightly later chronological fixed point, there is the base of his memorial at Delphi to the Spartan king Agesipolis, commissioned by the latter's father, the exiled king Pausanias, and probably set up not long after Agesipolis' death in 380. The epigram on the base has evidently been recut, but the original fourth-century signature of Kleon remains.[20]

Literary and archaeological evidence together show that, like most of the Polykleitan school, Kleon did a good deal of work at Olympia. Pausanias gives a detailed account of all the Zanes, and especially of the Ol. 98 set

---

[16] Pliny, *NH* xxxvi.35; the Hellenistic statue, M. Bieber, *Sculpture of the Hellenistic Age*[2] (Columbia, 1961), 82 f., Figs. 290–3. Daidalos of Bithynia (probably identical with Doidalsas), Eustath. on Dionys. Perieg. 793.

[17] Steph. Byz. s.v. Μονόγισσα.   [18] Paus. v.17.4.

[19] Paus. v.21.2–4.   [20] Marcadé, i, 60, Pl. xi.1.

which were the first of their kind; he says that two of them were by Kleon, while the authorship of the other four was unknown. Kleon's two were doubtless identified by his signature, and the base of one of them has been found.[21] According to Pausanias, these two were in the centre of the row of six, and the others had on their bases epigrams explaining the significance of the statues. It is possible, therefore, that Kleon made all six, but signed only two in order to leave room for the epigrams on the others, which were an important part of the monument.

Kleon is also credited by Pausanias with the following victor-statues: Alketos of Kleitor (boy boxer), Kritodamos of Kleitor (boy boxer), Deinolochos of Elis (boy runner), Hysmon of Elis (pentathlete), Lykinos of Heraia (boy runner). Hysmon's statue held what Pausanias calls 'old-fashioned' jumping-weights (the long-jump being one of the events which constituted the pentathlon). The base of Kritodamos' statue has been found, bearing Kleon's signature.[22] None of the victories concerned is dated.

Another statue by Kleon at Olympia was a bronze Aphrodite, one of many statues which stood in the Heraion.[23] His recorded activity is thus almost exclusively placed at Olympia, the only exception being the statue of Agesipolis at Delphi, and he seems, like Daidalos, to have had strong links with Elis, producing not only two statues of Eleian victors, but the Zanes which the Eleians were responsible for setting up. Pliny records that he made statues of philosophers, perhaps meaning portraits, though this is not definitely stated.[24] Kleon has also been credited with the authorship of the Youth from Antikythera, as a late work.[25] If this ascription is correct, his style must have developed from the fairly faithful adherence to Polykleitan principles which he shows in the early stages of his career (shown, for instance, by the Doryphoros-like stance of at least one of his Zanes) to something modified by other influences, perhaps that of Lysippos. It seems, therefore, that by the middle of the fourth century the Polykleitan school was in decline in the sense that its members were no longer producing works which conformed strictly to the master's Kanon; under these circumstances, it is hardly surprising that Kleon is its last known member.

[21] Marcadé, i, 60. For a possible copy of one of the Zanes, see Arnold, *Die Polykletnachfolge*, 204, Pl. 27a.

[22] Alketos, Paus. vi.9.2; Kritodamos, vi.8.5; Deinolochos, vi.1.4–5; Hysmon, vi.3.9–10; Lykinos, vi.10.9. Kritodamos' base, Marcadé, i, 61. Pausanias hesitates between calling the athlete 'Kritodamos' and 'Damokritos'; the base shows that the former is correct.

[23] Paus. v.17.3.　　　　　　[24] Pliny, *NH* xxxiv.87.

[25] Arnold, *Die Polykletnachfolge*, 207 ff., Pl. 27c considers this statue certainly in the Polykleitan tradition, though not purely so, and particularly close to Kleon. Since the statue is dated *c.* 340, he is also on chronological grounds the most likely of the known members of the school to have produced it.

One early fourth-century Sikyonian sculptor is known who was not a member of the school of Polykleitos — Damokritos, the pupil of Pison of Kalaureia, who worked on the Aigospotamoi dedication. Pausanias traces the school back through several generations to Kritios of Athens.[26] Damokritos made the Olympic victor-statue of Hippos of Elis, a boy boxer. According to Pliny he also made statues of philosophers, and a base now lost came from his statue of Lysis of Miletos (if the inscription is correctly recorded, Lysis was female, so this cannot have been an athlete-statue, but may have been a portrait).[27] Hippos' victory is undated, but an early fourth-century career for Damokritos is secured by his association with Pison. He was probably a rough contemporary of Daidalos and Kleon, whose teachers also worked on the Aigospotamoi monument.

[26] The school of Kritios, Paus. vi.3.5; Pison's work on the Aigospotamoi monument, Paus. x.9.8.
[27] Hippos of Elis, Paus. vi.3.5; philosophers, Pliny, *NH* xxxiv.87; base, *IGB* 316 f., No. 484. The inscription as recorded is not 4th-century, but it may have been recut. Cf. D. L. ix.49 for a sculptor 'Demokritos', perhaps the same.

3. Lysippos and his School

A. Lysippos

It can hardly be disputed that Lysippos was one of the most important figures in the history of Greek sculpture, being not only a remarkably prolific artist but the founder of a school which remained active for most of the third century BC, thus carrying on his style well into the Hellenistic period. Despite his importance, however, information about him is relatively sparse, and few copies of his works can be identified for certain, though many ascriptions have been made. A major source for Pliny's chapters on sculpture was Xenokrates, a member of the school of Lysippos and a practising sculptor as well as a writer on the subject, and it may have been from him that Pliny derived the view, detectable at several points in his work, that Lysippos was the supreme Greek sculptor, to whom all earlier practitioners of the art could be regarded as more or less imperfect forerunners.[1] But this view is conveyed to the reader in the form of an impression rather than a direct statement, and disappointingly few hard facts are offered in support of it.

Pliny and all other authors who mention Lysippos' nationality agree in calling him Sikyonian, and this is also consistent with the only signature of his which shows any trace of an ethnic.[2] The dates of his career are rather uncertain; his earliest dated work is the statue of Pelopidas dedicated by the Thessalians at Delphi, which should have been set up either after Pelopidas' expedition to Thessaly in 369, or after his death in 364.[3] Lysippos was therefore active in the late or possibly even the early 360s, and by that time was already sufficiently well known to secure a commission of some importance outside his native city. His earliest work known from literary evidence is probably the victor-statue of Troilos of Elis at Olympia, for which the *terminus post quem* is 01. 102 (372 BC). However, the dedicatory inscription of this statue is sometimes dated as late as *c.* 350 on epigraphical grounds. Troilos' victory may have been disputed, since he was Hellanodikes at the time, and Pausanias says that after this the Hellanodikai were forbidden to enter for the chariot-race — perhaps as a result of objections to the same man's being judge and competitor.[4]

---

[1] Pliny, *NH* xxxiv.83, D. L. iv.15. Cf. K. Jex-Blake and E. Sellers, *Pliny the Elder's Chapters on the History of Art*, rev. edn. (Chicago, 1968), xvi ff.

[2] From Thebes, Marcadé, *Signatures*, i, 66 f.

[3] Idem, i, 66, with discussion of date. A further fragment, *BCH* lxxxvii (1963), 206–8.

[4] Paus. vi.1.4–5; *Olympia*, v, No. 166. Marcadé, i, 71 f. accepts a date *c.* 370, apparently seeing no epigraphical objection to this.

If some such difficulty prevented the immediate erection of a victor-statue, it may not in the end have been made any earlier than the Pelopidas. As for the end of Lysippos' career, a *terminus post quem* of 316 is suggested by the story that he was commissioned by Kassander to design a special shape of jar for the export of wine from his new city of Kassandreia, which was founded in that year. A lost signature from a statue of 'King Seleukos' may take his career down to 306, when Seleukos and the other Diadochoi assumed the royal title, but this is rather less certain, as the statue concerned may have been a Roman copy, and the inscription not an accurate copy of the original, but composed with the benefit of hindsight.[5] If Lysippos really made a portrait of Seleukos as king, his career must have lasted upwards of sixty years, which is within the limits of possibility, but only just.

The only other work of Lysippos which can be very precisely dated is the victor-statue of the Theban boy pankratiast Korweidas. The victory cannot have taken place before 342, since the event was only introduced at the Pythian Games, where Korweidas won, in 346, and the name of the victor on that occasion is known; but it is unlikely to have taken place any later, since Thebes was occupied with the Chaironeia campaign in 338, and was totally destroyed by Alexander in 335. Thebes was restored in 316, and the inscription on the statue-base appears to date from this time, but it is commonly held to have been recut when the statue was set up again in the course of the restoration. If it was not made until after 316, it would be a very late work of Lysippos.[6]

Apart from these fairly precisely dated works by Lysippos, it is possible to assign *termini post quem* to two more — the Eros at Thespiai and the statue of Cheilon of Patras at Olympia. Thespiai was more or less deserted from 372 to 338, so the Eros is unlikely to have been dedicated until after the latter date, while Cheilon's statue was commissioned by the Achaians after his death in battle at Lamia in 322, and so must have been a relatively late work.[7] Lysippos' portraits and other works for Alexander should for the most part be dated during the latter's reign, though some may be earlier, since Pliny says that Lysippos made portraits of Alexander as a

[5] Wine-jars, Athen. xi.784c; Seleukos, Marcadé, i, 70. An excellent parallel for the misleading inscription in C. M. Robertson, *History of Greek Art* (London, 1975), 702 f. n. 40.

[6] Marcadé, i, 66 f.; boy's pankration at the Pythian Games, Paus. x.7.8. P. Moreno, *Lisippo* (Bari, 1974), 81 suggests that Korpheidas (his reading of the name) may = Iolaidas, the name of the first victor in Pausanias (his text is corrupt at this point).

[7] Thespiai, Xen. *Hell.* vi.3.1 and 5, Diod. xv.46.6, Paus. ix.14.2-4. It was destroyed (or at least partly depopulated) by the Thebans, and restored by Philip after Chaironeia (thus Hammond, *History of Greece*², 570, but not in any of the sources). Cheilon, Paus. vi.4.6-7 (hesitating between Chaironeia and Lamia as the scene of his death), vii.6.5 (decides on Lamia, quoting a local guide at Patras).

boy. However, it was presumably after Alexander's accession that Lysippos became his official sculptor; hence Pliny gives them the same *floruit*, 01. 113 (328 to 325 BC). It has sometimes been suggested that Lysippos fell out of favour with Alexander towards the end of his reign — the story of Lysippos' rebuke to Apelles for painting Alexander holding a thunderbolt, as if he were Zeus, suggests that he did not sympathize with attempts to represent Alexander as a more or less divine oriental monarch, and so may have been opposed to the king's own policy.[8] Hence it is possible that none of his works for Alexander should be dated in the very last years of the king's reign. It is perhaps noteworthy that after Alexander's death Lysippos appears to have found employment with those of his successors who retained close connections with Macedon and mainland Greece — Krateros and later Kassander. If his portrait of Seleukos is not accepted as dating from after 306, he may have spent the rest of his life in Greece.

For Lysippos' colossal statues of Zeus and Herakles at Taras, a date has been suggested between 334/3 and 331/0, when Alexander of Epeiros, the uncle of the Macedonian king, was giving military aid to the Tarentines.[9] These statues could thus be regarded as indirect products of Lysippos' association with Alexander, though not, presumably, actually commissioned by him.

Those works of Lysippos to which definite dates can be assigned have not, on the whole, survived in copies,[10] and those of which copies have been more or less certainly identified can at best be given relative dates based on their position in the supposed development of Lysippos' style — a rather unsafe criterion, in the absence of a sequence of absolutely dated works. The fact that Lysippos was, so far as is known, exclusively a worker in bronze has had the result that no original works by him have survived, with the possible exception of the reliefs on the base of his statue of Poulydamas at Olympia, which, if they are from his own hand, are isolated examples of his work in stone.[11] Hence his style must be judged entirely from copies, and how unreliable these can be is shown by the Herakles Farnese, which owes more of its appearance to the copyist Glykon than to Lysippos. On the strength of Pliny's remarks, the Apoxyomenos in the Vatican is identified as a copy of Lysippos' famous statue of this subject,

---

[8] Portraits of the boy Alexander, Pliny, *NH* xxxiv.63; *floruit*, *NH* xxxiv.51; rebuke to Apelles, Plut. *Mor.* 360d; its interpretation, Bieber, *Sculpture of the Hellenistic Age*[2], 48.

[9] Justin, xii.2, Livy, viii.17.9-10 and 24.1. Date, Beloch, *Gr. Gesch.* iii[2], 1, pp. 596 ff.

[10] There are several bases bearing Lysippos' signature, apart from those already mentioned, which can be at least loosely dated on epigraphical grounds (Marcadé, i, 68 ff.). None of the statues which stood on these is preserved.

[11] Paus. vi.5.1-9; *Olympia*, iii, Pl. lv.1-3.

and discussions of his style tend to centre on this work.[12] If the Apoxyo-menos is an example of his mature style, an earlier stage of his development may be represented by the statue of Agias from the Daochos group at Delphi, but this is a matter of much dispute. The case for associating the statue with Lysippos rests on the fact that he made a statue of Agias which stood at Pharsalos, with an inscription on its base very similar to that of the Delphi statue. It is chronologically possible that Lysippos made the Pharsalos statue early in his career (since Agias lived in the fifth century BC), and that it was copied for Daochos' monument at Delphi, which was dedicated between 338 and 334.[13] The Delphi statue is more or less Polykleitan in its pose and, at best, only 'looks forward to' the Apoxyo-menos; arguments as to whether this could represent even a very early work of Lysippos tend to hinge on the question whether one man's style could have changed sufficiently in the course of his career to permit him to produce both this and the Apoxyomenos.

The literary sources give little help in solving the question of Lysippos' early style, since he is said to have been self-taught, and therefore is not placed in a close relationship with any previous sculptor, traces of whose influence might have been looked for in his early works. According to Douris, Lysippos began his career as a bronze-smith, and was inspired by a remark of Eupompos, the founder of the Sikyonian school of painting, that one should imitate nature rather than other artists. Another story had it that Lysippos himself claimed that the Doryphoros of Polykleitos had been his master.[14] Since the most famous Sikyonian sculptors of the early fourth century were members of the school of Polykleitos, Lysippos could hardly have failed to be acquainted with the style which the Doryphoros exemplified, and may have begun by producing statues which conformed to it; in this respect the Agias from Delphi is the kind of work the young Lysippos might have been expected to produce. However, he was famous

[12] Pliny, *NH* xxxiv.62 and 65.

[13] Delphi inscription, *FdD* iii.4 460.2; Pharsalos base, Marcadé, i, 67 f.; date, Homolle, *BCH* xxi (1897), 595, J. Pouilloux, *FdD* ii, *La Region nord du sanctuaire* (Paris, 1960), 77. Opinions about the relationship between the Delphi Agias and Lysippos' statue range from that of F. P. Johnson, *Lysippos* (Durham, North Carolina, 1927), 125 ff., that there is no connection at all, through that of Robertson, *History of Greek Art*, 468 ff., that the Delphi statue may be a studio replica of an early work by Lysippos, to that of Bieber, *Sculpture of the Hellenistic Age*[2], 33, that Lysippos himself was responsible for the Delphi statue. Opinions also differ about the Daochos group as a whole; Bieber, loc. cit. considers it the work of several hands in a variety of styles, while Arnold, *Die Polykletnachfolge*, 210 ff., ascribes it to some very late members of the school of Polykleitos, strongly influenced by Lysippos.

[14] Douris, quoted Pliny, *NH* xxxiv.61; Doryphoros, Cic. *Brut.* 86.296. The con-text makes it possible to interpret Lysippos' remark as ironical – the Doryphoros taught him what *not* to do. Against this interpretation, Moreno, *Testimonianze per la teoria artistica di Lisippo* (Treviso, 1973), 88.

precisely for introducing a new system of proportions to replace that of Polykleitos, and the works commonly attributed to him have nothing Polykleitan about them.

It is reasonable to suppose that Lysippos began his career at Sikyon itself, where Pausanias saw statues of Zeus and Herakles by him in the Agora. It is also possible that his celebrated statue of Kairos stood here, though evidently not in the time of Pausanias, since he does not mention it. A representation of the Zeus has been identified on Sikyonian coins of the Roman Imperial period; it is a nude standing figure, of distinctly Lysippean proportions, but in its pose related to works of the Polykleitan school, perhaps specifically to one of Kleon's Zanes at Olympia, which suggests that it was an early work. The Herakles may have been the original of the Farnese type, since a figure of this type appears on Sikyonian coins of *c.* 300 BC.[15] The depiction of Herakles as growing weary towards the end of his Labours is a fairly rare subject in Greek art; one of the best-known examples is the Nemean Lion metope from Olympia, which resembles the Farnese type in giving an impression of despondency, although Herakles is here a young man and has only completed his first Labour. Since Lysippos worked at Olympia, it is possible that he saw the metope and derived from it the idea of representing Herakles in this state of mind, though he did not exactly copy either the subject or the pose.

Lysippos appears to have returned to the theme of the weary Herakles in another statue, the colossus at Taras, which later found its way to Constantinople. Herakles was shown unarmed, seated on a basket covered by the lion-skin, resting his head on his hand in an attitude of dejection. This pose is sometimes interpreted as representing his reaction to the task of cleaning the Augean stables, for which the basket would have been a useful implement but his normal weapons would not. Yet another Lysippean statue of a similar subject is known from an epigram. Herakles was again shown weaponless and dejected, deprived even of his lion-skin, a state which the poet explains as the result of an encounter with Eros.[16] By

---

[15] Zeus, Paus. ii.9.6; Herakles, Paus. ii.9.8; Kairos, Kallistratos, *Stat.* 6, entitled 'To the statue of Kairos at Sikyon'. Coins, Imhoof–Blumer and Gardner, *NCP* 29 f., No. 6, Pl. H x; Newell and Noe, *The Alexander Coinage of Sikyon*, 17, Nos. 27, 28, Pl. xviii.27.2. Another figure of Herakles which appears on Roman Imperial coins (*NCP* 30, No. 7, Pl. H xi) may represent the statue by Skopas at Sikyon (Paus. ii.10.1).

[16] Taras colossus, Niketas Choniatas, *De Alexio Isaacii Angeli Fr.* iii.4, pp. 687 f.; *De Signis Constantinopolitanis* 5, pp. 859 f.; he gives the sculptor's name as Lysimachos. Cf. Constantine Manasses, *Ekphr.* i, lines 21 ff. (Sternbach, *ÖJh.* v (1902), Beibl. col. 75). Significance of basket, e.g. Johnson, *Lysippos*, 194; but Marcadé, i, 73 associates it with the round chest on which Demeter sometimes sits. Epigram, *Anth. Gr.* xvi (*Plan.* iv), 103 (Tullius Geminus), cf. ibid., 104 (Philippos). Geminus' epigram also appeared on a lost base, once in Venice (cf. Marcadé, i, 70).

contrast, the Herakles Epitrapezios showed the hero in a lively and con-
vivial mood, but in a similar pose to the Taras colossus, sitting on a rock
covered by the lion-skin, but holding his club in one hand and a cup in
the other. A statuette, which purported to be the Epitrapezios of Lysippos,
was owned in the late first century AD by the collector Nonius Vindex,
and was given a colourful history according to which it had belonged
successively to Alexander, Hannibal, and Sulla. Unlike the Taras colossus,
which is known only from descriptions, this work is represented by several
copies, most of which are small, but one, the cult-statue from Alba Fucens,
is twice life-size. This raises the question whether the original was colossal,
from which, of course, it would follow that the statuette owned by Nonius
Vindex was of doubtful authenticity.[17] The copies vary considerably in
details, especially in the action of the arms, some having the club in the
left hand and the cup in the right, others the reverse. The Alba Fucens
statue also had some drapery about it, whereas most of the small copies
are nude. It is possible, therefore, that more than one original was involved,
which differed in size and in details of the pose.

Lysippos seems to have made an unusually large number of statues of
Herakles (besides those already mentioned, a series of the Labours for a
sanctuary at Alyzia in Akarnania).[18] However, while these form a large
number of the works by him which are known by name, they are only a
small proportion of the 1,500 works he is said to have produced.[19] His
range of subjects included gods, allegorical figures, portraits of both living
and dead persons, and animals.

Of his statues of gods, the Zeus at Taras was, like the Herakles, a
colossus, which defied Roman attempts to carry it off. It was forty cubits
tall, and was so balanced that it could be rocked with the hand but was
undisturbed by storms. No certain copy of it survives, and it is even uncertain whether the god was shown standing or seated. The other two
known statues of Zeus by Lysippos, the Zeus Nemeios at Argos and the
one at Megara which stood alongside some Muses by the same sculptor,
may both be represented on coins. Furthermore, the works at Megara may
be associated with a base bearing Lysippos' signature and a dedicatory
inscription. The lettering of this is dated *c.* 300, so it must have been a
very late work which stood upon the base, unless the inscription has been

---

[17] Statuette, Martial, ix.43 and 44, Stat. *Silv.* iv.6; the Alba Fucens statue and its
possible implications for the nature of the original Epitrapezios are discussed at
length by F. De Visscher, 'Héraklès Epitrapezios', *L'Ant. Class.* xxx (1961), 67–129,
where other copies of the type are also described and illustrated.

[18] Strabo, x.459; some copies have been identified, e.g. the group of Herakles
and the Hind in Palermo (Bieber, *Sculpture of the Hellenistic Age*², 36, Fig. 78).

[19] Pliny, *NH* xxxiv.37. The story that he put aside a gold piece for each work
completed may indicate what high prices he was able to command.

recut. The Zeus on the Megarian coins is in a pose similar to the god from Artemision, and has longer hair than one would normally expect to find on a late fourth-century statue; so if this is the statue by Lysippos, he may have been using a type of earlier origin.[20]

He also made a statue of Poseidon for the Korinthians, which may in fact have been the cult-statue in the temple at Isthmia. It is commonly identified as a type with the right foot raised on a rock or similar object, the right arm resting on the raised knee, and the trident in the left hand. This type is known in many copies, and also appears on coins of Demetrios Poliorketes, who, as head of the Korinthian League and effective controller of the Aegean, could appropriately use as a coin-device a statue of the sea-god from Korinth or Isthmia. The copies and most of the coins show the god bearded, but some of the coins give him a beardless, youthful face, probably that of Demetrios himself.[21]

Of the other statues of gods made by Lysippos, little is known except the fact of their existence. The Eros is commonly identified as a type, represented by several copies, in which the god is shown unstringing his bow. For the others – the Dionysos on Mount Helikon, the Helios in his chariot at Rhodes, and the Muses at Megara – even the identification of copies is doubtful. It should be noted that, except for the Muses, these are all male figures; the only other female figures ascribed to him are a portrait of the poetess Praxilla and a drunken flute-girl.[22] He evidently preferred, or at least was most famous for, male, often athletic types. In this respect he resembles Polykleitos and his followers.

Besides statues of familiar gods and heroes, for which, it seems, he sometimes used types which were already current, Lysippos made allegorical figures which seem to have been purely of his own devising. The most famous of these was the Kairos, which is known from a number of literary descriptions and copies, but there also exists a brief reference to a statue of Demos, which had no ears – the reason for this being, as the sculptor explained, that δῆμος ἀκοῇ οὔποτε τίθεται, αὐθαδείᾳ δὲ μᾶλλον. This may be identical with a statue of Demos seen by Pausanias at Athens, which he

[20] Zeus at Taras, Lucil. xvi, fr. 364 (Terzaghi³) (= Nonius, 201.16); Strabo, vi.278; Pliny, *NH* xxxiv.40. Zeus at Argos, Paus. ii.20.3; Imhoof–Blumer and Gardner, *NCP* 36, No. 11, Pl. K xxviii. Zeus at Megara, Paus. i.43.6; *NCP* 5, No. 4, Pl. A iv. Base, Marcadé, i, 69 f., cf. Loewy, *AM* x (1885), 150.
[21] The Poseidon mentioned, but not described, Lucian, *Iupp. Trag.* 9; copies discussed by Picard, *La Sculpture*, iv.2, pp. 491 ff.; coins, e.g. E. T. Newell, *The Coinages of Demetrios Poliorketes* (London, 1927), Pl. vii, Nos. 13 and 17 (bearded), Pl. viii, Nos. 4 and 6 (beardless).
[22] Eros, Paus. ix.27.3, cf. Picard, iv.2, pp. 534 ff.; Dionysos, Paus. ix.30.1, cf. Lucian, *Iupp. Trag.* 12; Helios, Pliny, *NH* xxxiv.63; Muses, Paus. i.43.6; Praxilla, Tatian, *C. Graec.* 33 (p. 34, ed. Schwartz); drunken flute-girl, Pliny, *NH* xxxiv.63.

says was by Lyson.[23] But this statue stood in the Bouleuterion at Athens and thus, it might be said, kept watch on the functioning of an important part of the Athenian democracy, so it is unlikely that Demos would have been respected in such an unflattering light. Lysippos' Demos could perhaps more appropriately have been set up at Sikyon, where the *demos* was anti-Macedonian, and so could be insulted with impunity while Sikyon was ruled by pro-Macedonian tyrants — perhaps especially after the crushing of Euphron's revolt in 322.

The statues by Lysippos which are best attested as having been made for Alexander are his portraits of Alexander himself and members of his circle. One such portrait is particularly well known from descriptions — that of the king gazing up at the sky in what was apparently a characteristic pose of his. It was this work, according to Plutarch, which pleased Alexander so much that he made Lysippos his official sculptor. It is often identified with the statue of Alexander holding a spear, which Lysippos contrasted with Apelles' painting of the king as Zeus. Several copies of the whole statue have been identified, and several busts of Alexander are also held to have been derived from it.[24] It has sometimes been suggested that Lysippos gave Alexander's features to certain divine statues, such as the Herakles Epitrapezios and the Helios at Rhodes; this, however, seems to be only a slightly different form of the artistic flattery for which he condemned Apelles. In any case, most of the copies of the Herakles Epitrapezios represent a bearded figure, whereas Alexander was clean-shaven. However, Herakles is often shown gazing upward in a manner reminiscent of Alexander's characteristic posture, and this may have been intended as a more subtle compliment to the king.[25] Another portrait of Alexander may have been included in the memorial to the Companions killed at the Granikos, which consisted of a group of equestrian portraits of the dead men. It was set up at Dion in Macedonia, and later taken to Rome; it was probably made not long after the battle in 334 BC, and its location perhaps indicates that Lysippos did not accompany Alexander to the East, but remained behind in Macedon.[26] After Alexander's death, Lysippos and Leochares were jointly commissioned by Krateros to make a group for dedication at Delphi, representing the occasion when he had saved

[23] *Gnomologium Vaticanum*, No. 399 (*Wiener Stud.* xi (1889), 62); Paus. i.3.5. Lyson is otherwise known, Pliny, *NH* xxxiv.91, so Pausanias was not necessarily simply making a mistake for 'Lysippos'.
[24] Plut. *Mor.* 335a–b and f, 360d (cf. *Anth. Gr.* xvi (*Plan.* iv), 120; Plut. *Alex.* 4.1–2; Tzetz. *Chil.* xi.90 ff. (ed. Leone). Copies, Picard, *La Sculpture*, iv.2, pp. 717 ff.
[25] Picard, *RA* 1911, 1, pp. 265 ff.; *La Sculpture*, iv.2, pp. 522 ff.
[26] Pliny, *NH* xxxiv.64; Arrian, *Anab.* i.16.4; Plut. *Alex.* 16.15–16; Vell. Paterc. i.11.3–4 (the only source which mentions a portrait of Alexander in the group); Justin, xi.6.13. Possible copy of one of the figures, Johnson, *Lysippos*, Pl. 48a.

Alexander's life during a lion-hunt. Echoes of this work have been recognized in a relief from Messene and in the Lion-hunt mosaic from Pella, but these are too unlike for both to be accurate representations of the group. The subject, showing Alexander as mortal and fallible, would perhaps have been congenial to Lysippos; a somewhat critical attitude to his patron is suggested not only by his disapproval of Apelles' flattery but by the story that the Kairos was made as a diplomatic rebuke to Alexander for letting slip an opportunity.[27]

Besides portraits of living persons, Lysippos made several of historical figures — Sokrates, the fifth-century Sikyonian poetess Praxilla, and Aisop and the Seven Sages. Two of his athletic statues also represented men of the previous century, the Agias and the Poulydamas at Olympia. The reliefs on the base of Poulydamas' statue represented some of his famous exploits, such as the exhibition of wrestling which he gave before the Great King. Lysippos' other victor-statues are known or supposed to have been made for contemporaries, though Cheilon's was not made until after the athlete's death. In producing portraits of living persons, Lysippos may have made use of the technique, invented by his brother Lysistratos, of taking plaster moulds of the face, a process which naturally tended to favour the production of realistic rather than idealized portraits. A rather cryptic remark attributed to Lysippos, that other sculptors represented men as they were, but he showed them as they seemed to be, may refer to this increased possibility of realism in sculpture.[28]

This and other recorded remarks of Lysippos, such as the claim that the Doryphoros was his teacher, suggests that he had devoted some thought to the relationship between his style and that of his predecessors. Unlike Polykleitos, however, he is not recorded as having treated one of his statues in particular as embodying his new principles of style and proportion in their purest form, nor as having written a treatise on the subject. The features of his style mentioned by Pliny (probably using Xenokrates as a source) which are most likely to remain recognizable in copies are the relative smallness of the head and slenderness of the body; his careful treatment of the hair no doubt involved a great deal of fine work on the bronze after casting, and could hardly have been reproduced

[27] Krateros group, Pliny, *NH* xxxiv.64; Plut. *Alex.* 40.5; the dedicatory inscription (*FdD* iii.4, No. 137) shows that it was set up by Krateros' son, probably after his father's death in 321. Messene relief, Picard, *La Sculpture*, iv.2, pp. 741 ff., Figs. 314–15; mosaic, C. M. Robertson, *Greek Painting* (Geneva, 1959), 169. Kairos story, Tzetz. *Chil.* viii.422, x.257–67. (ed. Leone).

[28] Sokrates, D. L. ii.43; Praxilla, Tatian, *C. Graec.* 33 (p. 34 ed. Schwartz); Aisop, *Anth. Gr.* xvi (*Plan.* iv), 332 (Agathias). Lysistratos, Pliny, *NH* xxxv.153. He appears to have been considerably overshadowed by his brother, since Pliny gives him the same *floruit* (*NH* xxxiv.51) and only one statue by him is known — a portrait of 'wise' Melanippe (Tatian, *C. Graec.* 33 (p. 35 ed. Schwartz)). Lysippos' remark, Pliny, *NH* xxxiv.65.

even by the most conscientious copyist in marble. As for his συμμετρία, a word for which Pliny could find no Latin translation, it is hard to define what this quality was, let alone to detect it in surviving copies.[29] Since it was a quality which Lysippos shared with his predecessors in spite of the radical changes which he had made in their system of proportions, it was perhaps concerned with the relationships of balance and contrast between the various parts of the human body, another matter which preoccupied Polykleitos and his school. Lysippos dealt with this in a different way from the Polykleitans, in that, instead of treating the body as two contrasted vertical halves, as they often did, he chose in many cases to create a strong horizontal emphasis by bringing one or both arms across the torso, and, instead of placing the weight firmly on one foot and leaving the other free, he frequently attempted to show the figure in the act of transferring its weight from one foot to the other. The Apoxyomenos exhibits both these features, and another statue attributed to Lysippos, a figure of a dancing girl preserved in several copies, is in an even more momentary pose. This statue also shows another characteristic which is found to some extent in Lysippos' works, but much more in those of his pupils – the composition which offers more than one satisfactory viewpoint.[30] Even works such as the Apoxyomenos, which appear to have been designed to be seen from one direction only, represent a considerable departure from the rather flat design of most statues of the Polykleitan school. These advances in composition and in the rendering of movement appear to have been the achievements in which Lysippos was believed to have excelled all his predecessors and brought Greek sculpture to perfection.

B. The School of Lysippos

Lysippos is known to have had several pupils, including his own sons, and these in turn taught other sculptors, thus keeping the school in existence for at least two generations more. The majority of these artists were Sikyonians by birth, and seem to have confined their activity to mainland Greece, with certain notable exceptions such as Eutychides' Tyche at Antioch. The last known member of the school, Thoinias, is found working at Sikyon itself, which evidently remained the headquarters of the school.

Of the sons of Lysippos, Daippos, Boidas, and Euthykrates, relatively little is known. Daippos appears to have specialized in athletic sculpture, since his only known works are two Olympic victor-statues and a Perixyomenos. Boidas' only known work is an *adorans*, commonly identified with a bronze statue of a praying boy in Berlin. The third brother, Euthykrates,

[29] Pliny, *NH* xxxiv.65.
[30] The original may have been Lysippos' drunken flute-girl (Pliny, *NH* xxxiv.63); C. M. Robertson, *History of Greek Art*, 468 and 704 n. 53.

is by far the best attested in the sources, perhaps because he was the most highly thought of by later art historians. His known works include an Alexander, which makes it likely that he was active before 323, and other subjects also treated by Lysippos; a Herakles, a cavalry battle, and various animals. He is also credited with an image of Trophonios at Lebadeia, a group of Thespiades, and several portraits of women. Pliny says that he imitated his father's *constantia* rather than his *elegantia*, and that he favoured a rather austere style.[1] This suggests that he may have imitated Lysippos' simpler and more traditional works rather than his more elaborate decorative pieces, and in this he seems to have been exceptional among the members of the school.

The most famous of the other pupils of Lysippos appears to have been Eutychides, whose principal work was the statue of Tyche at Antioch. This must date from about the time of the foundation of Antioch, perhaps from 01. 121 (296 to 293 BC), which Pliny gives as Eutychides' *floruit*. The statue was apparently colossal, though all the copies are small, and showed Tyche sitting on a rock with the river Orontes emerging from under her feet. She was heavily draped and wore the turreted crown which became the standard attribute of Tyche. The pose is a complicated one which, with the aid of the lines of the drapery, offers several interesting viewpoints; this perhaps reflects the fact that the statue stood in the open, not in a temple, and so could be approached from several directions. This was the first of the local Tychai whose cults grew up in the Hellenistic period, and to some extent set the pattern for later representations of the goddess. A colossal head of Tyche found at Sikyon may be a copy of a local cult-statue by Eutychides or another member of the school of Lysippos.[2] (See Plate 7.) Eutychides is also said to have made a statue of the river Eurotas 'more liquid than the river itself', which perhaps bore some resemblance to the Orontes under the feet of the Tyche, a victor-statue at Olympia, and a 'Liber Pater' (i.e. a Dionysos). The latter is mentioned in Pliny's section on sculpture in stone, and so was evidently in that material rather than bronze. Eutychides was also a painter, and was credited with a picture of Nike driving a chariot.[3] His pupil, Kantharos son of Alexis, was apparently a sculptor of some merit, but not famous

[1] Daippos, Paus. vi.2.6 and 16.3, Pliny, *NH* xxxiv.87; Boidas, Pliny, *NH* xxxiv.73, cf. e.g. Bieber, *Sculpture of the Hellenistic Age*[2], Fig. 93; Euthykrates, Pliny, *NH* xxxiv.66, Tatian, *C. Graec.* 33 (p. 34 ed. Schwartz).

[2] *Floruit*, Pliny, *NH* xxxiv.51 (along with other pupils of Lysippos); Tyche, Paus. vi.2.7, Joh. Malal. *Chron.* xi.276, apparently also viii.200 f.; copies, T. Dohrn, *Die Tyche von Antiochia* (Berlin, 1960), 13–29; Sikyon Tyche, *PAE.* 1935, pp. 82 f., No. 6 and 81, Fig. 14, said to be Roman, pre-Hadrianic.

[3] Pliny, *NH* xxxiv.78, cf. *Anth. Gr.* ix.709 (Philippos); Paus. vi.2.6–7; Pliny, *NH* xxxvi.34, xxxv.141.

for any one statue in particular. His only known works are Olympic victor-statues.[4]

In the second generation, a leading figure in the school of Lysippos was Euthykrates' pupil Teisikrates, who is said to have been stylistically closer than his master to the other members of the school. He made a portrait of Demetrios Poliorketes, several copies of which have been identified, including a statuette from Herculaneum, which shows Demetrios standing with one foot raised on a rock, in a pose very similar to that of the Poseidon attributed to Lysippos, and gazing upwards in the manner characteristic of Alexander, which Lysippos rendered so well. A head identified as a portrait of Demetrios, found at Sikyon itself, may be a copy of this work, but it lacks the upward gaze, and the top of the head is missing, where might have been found the little horns which Demetrios wears both in Teisikrates' portrait and on coins. (See Plate 8.) According to Plutarch, no artist was ever able to do justice to Demetrios' good looks, but if Teisikrates used Lysistratos' technique of taking moulds from the face, he may at least have come nearest to producing an accurate rendering of his subject's features.[5] Teisikrates' other known works are a portrait of Peukestes, who saved Alexander's life, an old man of Thebes, and a chariot, to which one Piston later added the figure of a woman. A base found at Eretria belonged to his statue of Aischylos son of Antandridas, commissioned by the Delphians after Aischylos had held the office of *Hieromnemon* in 273/2. Three signatures of his have also been found at sites in Boiotia, two of which give his father's name as Thoinias.[6]

Teisikrates had two sons, Thoinias and Arkesilaos. Arkesilaos became a painter, but Thoinias followed his father's profession. He is, however, known only from the survival of several of his signatures, not from any literary source. These signatures have been found at Sikyon itself, various sites in Boiotia, and Delos.[7] He appears to have continued, to some extent, his father's association with the Antigonid dynasty, since he made (and possibly dedicated) a statue of Philip V at Sikyon. This work should be dated *c.* 220, when Philip had just become king and was still on friendly terms with Aratos. Thoinias' earliest dated work is his statue of the poet

---

[4] Pliny, *NH* xxxiv.85, Paus. vi.3.6 and 17.7.

[5] Pliny, *NH* xxxiv.67; copies, Picard, *RA* xxii (1944), 5–37; Sikyon head, *PAE*, 1935, p. 82, No. 5, 81, Fig. 13; Plut. *Dem.* 2.2.

[6] Peukestes, Pliny, *NH* xxxiv.67, cf. Arrian, *Anab.* vi.10.1–2, Plut. *Alex.* 63.7–8, Curt. ix.5.14–18; Eretria base, *ADelt.* xvii (1961–2), A 211–14 (for date, cf. Daux, *Chronologie delphique* (*FD* iii suppl., Paris, 1943), 34); other bases, *IG* vii.267 (from Oropos), 2470 (from Thebes); *ADelt.* xvi (1960), B 147, *Rev. Phil.* xxxix (1965), 263, *SEG* xxii, No. 416, *ADelt.* xxv (1970), A 138 f (from Thebes).

[7] Arkesilaos, Pliny, *NH* xxxv.146, Paus. i.1.3; Thoinias, Marcadé, *Signatures*, ii, 128–30. For the Delos base, cf. *SEG* xix, 520.

Herakleitos of Halikarnassos in the Amphiareion at Oropos, which is dated *c.* 240. Thus his career falls roughly into the third quarter of the third century, making him the latest known direct artistic descendant of Lysippos. Since none of his statues has survived, it is not possible to form an opinion about his style; but if he continued to follow Lysippos as faithfully as his father had done, his contemporaries perhaps considered him rather old-fashioned. This may account for his failure to find a place in the early literature of Greek art, unless this was simply due to the fact that he was active after Ol. 121 (296 to 293 BC), the date when, according to Pliny, 'art came to an end'.[8]

There remains Xenokrates, described by Pliny as a pupil of either Euthykrates or Teisikrates, a prolific sculptor and author of a book on the subject, and perhaps also a painter, since he wrote on this art as well. No statues attributable to him survive, and Pliny does not mention any of his works by name. A number of signatures of Xenokrates survive, two of which come from Oropos, where Teisikrates and Thoinias also worked. In one he is called Athenian, which gives rise to doubt whether Pliny's Xenokrates is meant, since he is generally assumed to have been Sikyonian, although Pliny does not actually say so. Xenokrates is commonly held to have been the source for many passages in Pliny which tend to glorify Sikyonian artists, especially Lysippos and his contemporaries in the Sikyonian school of painting, Apelles and Pausias.[9] In both cases, the artists are placed in an order of development, which is not necessarily chronologically correct, towards the successful rendering of nature. Xenokrates probably ended his work with the first generation of Lysippos' pupils in sculpture and with the pupils of Pausias in painting, and it was possibly for this reason that Pliny regarded the history of Greek sculpture as ending with this generation; for chronological reasons, Xenokrates could not have carried his work much beyond this date, and may not have wished to do so, since for him sculpture had reached its perfection with Lysippos, and its subsequent history could only be one of decline.

---

[8] Statue of Philip, Marcadé, ii, 129 f., cf. Plut. *Arat.* 47–52; Herakleitos, cf. Strabo, xiv.656, D. L. ix.17, Kallim. *Epig.* 2 (Pfeiffer); 01. 121, Pliny, *NH* xxxiv.51–2.

[9] Pliny, *NH* xxxiv.83; Pliny cites books by him *De Toreutice* (*NH* i, list of sources for xxxiv) and *De Pictura* (*NH* xxxv.68); cf. D. L. iv.15 and perhaps vii.188 (Wilamowitz, *Antigonos von Karystos* (Berlin, 1881), 8 n. 3). Bases, *IG* vii, 336 (from Oropos), 332 (from Oropos); *IG* ix.1, No. 131 (from Elateia); *IGB* 154k, 1 (Z) (from Attalos' victory-monument). Identity with Pliny's Xenokrates accepted by B. Schweitzer, *Xenokrates von Athen* (Halle, 1932), 4 f. His work discussed by Jex-Blake and Sellers, *The Elder Pliny's Chapters on the History of Art*, xvi–xxxvi, A. Kalkmann, *Die Quellen der Kunstgeschichte des Plinius* (Berlin, 1898), 69–81, Schweitzer, *Xenokrates von Athen*, J. J. Pollitt, *The Ancient View of Greek Art* (New Haven, 1974), 74–7. Pliny cites him by name only once (*NH* xxxv.68), in a passage which, as it happens, praises the non-Sikyonian Parrhasios.

One Sikyonian sculptor who was active around 300 BC, Daitondas, is not known to have belonged to the school of Lysippos. His date is fixed by Pausanias' description of his victor-statue of Theotimos, whose father served under Alexander, and by two bases bearing his signature. One of these comes from Thebes, which calls to mind the activity of Teisikrates and Thoinias in Boiotia. Perhaps he was, like them, a member of the school of Lysippos, and it is pure accident that the fact has not been recorded. The same may be true of the sculptor Menaichmos, if he was identical with the late fourth-century Sikyonian historian of that name.[10]

[10]   Daitondas, Paus. vi.17.5, Marcadé, i, 25; Menaichmos, *FGH* 131, esp. T.2.

4. Sikyonian Painting and Mosaics

According to ancient sources, Sikyon was a major centre of painting from the very beginnings of the art; but, as with other branches of art, the amount of detailed evidence offered in support of this view is relatively small. The fourth-century and later Sikyonian school of painting is well attested, with names of individual artists and descriptions of some of their works, which it may therefore be possible to identify in copies. For earlier periods, however, the information is much less definite.

Pliny's account of the origin of painting makes the art begin with the drawing of an outline round a man's shadow, which, he says, some Greeks claimed was first done at Sikyon, others at Korinth. Both the procedure and the places with which its invention was associated call to mind Pliny's account of the origin of clay-modelling, and the two arts are more explicitly put together by Athenagoras, who credits the invention of *graphike* (which he distinguishes from *skiagraphia*, the difference apparently being that *graphike* involved painting within the outlines) to Kraton of Sikyon.[1] This name does not appear in Pliny, who instead mentions Telephanes of Sikyon as one of the first exponents, though not the inventor, of line-drawing. He is said to have used no colour, but to have shown some internal lines in his figures as well as the outlines, and to have added inscriptions naming his subjects. On the scheme of development outlined by Pliny, Kraton should represent a later stage than Telephanes, since he evidently used colour; but since the two accounts differ considerably in the developments they describe and the personalities to whom they refer, perhaps it is unwise to try to amalgamate them. No individual work of Telephanes is mentioned, but Kraton is said to have painted the shadows of a man and a woman on a whitened board.

In the absence of any vase-paintings which can securely be assigned to a Sikyonian school, there is little possibility of detecting a distinctive Sikyonian style of panel-painting in the archaic period. The wooden *pinakes* from Pitsa come from a site which is geographically close to Sikyon, but appear to be of Korinthian origin. They reflect a later stage in Pliny's scheme of the development of painting than that to which Telephanes belongs, since they show such features as the differentiation of the sexes by skin colour, an invention which Pliny ascribes to Eumaros of Athens, and the later *pinakes* C and D show an increased complexity of pose and drapery such as Pliny says was introduced by Eumaros' successor,

[1] Pliny, *NH* xxxv.15–16; Athenagoras, *Leg. pro Christ.* 17.3.

Kimon of Kleonai.[2] The white ground of the *pinakes* also recalls Kraton's work as described by Athenagoras. The earliest of the *pinakes* are dated in the 530s, and the latest *c.* 500; this suggests that Eumaros and Kimon were active in the second half of the sixth century, and Telephanes (and perhaps Kraton too) in the first half of the century, or even earlier.

After the early Sikyonian painters, there follows a long blank period until the appearance of Eupompos, the founder of the fourth-century Sikyonian school. Pliny makes him a contemporary of Zeuxis, who was active at the end of the fifth century and the beginning of the fourth. This may in fact be a slightly early date for Eupompos, whose pupil Pamphilos was active in the mid-fourth century. He may have survived long enough to meet the young Lysippos, if the anecdote about his influence on Lysippos' style implies direct personal contact. This anecdote provides the only information we have about Eupompos' style, and only one painting by him is recorded – an athletic victor holding a palm.[3] As Pliny recognized, his artistic importance can be deduced from the fact that he founded a school which lasted for several generations, but it would seem that few of his own works survived, perhaps because they were less highly esteemed than those of his successors.

Pamphilos, Eupompos' pupil, was not a Sikyonian by birth, but an Amphipolitan. One of his pictures, 'proelium ad Phliuntem ac victoria Atheniensium', is generally supposed to have represented the capture of Thyamia by Chares and the Phieiasians in 366. The choice of a Sikyonian defeat as a subject can best be explained by the supposition that Pamphilos or his patron was an enemy of Euphron, whose fall was partly brought about by the defeat at Thyamia. The only other known paintings by Pamphilos are a family group and an 'Odysseus on the raft', but it is known that he painted in encaustic as well as tempera, and that Aratos enthusiastically collected his works and sent them to Ptolemy. Pliny's account of Pamphilos, perhaps using a treatise by him as a source, concentrates on his contributions to the theory of painting. He was a learned man himself, and insisted that arithmetic and geometry were essential studies for aspiring artists. Perhaps because the training he offered included tuition in these subjects, he charged his pupils the high fee of a talent, which no doubt had the advantage, from his point of view, of allowing him to take a relatively small number of promising pupils. Three are known by name – Apelles, Melanthios, and Pausias – of whom Apelles at least was not a native of Sikyon, but was attracted thither when he was already an established artist

---

[2] *Pinakes*, *EAA* vi, 200 ff.; Eumaros and Kimon, Pliny, *NH* xxxv.56.

[3] Eupompos' works and school, Pliny, *NH* xxxv.75; his date, *NH* xxxv.64; Lysippos story, *NH* xxxv.61.

by the fame of Pamphilos' school. Pamphilos also appears to have possessed considerable influence inside Sikyon, since he was able to bring it about that free-born boys were taught drawing and painting as a normal part of their education.[4] Perhaps he was enabled to do this by the support of a powerful patron.

Little is known about Melanthios apart from the fact that he was Pamphilos' pupil and wrote a treatise on painting. Although his pictures were famous and much sought after by collectors, the only one known by name is a portrait of the tyrant Aristratos with a chariot driven by Nike, painted by Melanthios and all his school, including Apelles. This painting caused a crisis of conscience for Aratos, who was committed to destroying the monuments of the Sikyonian tyrants, but wished to preserve this one for the sake of its artistic merits. He finally accepted a compromise whereby the figure of Aristratos was painted out (all but the feet, which remained visible under the chariot) and a palm-tree substituted. A little can be discovered about Melanthios' style, which was apparently closely related to that of his master Pamphilos. Quintilian places them together as the painters who excelled in *ratio* (as opposed, for instance, to the *gratia* of Apelles), and Pliny says that Apelles acknowledged Melanthios as his superior in composition. The painter himself is said to have asserted that works of art, like people's characters, are the better for some αὐθάδεια and σκληρότης.[5] It seems that he followed Pamphilos in constructing his pictures on a mathematical basis, ignoring or even deliberately avoiding the possibility of more immediate visual appeal. No pupils of his are known by name, though the account of Aristratos' portrait suggests that he had some.

Unlike the painters so far discussed, Pausias was primarily a worker in encaustic, and was taught first by his father Bryes, who is otherwise unknown, and later by Pamphilos. The encaustic technique appears to

---

[4] Pamphilos' works and school, Pliny, *NH* xxxv.76-7, Suda, s.v. Πάμφιλος (where the painter appears to have been confused with another man), also s.v. Ἀπελλῆς; materials, Pliny, *NH* xxxv.123; treatise, Jex-Blake and Sellers, *The Elder Pliny's Chapters on the History of Art*, xlii; export to Ptolemy, Plut. *Arat.* 12.6-13.1, cf. Athen. v.196e. The 'Herakleidai of Pamphilos' (Ar. *Plut.* 385 and Schol.) seems to have been a play, not a painting (cf. L. H. Jeffery, 'The battle of Oinoe in the Stoa Poikile: a problem in Greek art and history', *BSA* lx (1965), 46 f., quoting Robertson). E. C. Keuls, *Plato and Greek Painting*, (Leiden, 1978), 139-50 discusses the theory of the Sikyonian school, esp. Pamphilos, and suggests that some aspects of it, especially the practical application of mathematics to painting, were attacked by Plato.

[5] Melanthios' treatise, Pliny, *NH* i, list of sources for xxxv, D. L. iv.18, Vitruv. vii, *praef.* 14 ('Melampus' in text); high value of his paintings, Pliny, *NH* xxxv.50; Aristratos portrait, Plut. *Arat.* 13.2-5 (quoting Polemon as source for at least part of the story); style, Quint. xii.10.6, Pliny, *NH* xxxv.80, D. L. iv.18.

have originated as a method of colouring marble statues, and was only later used for panel-paintings; Pausias, so Pliny says, was the first great painter to use it (for Pamphilos it was apparently only a sideline). So far was he a specialist that when he worked with the brush, on the restoration of some murals by Polygnotos at Thespiai, he was considered relatively unsuccessful, 'quoniam non suo genere certasset'. He also used encaustic for architectural decoration, being, according to Pliny, the first to paint coffered ceilings and to make customary the decoration of vaults.[6] Most of his panel-paintings were small, and boys were his favourite subject. One such picture was known as ἡμερήσιος because he had painted it in a day, to refute critics who claimed that the encaustic method was excessively slow. His pornographic pictures were probably also small, like those of Parrhasios, who seems to have invented the genre. He also painted several flower-pictures, inspired by the work of his mistress Glykera, who was supposed to have invented garlands made from several kinds of flowers; similarly, Pausias represented a variety of flowers in his paintings. The most famous of these was a portrait of Glykera holding a wreath, known as the Garland-weaver or Garland-seller. A copy of this painting (or possibly a replica by Pausias himself) was sold for two talents in the first century BC. Although none of these paintings now survives, we can obtain some idea of their subject-matter from floral decorations on vases and mosaic floors which correspond in their design to what is known of Pausias' paintings.[7] He also painted large pictures, one of which, a 'sacrifice of oxen' which Pliny saw in Rome, incorporated an important innovation in the use of foreshortening, whereby an ox seen end-on was successfully rendered although Pausias denied himself the trick used by earlier painters to give an impression of depth, the use of light colours for objects which were intended to stand out in the picture, and dark for those which should recede; here the ox was all black, but stood out none the less. This picture was evidently extremely famous, and although no direct copies of it survive, echoes of it can perhaps be detected in a number of Roman paintings and mosaics. Pausanias saw other paintings by Pausias in the

[6] Pliny, *NH* xxxv.123-7; origin and method of encaustic, C. M. Robertson, *History of Greek Art*, 485; coffers and vaults, idem, 487 (including examples of painted coffers earlier than Pausias, thus refuting Pliny's claim that he was the first to practise this type of decoration); a well-preserved Hellenistic vault painted with 'Pausian florals' in a tomb at Lefkadia in western Macedonia, *AAA* vi (1973), 87–92 and Colour Pl. 1.

[7] Pornography, Athen. xiii.567b, cf. Pliny, *NH* xxxv.72 and Fronto, *Ad M. Ant. Imp. de Eloq.* i.1 (Van den Hout, p. 131); Glykera, Pliny, *NH* xxxv.125, xxi.4 (where she and Pausias are dated after 01. 100 (380 to 377 BC)); 'Pausian florals' in mosaics, see pp. 154–156; on vases, e.g. H. Jucker, *Bildnis im Blätterkelch* (Olten, 1961), figs. 126–8; also in metalwork, e.g. *Met. Mus. Bull.* xxxii.5 (1973/4), No. 171, Pl. 31, and textiles, e.g. *AAA* x (1977), Colour Pl. 1.

Tholos at Epidauros — an Eros who had laid aside his bow and arrows and taken up the lyre, and a Methe (Drunkenness) drinking from a glass bowl through which her face could be seen. This work again finds echoes in Roman painting, in the transparent glass vessels which appear in still-lifes from Pompeii and Herculaneum.[8]

Pausias had at least two pupils, including his son Aristolaos, whom Pliny numbers among the 'most severe' painters. The list of his works includes a sacrifice of oxen, which suggests that he attempted to improve upon his father's treatment of the subject, and several others have an Athenian flavour — a Perikles, a Theseus, and a picture of the Attic *demos*. On the other hand, the obvious association for his Epameinondas is with Thebes, and his Medeia and 'Virtus' have no particular local connections.[9] There are no known copies of any of these paintings. Pausias' other pupil, Nikophanes, is the subject of conflicting pieces of information. At one point Pliny describes his work as elegant and attractive, but elsewhere says that he was very much a painters' painter, a careful worker but inclined to use over-harsh colours, especially yellow. Here he is contrasted with the universally popular Sokrates, perhaps a fellow-pupil. One of these two is said to have painted a group of Asklepios and his daughters, and a figure of Oknos twisting a rope which was being eaten by an ass. No doubt it was the 'elegant' Nikophanes whom Polemon considered a good painter of obscene pictures; the choice of subject-matter links him to Pausias, and if there were in fact two painters named Nikophanes to whom these two pieces of information apply, it was probably the 'elegant' one who was Pausias' pupil.[10]

The direct descent of the Sikyonian school from Eupompos comes to an end with the pupils of Pausias; several other Sikyonian painters are known, but no connection can be traced between them and the main school. There is, for instance, Eutychides, who must have been roughly contemporary with the pupils of Pausias, but is not known to have had anything to do with them. However, the subject of his one known painting, Nike driving a chariot, is reminiscent of the portrait of Aristratos by Melanthios and his circle, which in Eutychides' time was presumably to be seen at Sikyon in its original state, and which may have helped to inspire him. Since only this one painting by him is known as against four statues, it seems that he remained primarily a sculptor.[11]

[8] Echoes of Pausias' ox, e.g. G. C. Picard, *Roman Painting* (London, 1970), Fig. lii, S. di Neuhoff, *Ancient Corinth and its Museum* (Athens, 1973), Pl. 23; Epidauros paintings, Paus. ii.27.3; glass vessels, e.g. A. Maiuri, *Roman Painting* (Geneva, 1953), 134 and 136.

[9] Pliny, *NH* xxxv.137.

[10] Pliny, *NH* xxxv.111 and 137; Athen. xiii.567b (quoting Polemon); cf. also Plut. *Mor.* 18b, where the text has Χαιρεφάνης.

[11] Pliny, *NH* xxxv.141.

Among the public buildings in the new city of Demetrias-Sikyon was an art gallery built by Demetrios' mistress Lamia. It was probably in this gallery that works by the fourth-century masters, such as the portrait of Aristratos, were kept; a description of it was written by Polemon in the second century BC. The pictures were sold in 56 BC to pay off the Sikyonian national debt, and were taken to Rome, so it is possible that some of the works by Sikyonian masters which Pliny saw in Rome, such as Pausias' 'sacrifice of oxen', had once been in this gallery.[12] Regrettably, only a few fragments of Polemon's work survive, and the dispersal of the paintings in the first century BC left nothing to be described by Pausanias, so the contents of the gallery can only be guessed at; but the fact that it was established at all shows the high esteem in which Sikyonian painting was held at this time.

Half a century later, in the time of Aratos, fourth–century Sikyonian paintings were still held in high esteem as collectors' items, but there was also a flourishing contemporary school of painting. Perhaps the discontinuity between this and the fourth–century school is less than it appears in the sources, where, as in the case of sculpture, the ending of Xenokrates' treatise at a date in the early third century may have produced the appearance of a break in artistic activity where in fact there was none. The leader of the third-century school was Nealkes, a personal friend of Aratos. It was he who persuaded Aratos to spare the portrait of Aristratos on condition that the offending figure was removed, and who carried out the necessary alteration. A number of original works by Nealkes are also known; a groom holding a racehorse, an Aphrodite, and a naval battle between the Persians and Egyptians, in which he indicated that the scene was the Nile rather than the open sea by painting an ass drinking on the bank and a crocodile lying in wait for it. Concerning his picture of the racehorse, the story is told that after repeated unsuccessful attempts to render the foam at the animal's mouth, the artist in disgust threw his sponge at the offending spot, and thereby accidentally produced exactly the effect he wanted. Nealkes' daughter Anaxandra became a painter, as did his colour-grinder Erigonos, who had a famous pupil of his own, Pasias. The Sikyonian Xenon, whose teacher is called Neokles by Pliny, may also in reality have been a pupil of Nealkes.[13]

---

[12] Athen. xiii.577c quotes Polemon's Περὶ τῆς ἐν Σικυῶνι ποικίλης στόας (on the foundation of the gallery by Lamia), and xiii.567b his Περὶ τῶν ἐν Σικυῶνι πινάκων, which may be the same work. Sale of pictures, Pliny, *NH* xxxv.127.

[13] Nealkes, Pliny, *NH* xxxv.142, 102–4 (where the story about the racehorse is told alongside a similar one about a dog by Protogenes); the same story told of an unnamed artist, Plut. *Mor.* 99b, Val. Max. viii.11 ext. 7; and of Apelles, Dio Chrys. *Orat.* lxiii.4–5, Sext. Emp. *Pyrrh. Hypoth.* i.28. Anaxandra, Clem. Alex. *Strom.* iv.19.122.4; Erigonos and Pasias, Pliny, *NH* xxxv.145; Xenon, ibid., 146.

Other painters are also known to have worked for Aratos, and so should probably be grouped with Nealkes and his school, though no direct connection between them is attested. These are Leontiskos, who painted Aratos as a victor with a trophy, and also a woman playing the kithara, and Timanthes, who painted Aratos' battle at Pellene *c.* 240. Arkesilaos, the son of the sculptor Teisikrates, must also have been active at about this time, but his only known work was in Athens — a painting of Leosthenes, who led Athens into the Lamian War, and his children, which Pausanias saw in the sanctuary of Zeus and Athena at Peiraieus.[14]

Although the lack of information about these third-century painters may be partly due to the loss of the literature which dealt with them, especially Polemon's work on the Sikyon art gallery, what little is known suggests that they were in any case inferior to their predecessors and of less interest to later collectors and critics. Pliny lists them among artists of the second rank, and Fronto's judgement that Nealkes was incapable of painting 'magnifica' points the same way.[15] Aratos is said to have sought out works by Pamphilos and Melanthios, by then a hundred years old or more, to send to Ptolemy, rather than those of Nealkes and other contemporaries.

Some very obscure Sikyonian painters, of whom no more is known than their names and ethnic, may belong to the third-century group; the Mnasitheos mentioned by Pliny, and the Thales who is called a genius, but known only as the philosopher's namesake.[16] But it is equally possible that they belonged to the fourth century, since even in this relatively well-documented period painters such as Pausias' father Bryes could remain almost unknown.

Plainly, it was the fourth-century painters who made the reputation of the Sikyonian school, and provided justification for remarks such as Pliny's that Sikyon was 'for a long time the home of painting'.[17] The preservation of many of their works in the local art gallery no doubt served to maintain their fame and that of their city, and also to inspire their successors; but these may also have suffered by the comparison, both in others' opinion and in their own.

Although no original Sikyonian paintings survive, some evidence for

[14] Leontiskos, Pliny, *NH* xxxv.141; Timanthes, Plut. *Arat.* 32.6 (possibly the same who went with Aratos on an embassy to Ptolemy, ibid., 12.3); Arkesilaos, Paus. i.1.3.
[15] Pliny, *NH* xxxv.138 (introducing the alphabetical list in which they appear); Fronto, *Ad M. Ant. Imp. de Eloq.* i.1 (Van den Hout, p. 131).
[16] Mnasitheos, Pliny, *NH* xxxv.146 (possibly identical with the man who helped Aratos capture Sikyon, Plut. *Arat.* 7.4 and 6); Thales, D. L. i.38 (he distinguishes two, the Sikyonian and one mentioned by Douris in his work on painting).
[17] *NH* xxxv.127 (in the course of his discussion of Pausias).

their style may be given by the third-century painted grave-stelai from Pagasai in Thessaly. The link between the two sites is provided by Pausanias, who saw a grave-monument with painted decoration at Sikyon. This, he says, was not of the usual local form, but was so designed that the architecture fitted the painting, which was very fine. Hence it seems likely that the painting was the most important part of the monument, probably a portrait of the person commemorated, as on the Pagasai stelai. Even the subject of the Sikyon monument, Xenodike who died in childbirth, can be paralleled at Pagasai, where the stele of Hediste shows the dead woman lying in bed surrounded by attendants, including a nurse holding the baby.[18] However, because of the stress which Pausanias lays upon the exceptional nature of Xenodike's monument, it is not easy to decide whether painting was commonly used in this way at Sikyon, though in view of the popularity of the art there this is likely enough. As described by Pausanias, the normal Sikyonian monument was a stone structure consisting of a base supporting columns and a pediment-like top, with a brief inscription consisting of the name of the dead person and '$\chi\alpha\hat{\iota}\rho\epsilon$'. Stelai bearing such inscriptions and foundations of more substantial monuments have been found at Sikyon, and representations of the structures described by Pausanias have been identified on local coins, which show a *naiskos*-like structure, apparently containing a statue, on a tall cylindrical base, flanked by herms and cypresses.[19] Such structures could have sheltered paintings as well as statues, and it has been suggested that many such once existed, but were removed in 56 BC, leaving only Xenodike's monument to be seen by Pausanias. A painted monument is known to have existed at Sikyon in the fourth century — that of Telestes, which Aristratos commissioned from Nikomachos — but the form of this is unknown. There is no evidence that any of the famous masters of the Sikyonian school painted grave–stelai, though it has been suggested that Pausias' small pictures of boys, and even his portrait of Glykera, were of this nature.[20]

The paintings once at Sikyon may have disappeared, but there remain some fine specimens of the related art of mosaic, some of which are closely

---

[18] Paus. ii.7.3; A. S. Arvanitopoulos, Γραπταὶ στῆλαι Δημητριάδος–Παγασῶν (Athens, 1928), 147–9, Pl. ii, dated mid-3rd century BC. There is no evidence of date for Xenodike's stele.

[19] Form of monuments, Paus. ii.7.2; epitaphs, e.g. M. L. Earle, 'New Sicyonian inscriptions', *CR* vi (1892), 134 f.; coins, *NCP* 28, No. 1, Pl. H i–ii; foundations, *PAE* 1908, pp. 150 f., *ADelt.* xxii (1967), B 164 f., Pls. 124*a*–*β*.

[20] Arvanitopoulos, *AE* 1908, 23–31 and 39 f. Since the stelai are painted in encaustic, Pausias is the obvious artist with whom to associate them.

connected both with mosaics from other sites and with known paintings, especially the flower-pieces of Pausias. The earliest mosaics can be dated shortly before 400 BC, and are thus among the earliest specimens of the art in Greece. They are made from natural pebbles, and consequently have a very limited range of colours; the early ones are black and white only, the later also use red. The resulting two-colour effect, with the design normally in white on a dark ground, is strongly reminiscent of red-figure vase-painting. The best-preserved of the early floors has two con-centric circular friezes round a central rosette, the inner frieze containing animals, the outer galloping centaurs. (See Plate 17.) The corners are filled with a palmette pattern. Rather more than half of this floor is preserved intact in the Sikyon Museum. There are also some fragments which appear to belong to another floor of similar design, showing a griffin attacking another animal. Another floor of more complicated design than these is represented by several fragments. It apparently consisted of a circular centrepiece, which is entirely lost, surrounded by a wave-pattern in black. The circle was placed in a white square, the corners of which were filled with figures of which one is preserved – a man, rendered in 'black-figure', with red hair. The whole was surrounded by a black border with animals in white. (See Plates 9, 10, 11, 12.) The use of red suggests that this mosaic is somewhat later in date than those previously mentioned, and comparison with other floors from Sikyon and elsewhere suggests that the lost centrepiece may have contained a 'Pausian' floral pattern, which would bring the likely date well down in the fourth century. A different design again is found in a mosaic from Kokkinia in the coastal plain, with a centrepiece of florals round a gorgoneion, and animals in the corners. The entry-panel is preserved, showing a row of vases on a table. Here too some red is used for details, and the piece is dated to the first quarter of the fourth century.[21] The other two mosaics from Sikyon are

---

[21] Orlandos, *PAE* 1938 p. 123, 1941-4 pp. 59 f. dates all the Sikyon mosaics in the first half of the fourth century or even earlier; Robertson, *JHS* lxxxv (1965) 83 f., lxxxvii (1967) 134 dates the animal mosaics between those at Olynthos (des-troyed 348) and at Pella, and the florals in the second half of the fourth century. A black-and-white animal mosaic from Korinth, very similar to the Sikyon ones, appears firmly dated by its context *c*. 400, if not earlier (*AJA* xli (1937) 546 f.). Centaur mosaic, *PAE* 1938 p. 123, 122 fig. 3; *JHS* lix (1939) 198, pl. 13c; *EAA* v 209 fig. 294; *JHS* lxxxv (1965) 83; *BCH* c (1976) 582, fig. 8. Griffin fragment, *BCH* c (1976) 583 fig. 10 (upside down and misinterpreted as a swan). Fragments with red-haired man, *PAE* 1935 pp. 82-3 figs. 15-17, 1936 p. 94 figs. 8-9; *JHS* lxxxv (1965) 83; *BCH* c (1976) 583 fig. 9. Kokkinia mosaic, *ADelt.* xxii (1967) B 165; *BCH* c (1976) 572-581. Other mosaics, said to be similar to those from Olynthos, are reported to have been found west of the Asopos, where the new Korinth-Patras road crosses the river, *ADelt.* xxi (1966) B 124. Some fragments now in the Sikyon Museum, with a meander-patterned border, may come from this site.

dated to the second half of the fourth century, since they have 'Pausian' floral patterns, with relatively generous use of red. One is fragmentary, the other intact.[22] The fragmentary one is reconstructed to give a circular centrepiece of florals arranged symmetrically round a central rosette, the whole surrounded by wave-pattern, with animals in the corners or in an outer border. The complete floor is of rather different design, with the florals occupying the whole square, and the effect, although still symmetrical, is more naturalistic, since the individual flowers are strongly foreshortened and grow from curling stems. (See Plates 14, 15, 16.) There is a griffin on the entry-panel. (See Plate 13.) This floor represents the 'Pausian floral' *par excellence* — a complex pattern of vegetation naturalistically rendered, but with the fundamentally unnatural feature that different types of flower are shown growing on the same stem.

A number of other 'Pausian floral' mosaics are known, most of which come from sites in Macedonia. One which shows particularly striking resemblances to the specimens from Sikyon was found in the palace at Verghina. It has a circular floral pattern with a central sixteen-pointed rosette (this feature is particularly close to the Sikyon mosaic), the whole surrounded by a border of meander and wave-pattern, while the corners of the square are occupied by further florals and female figures which merge into the vegetation below the waist.[23] These call to mind Pausias' painting of Glykera with the garland, though he can hardly have shown her weaving her own body into it. Another mosaic, from a circular building at Pella, has a floral centre surrounded by wave-pattern, and an outer frieze of animals, similar to those in the early mosaics from Sikyon. Florals also appear as border-patterns in the Lion-hunt and Stag-hunt mosaics from Pella.[24] That of the Stag-hunt is well-preserved; in it the stems start from diagonally opposite corners and spread out along the two adjacent sides, bearing a variety of flowers, leaves, and coiled tendrils.

The numerous affinities between the Macedonian and Sikyonian mosaics raise interesting speculations about the origin of the craftsmen who made them. The only name known is that of Gnosis, who signed the Pella Stag-hunt without giving his ethnic. The place of origin of the art of mosaic in Greece is debatable, though Macedonia is sometimes favoured;[25] but the

[22] Fragmentary mosaic, *PAE* 1941–4 p. 59 f. fig. 4; *JHS* lxxxvii (1967) 134 no. 2. Intact mosaic, *PAE* 1941–4 p. 59 fig. 3 (upside down); *BCH* lxiv/lxv (1940/1) 241 fig. 7; *JHS* lxxxvii (1967) 133 f. no. 1, pl. xxiv; *BCH* c (1976) 585 figs. 11–12.

[23] *Ancient Macedonia* (ed. Laourdas and Makaronas) pl. xvii.

[24] Circular floor, *Ancient Macedonia* pl. xviii; lion-hunt, *Archaeology* xi (1958), lower pl. on p. 253; stag-hunt, *Ancient Macedonia* pl. xiii. Another 'Pausian floral' mosaic from Epidamnos, *ÖJh.* xxi–xxii (1922–4) Beibl. 203–14, figs. 122–3; Rumpf, *MuZ* 139 fig. 16; *Konferenca e Parë e Studimeve Albanologjike* 460 f. and fig. 1.

[25] Robertson, *History of Greek Art* 486 f.

earliest mosaics from Sikyon date from before any known connection between that state and Macedon, and so may have established an independent local tradition. The especially close resemblance between the floor from Verghina and the latest one from Sikyon makes it possible that one imitated the other, but it is uncertain which way round the imitation was; a Sikyonian partisan of Macedon having a floor made in imitation of one in his master's palace, or a Sikyonian craftsman bringing to the Macedonian court a style of decoration already established in his native city?

5. Sikyonian Literature and Music

Sikyon must have been the scene of literary and musical activity from a very early date, since by the time of Kleisthenes such events as contests of rhapsodes and the tragic choruses in honour of Adrastos were already well established. Kleisthenes abolished the contests and transferred the choruses to the cult of Dionysos, in the process no doubt seeing to it that instead of the deeds of Adrastos they dealt with other mythical subjects which he did not find politically offensive. It is not possible to draw any conclusions about the form of the choruses or the manner in which the subject-matter was treated. Since Herodotos is the only author who refers to them, their later history is a matter for speculation; were they transferred back to Adrastos when his cult was revived at the end of the sixth century, or left with Dionysos? The latter appears more likely, since by the time Pausanias visited Sikyon the cult of Adrastos had disappeared, leaving Dionysos as the god in charge of the theatre, near which his temple stood, and having as one of the principal features of his cult a torchlight procession with 'local hymns'. These in particular, and the theatrical performances in general, look like the descendants of Adrastos' choruses.[1] Since the cult-image with which the procession and hymns were associated were of very early date, it seems likely that the connection had been made in the time of Kleisthenes and had remained unbroken thereafter.

The rhapsodic contests are even harder to trace, since Kleisthenes simply abolished them. Herodotos does not say in honour of what god or hero they were held, though he keeps them firmly distinct from the ceremonies of the Adrastos cult. It is possible that they were dedicated to Apollo, and that the Pythia which Kleisthenes founded were designed to replace them. However, when it was later suggested that there had been Pythia at Sikyon before Kleisthenes, it was assumed that they had been athletic rather than musical contests. Some kind of musical contest existed at Sikyon in the fourth century BC, when the kitharode Stratonikos won a victory there. Since he celebrated this with a dedication in the Asklepieion, it seems reasonable to suppose that the contest was sacred to Asklepios, and so cannot have originated until his cult was introduced to Sikyon. However, there is some evidence that Asklepios replaced an earlier healing god, Apollo Karneios, to whom many features of the cult, including the

---

[1] Kleisthenes, Hdt. v.67.1 and 5; Dionysos cult, Paus. ii.7.5–6.

musical contest, may originally have belonged.[2] If the contests abolished
by Kleisthenes were Karneia, they could have been revived at the time
when other aspects of his anti-Argive policy were abandoned.

A musical event, again associated with Dionysos, concerning which
there is more detailed information, is the performance by the *phallophoroi*.
This, along with similar performances which took place in other Greek
cities, is described by Semos of Delos, who appears to have lived at the end
of the third century BC. They wore a headdress of *herpyllon* and *paideros*,
plants which were more or less peculiar to Sikyon, crowned with a wreath
of violets and ivy, and thick cloaks. One man, who was smeared with soot,
carried the phallos. They entered the theatre in procession, singing a hymn
to Dionysos of which Semos quotes the opening, in which the god is
assured that what follows will be totally new and never previously sung.
After this they picked out members of the audience for abuse.[3] The
date at which the rite originated is unknown.

In the hero-cult of Aratos, set up after his death at the end of the third
century BC, his birthday was observed as a festival which had a musical
element in the shape of a song with kithara accompaniment performed by
the Artists of Dionysos. The content of the song is not known; if it dealt
with the deeds of Aratos there would be an obvious parallel with the pre-
Kleisthenic Adrastos choruses. Plutarch, who describes the cult in detail,
says that many of its rites had fallen into disuse by his time, so it is possible
that he had never actually heard the song.[4] Further evidence for the
activity of the Sikyonian Artists of Dionysos is provided by their participation in the Soteria at Delphi, where many Sikyonians figure in the lists
of contestants.[5]

We can thus see a tradition of literary and musical activity at Sikyon
commencing before the reign of Kleisthenes, and continuing well into the
Hellenistic period. Not surprisingly, Sikyon is known to have produced a
number of more or less famous composers and performers, and also to
have been credited in antiquity with various innovations in this as in other
artistic fields. There is also some evidence for a Sikyonian tradition of the
history of music, formulated in the fourth century BC and, in its treatment of the subject, to some extent resembling the later work of Xenokrates
on sculpture and painting. This tradition was embodied in the so-called
Sikyonische Anagraphe and in the works of Menaichmos, both of which

[2] Pythia, Pind. *Nem.* ix.9; Stratonikos, Athen. viii.351e–f; his date, see Gow,
Machon 80 f.; musical contests at Spartan Karneia, cf. Athen. xiv.635e.
[3] *FGH* 396 F 24; date, Jacoby *RE* 2 iiA col. 1357 f.
[4] Plut. *Arat.* 53.5–6.
[5] Nachtergael, *Les Galates en Grèce et les Sôtéria de Delphes* Actes 2–11, 58–68.

are known only from a few fragments. Other ancient references to Sikyonian musicians and their technical innovations may ultimately be derived from one or other of these sources, but are not definitely identified as such.

The local tradition represented by the *Anagraphe* traced the art of singing to the kithara back to Amphion, who was claimed as a Sikyonian through his mother's connection with Epopeus. As well as such mythological characters, the work made reference to historical persons such as the aulete Sakadas of Argos, and gave a chronology based on the list of Priestesses of Argive Hera. It must therefore have been written after the compilation of this list by Hellanikos in the second half of the fifth century, but before the mid-fourth century, when it was quoted by Herakleides Pontikos.[6] No author is named — it is referred to simply as 'the document preserved at Sikyon' — and it is unlikely to have been the work of Menaichmos, who is said to have lived in the time of the Diadochoi.

If all the references to Menaichmos really relate to the same man, he must have been extremely talented and versatile, and should be considered an important author and minor artist. He is credited with a *History of Alexander*, a *History of Sikyon*, a *Pythikos* (apparently dealing with the Delphic rather than the Sikyonian Pythia), an *On Craftsmen* and an *On Metal-work* which was used as a source by Pliny. He also made a statue of a calf, apparently being attacked by a man. It may have been a piece of decorative metal-work, such as a cup with relief decoration, rather than a large free-standing statue, since it was classified as a work of *toreutike*. Fragments survive from several of his literary works, those from the *On Craftsmen* dealing mainly with musical inventions.[7] The tendency to turn the history of an art into a catalogue of inventions and technical advances is shared with Xenokrates and with what is known of the *Anagraphe*.

Much information about Sikyonian musicians is found in Athenaios; some of these items deal with inventions, and so may ultimately be derived from Menaichmos or the *Anagraphe*. Thus Lysander of Sikyon is said to have originated the art of solo kithara-playing (here Philochoros is quoted in opposition to Menaichmos, who ascribed this invention to somebody else), and Epigonos, who migrated from Ambrakia to Sikyon, is made the inventor of a new type of instrument with forty strings which was called *epigoneion* after him. The exact nature of this instrument is uncertain, but the name should perhaps be seen as a pun on γόνυ as well as a reference

---

[6] *FGH* 550. The fragments, and some information about the work, are preserved in [Plut.] *De Mus.* 1131f–1132a, 1134b.

[7] *FGH* 131.

to its inventor, suggesting that the instrument was played on the knee.[8] Epigonos had pupils, who are not known by name but as a group, who were the first to practise ἔναυλον κιθάρισιν (less likely duets for kithara and aulos than a technique of kithara-playing which produced an aulos-like tone), which had been invented by Lysander. Lysander is also credited with a number of other innovations whose exact nature is obscure, especially with being the first to 'substitute one instrument for another' and to perform with a chorus. Epigonos and Lysander are shadowy figures of whom little can be said beyond the bare statements about their inventions in the sources, but the suggested dating of Epigonos in the sixth century would bring them into a possible association with Kleisthenes. All that is known for certain about instrumental music at the Orthagorid court is that an aulos-player performed at the banquet which Kleisthenes gave for Agariste's suitors, and found himself accompanying Hippokleides' exhibition of dancing, but in the wider field of *mousike* there is the example of Ibykos to show that foreign artists came to work for Kleisthenes, and Epigonos may have been another such. Ibykos is also credited with the invention of an instrument, the *sambyke*, so it seems that he and Epigonos shared an interest in this aspect of their art.[9]

A highly successful Sikyonian musician who can certainly be dated in the time of Kleisthenes is the aulos-player Pythokritos son of Kallinikos, who won six successive Pythian victories immediately after Sakadas. Since Sakadas is known to have won at the first three Pythian Games after the Sacred War (586, 582, 578), Pythokritos' victories must be dated 574 to 554, so that the beginning of his career falls well within the reign of Kleisthenes. He also provided the musical accompaniment to the pentathlon at Olympia, and consequently had a monument there, which was seen by Pausanias.[10] Sikyonians continued to be successful in musical and dramatic contests in later times; they appear not only at the Soteria at Delphi, but at Athens, Oropos, and even Delos.[11]

The Sikyonians also had a certain reputation for dancing, being credited by some with the invention of dances involving the throwing of a ball, such as we find performed by Nausikaa and her companions in the *Odyssey*.

[8] Lysander, Athen. xiv.637f–638a; Epigonos, Athen. iv.183c–d, Pollux, iv.59; epigoneion, Sachs, *History of Musical Instruments* 137.

[9] Epigonos' pupils, Athen. xiv.637f–638a; his date, *RE* vi 69 s.v. Epigonos 7; Kleisthenes' banquet, Hdt. vi.129.2 (the after-dinner conversation was also about *mousike*, perhaps indicating Kleisthenes' interest in the subject); *sambyke*, Athen. iv.175d–e, Suda s.v. Ἴβυκος and Σαμβύκαι.

[10] Paus. vi.14.9–10. For Sakadas' Pythian victories, cf. Paus. x.7.4.

[11] Athens, *IG* ii² 3045, 3055, 3068, 3069, 2078; Oropos, *IG* vii 414 lines 4–5; Delos, *IG* xi.2 no. 108 line 23.

There was also a local type of dance known as *aleter*, which was considered 'serious' as opposed to the licentious *kordax*. It was perhaps by contrast with this kind of dance that Hippokleides' exhibition appeared so indecent to Kleisthenes. Athenaios records an inscription in the sanctuary of the Muses on Mount Helikon set up by Bakchiadas of Sikyon, who had danced and trained a chorus of men for a festival there. The inscription is described as 'ancient', but its exact date is uncertain.[12]

Sikyon produced a number of native poets as well as the immigrant Ibykos, but little of their work now survives. Praxilla, who lived in the mid-fifth century BC, composed a number of well-known *skolia* among other poems, including one on Adonis in which, on being asked in Hades what he missed most from his life on earth, he replied 'the sun, the stars, the moon, *sikyoi* in season, apples and pears'. This noteworthy example of bathos, as critics considered it, gave rise to the proverb 'sillier than Praxilla's Adonis'.[13] The only other Sikyonian poet of whose work much is known is the comic author Machon, who apparently spent most of his working life at Alexandria, where he was buried. Besides plays, of which very few fragments are preserved, he wrote a work called Χρεῖαι, a collection of witticisms by famous hetairai, musicians, and others, from which Athenaios quotes extensively. Some of these anecdotes may have originated at Sikyon, or at least have been current there, such as those about Demetrios Poliorketes and Lamia, but the majority have an Athenian background and were perhaps widely circulated in the Greek world, including Alexandria. Machon probably lived in the first half of the third century BC.[14]

Other Sikyonian poets were Sophilos, an author of Middle Comedy, Axiopistos, who wrote works called *Kanon* and *Gnomai* which were falsely attributed to Epicharmos, and Tyndarichos, who wrote a verse treatise on cookery. There are no surviving fragments of the latter two authors. Tragedy is represented by Neophron's *Medeia*, which is said to have served as a source for Euripides' play of the same name, or even to have been identical with it; but this author is also said to have been a contemporary of Alexander, and the surviving fragments of his play, which are not remarkable for their literary quality, look like attempts to rewrite Euripides' *Medeia* in accordance with the criticisms of Aristotle. Neophron is said to have written 120 tragedies in all, and to have been the first to bring on to the stage *paidagogoi* and the torturing of slaves. Perhaps more important, but not represented by any fragments, is Epigenes, who is said

---

[12] Athen. i.14d, cf. *Od.* vi.100; Athen. xiv.631d, cf. xiv.628c–d; Athen. xiv.629a.
[13] Fragments collected in Page, *Poetae Melici Graeci* 747–54.
[14] Athen. vi.241f–242a, xiv.664a; his epitaph, *Anth. Pal.* vii.708 (Dioskorides); fragments collected in Gow, *Machon*.

to have lived before Thespis (who was variously described as his second or sixteenth successor) and to have been the inventor of tragedy, or at least of the kind which dealt with non-Dionysiac subjects. It may have been on his account that the claim was made that tragedy originated at Sikyon; the Suda says that his non-Dionysiac tragedy was written in honour of Dionysos, which would place his activity in or after the reign of Kleisthenes. Ariphron wrote a Paian to Hygieia which is preserved by Athenaios and in inscriptions from Athens and Epidauros; he is probably identical with the Ariphron who appears as *chorodidaskalos* in an early fourth-century Attic inscription. Several works by the epigrammatist Mnasalkes are preserved in the *Greek Anthology*, and he is apparently identical with the Mnasalkes son of Mnasippos honoured in a decree from the Amphiareion at Oropos, which is dated in the third quarter of the third century. He is said to have been a native of Plataiai, a village in Sikyonia.[15]

Very little is known about Sikyonian prose writers apart from Menaichmos, the unknown author of the *Anagraphe*, and Aratos, whose memoirs were used as a source by Polybios and Plutarch. Others are mere names, such as Aristarchos, used by Pliny as a source on geographical matters, Diogenes, author of Τὰ περὶ Πελοπόννησον, Euphronidas, a Korinthian or Sikyonian grammarian who was said to have been the teacher of Aristophanes of Byzantion, and Herakleitos, who wrote *On Stones*. The second-century periegete Polemon was sometimes, probably wrongly, called a Sikyonian, perhaps because of his interest in the local art gallery, and Sikyon was also one of the suggested places of origin of the historian Phylarchos. A *Sikyonian Constitution* was among the works of this nature associated with Aristotle, which perhaps used local sources, especially for the historical part.[16]

A number of poets, although not of Sikyonian origin, were associated with the city in one way or another. Thus it is recorded that the Sikyonian Treasury at Delphi contained a golden book dedicated by Aristomache of Erythrai, an epic poetess who won two victories at Isthmia. The Athenian

[15] Sophilos, Suda, s.v. Σώφιλος, fragments in Kock, ii, 444–7; Axiopistos, Athen. xiv.648d; Tyndarichos, Athen. xiv.662c–d, Pollux vi.71; Neophron, Suda, s.v. Νεοφρῶν, D.L. ii.134, fragments in Argum. Eur. *Med.* and Schol. 666, 1387, Stob. *Floril.* iii.20.33, cf. W. Schmid and O. Stählin, *Geschichte der griechische Litteratur* (Munich, 1929–48), i. 3, pp. 370 f.; Epigenes, Suda, s.v. Θέσπις and οὐδὲν πρὸς τὸν Διόνυσον, Phot. *Lex.* 357.5, cf. Zenob. v.40; tragedy at Sikyon, Themistios, *Or.* xxvii.337b; Ariphron, Athen. xv.702a–b, *IG* ii², 4533, *IG* iv², 1, No. 132, cf. *IG* ii², 3092; Mnasalkes, Strabo, ix.412, *IG* vii, 395, epigrams collected in A. S. F. Gow and D. L. Page, *The Greek Anthology: Hellenistic Epigrams* (Cambridge, 1965).
[16] Aristarchos, Pliny, *NH* i, list of sources for v; Diogenes, D.L. vi.81; Euphronidas, Suda, s.v. Ἀριστοφάνης Βυζάντιος; Herakleitos, [Plut.] *De Fluv.* xiii.4; Polemon, Athen. vi.234d; Phylarchos, Suda, s.v. Φύλαρχος; Aristotelian *Constitution*, Arist. fr. 580 Rose.

comic author Eupolis was buried at Sikyon, and the dithyrambic poet Telestes of Selinous had a monument there set up by Aristratos. Sophokles had a Sikyonian mistress, Theoris, by whom he had a son Ariston, and wrote a play entitled *Thyestes at Sikyon*, which apparently dealt with the meeting of Thyestes and Pelopia which resulted in the birth of Aigisthos. Ariston's son Sophokles also wrote tragedies. Both Alexis and Menander wrote comedies entitled *The Sikyonian*; a substantial part of Menander's play is preserved.[17] The Sikyonian of the title (who in fact turns out to be of Athenian origin) is a commander of mercenaries who has been serving in Karia – perhaps an occupation frequently resorted to by Sikyonians who had to leave their native city. However, it is not obvious from the surviving fragments of the play that it was essential to the plot that he should come from Sikyon rather than any other Greek city.

[17] Aristomache, Plut. *Mor.* 675b; Eupolis, Paus. ii.7.3; Telestes, Pliny, *NH* xxxv. 109; Theoris, Suda, s.v. Ἰοφῶν, Hesych. s.v. Θεωρίς, Athen. xiii.592a–b; *Thyestes at Sikyon*, frs. 226–47 Nauck, cf. Hygin. *Fab.* 88; Sophokles II, Snell, *Trag. Graec. Frag.* i, No. 62; Alexis, fr. 206, Kock, Edmonds; Menander, see A. W. Gomme and F. H. Sandbach, *Menander – a Commentary* (Oxford, 1973), 632–6.

Select Bibliography

Adler, F. and others, *Olympia*, ii, *Die Baudenkmaler*, Asher, Berlin, 1892.

Andrewes, A., *The Greek Tyrants*, 3rd edn., London, 1960.

Androutsopoulos, G. D., "Ἐπιγραφὰι ἐκ Καμαρίου Κορινθίας', Πολέμων iii (1947/8), 50–2.

Arnold, D., *Die Polykletnachfolge*, Berlin, 1969.

Arvanitopoulos, A. S., 'Ἀνασκαφαὶ καὶ ἐρεύναι ἐν Σικυῶνι κὰι Θεσσαλίᾳ' *PAE* 1908, 145–152.

Barron, J. P., 'The Son of Hyllis', *CR* n.s. xi (lxxxv) (1961), 185–7.

—— 'The Sixth-century Tyranny at Samos', *CQ* n.s. xiv (1964), 210–29.

—— 'Ibycus: To Polycrates', *BICS* xvi (1969), 119–49.

Bieber, M., *The Sculpture of The Hellenistic Age*, revised edn., Columbia, 1961.

Brownson, C. L. and Young, C. H., 'Further Excavations at the Theatre of Sicyon in 1891', *AJA* viii (1893), 397–409, Pl. xiii.

Charitonides, S., 'Σικυών', *ADelt* xxi (1966), B 124.

Congdon, L. O. K., 'Greek Caryatid Mirrors', unpublished thesis, Harvard, 1963.

Denicolai, M., 'La genealogia dei tiranni di Sicione secondo un nuovo frammento storico', *Atti della reale accademia delle scienze di Torino*, li (1916), 1219–28.

Dinsmoor, W. B., 'Studies of the Delphian Treasuries', *BCH* xxxvi (1912), 439–95.

Earle, M. L., 'Excavations at the Theatre of Sicyon: ii Supplementary Report of the Excavations', *AJA* v (1889), 286–92.

—— 'iii A Sicyonian Statue', ibid., 292–303, Pl. viii.

—— 'Supplementary Excavations at the Theatre of Sicyon in 1891', *AJA* vii (1891), 281–2.

—— 'Excavations in the Theatre at Sicyon in 1891', *AJA* viii (1893), 388–96, Pl. xiii.

—— 'New Sicyonian Inscriptions', *CR* vi (1892), 132–5.

Fiechter, W., *Das Theater in Sikyon*, Stuttgart, 1931.

Forrest, W. G., 'The First Sacred War', *BCH* lxxx (1956), 33–52.

Fossum, A., 'The Theatre at Sikyon', *AJA* ix (1905), 263–76, Pls. viii–ix.

Frolov, E., 'Die Späte Tyrannis im Balkanischen Griechenland: iv Peloponnes 1 Die Tyrannis des Euphron in Sikyon', *Hellenische Poleis* (ed. H. Welskopf), 376–88, Berlin, 1974.

Gitti, A., 'Clistene di Sicione e le sue riforme: studia sulla storia arcaica di Sicione', *Atti della r. accad. naz. dei Lincei* vi.2 (1926–9), 535–623.

Hammond, N. G. L., 'The Family of Orthagoras', *CQ* n.s. vi (1956), 45–53.

Imhoof-Blumer, F., and Gardner, P., *Numismatic Commentary on Pausanias*, reprinted from *JHS* vi (1885), vii (1886), viii (1887).

Jeffery, L. H., *Local Scripts of Archaic Greece*, Oxford, 1961.

Jex-Blake, K., and Sellers, E., *Pliny the Elder's Chapters on the History of Art*, revised edn., Chicago, 1968.

Johansen, K. Friis, *Les vases sicyoniens*, Paris and Copenhagen, 1923.

166   Select Bibliography

Johnson, F. P., *Lysippos*, Duke University, 1927.
Kekule von Stradonowitz, R., 'Über den Apoll des Kanachos', *Sitzungsber. der Königlich preussischen Akad. der Wissenschaften* 1904, xxiii–xxiv (28 Apr. 1904), 786–801.
Krystalli, K., 'Σικυών', *ADelt* xxii (1967), B 164–6.
La Coste-Messelière, P., *Au Musée de Delphes*, Paris, 1936.
Langlotz, E., *Frühgriechische Bildhauerschulen*, Nürnberg, 1927.
Leahy, D. M., 'The Bones of Tisamenos', *Historia* iv (1955), 26–38.
— — 'Chilon and Aischines: a further consideration of Rylands Greek Papyrus Fr. 18', *Bull. John Rylands Library* xxxviii (1956), 406–35.
— — 'Chilon and Aischines again', *Phoenix* xiii (1959), 31–7.
— — 'The Dating of the Orthagorid Dynasty', *Historia* xvii (1968), 1–23.
Lenchantin de Gubernatis, M., 'Il nuovo storico di Sicione e la dinastia degli Ortagoridi', *Atti della reale accademia delle scienze di Torino*, li (1916), 290–305.
— — 'I nuovi frammenti di Eforo e lo storico di Sicione', *Boll. Fil. Class.* xxv (1918–19), 127–31, 141–3.
Linfert, A., *Von Polyklet zu Lysipp: Polyklets Schule und ihr Verhältnis zu Skopas von Paros*, Freiburg University, 1966.
Lippold, G., 'Sikyon', *RE* ii, A 2528–2549.
Marcadé, J., *Receuil des signatures de sculpteurs grecs*, 2 vols., Paris 1953 and 1957.
Meloni, P., 'La tirannide di Eufrone I in Sicione', *Riv. Fil.* n.s. xxix (1951), 10–33.
Momigliano, A., 'La genealogia degli Ortagoridi', *Atene e Roma* n.s. x (1929), 145–53.
McGregor, H. F., 'Cleisthenes of Sicyon and the Panhellenic Festivals', *TAPA* lxxii (1941), 266–87.
McMurtry, W. J., 'Excavations at the Theatre of Sicyon: i General Report of the Excavations', *AJA* v (1889), 267–86, Pls. vi, vii, ix.
Odelberg, P., *Sacra Corinthia, Sicyonia, Phliasia*, Upsala, 1896.
Oost, S. I., 'Two notes on the Orthagorids of Sicyon: i Andreas and Orthagoras, Mageiroi. ii Cleisthenes the King', *CP* lxix (1974), 118–20.
Orlandos, A., 'Ἀνασκαφαὶ Σικυῶνος', *PAE* 1932, 63–76.
— — 'Ἀνασκαφαὶ Σικυῶνος', *PAE* 1933, 81–90.
— — 'Ἀνασκαφαὶ Σικυῶνος', *PAE* 1934, 116–22.
— — 'Ἀνασκαφαὶ Σικυῶνος', *PAE* 1935, 73–83.
— — 'Ἀνασκαφαὶ Σικυῶνος', *PAE* 1936, 86–94.
— — 'Ἀνασκαφαὶ Σικυῶνος', *PAE* 1937, 94–6.
— — 'Ἀνασκαφαὶ Σικυῶνος', *PAE* 1938, 120–3.
— — 'Ἀνασκαφαὶ Σικυῶνος', *PAE* 1939, 100–2.
— — 'Ἀνασκαφαὶ Σικυῶνος', *PAE* 1941–4, 56–60.
— — 'Ἀνασκαφαὶ Σικυῶνος', *PAE* 1951, 187–91.
— — 'Ἀνασκαφαὶ Σικυῶνος', *PAE* 1952, 387–95.
— — 'Ἀνασκαφαὶ Σικυῶνος', *PAE* 1953, 184–90.
— — 'Ἀνασκαφαὶ Σικυῶνος', *PAE* 1954, 218–31.
— — 'La Fontaine de Sicyone', *AJA* xxxviii (1934), 153–7.
— — 'Ἐπιγραφαὶ τῆς Σικυῶνος', Ἑλληνικά x (1937–8), 5–18.
— — 'Pitsa', *EAA* vi, 200–6.

Parke, H. W., and Boardman, J., 'The Struggle for the Tripod and the First Sacred War', *JHS* lxxvii (1957), 276–82.

Pfister, F., 'Die Lokalhistorie von Sikyon bei Menaichmos, Pausanias und den Chronographen', *Rhein. Mus.* lxviii (1913), 529–37.

Pharaklas, N., Σικυώνια, Athens Technological Organization/Athens Center of Ekistics, 1971.

Philadelpheus, A., 'Ἀνασκαφαὶ Σικυῶνος', *ADelt* x (1926), 46–50.

—— 'Ἀρχαιολογικὴ συλλογὴ Σικυῶνος', *ADelt* x (1926) παράρτημα, 17–23.

—— 'Note sur le Bouleuterion (?) de Sicyone', *BCH* 1 (1926), 174–82.

Philippson, A., *Der Peloponnes*, Berlin 1892.

—— and Kirsten, E., *Die Griechischen Landschaften: iii Der Peloponnes: 1. Der Osten und Norden der Halbinsel*, Klostermann–Frankfurt, 1959.

Picard, C., 'Teisicrates de Sicyone et l'iconographie de Demetrios Poliorcetes', *RA* xxii (1944), 2, 5–37.

Pomtow, E., 'Die Alte Tholos und das Schatzhaus der Sikyonier zu Delphi', *Zeitschr. für Gesch. der Architektur* ii (1910), 97–143, 153–92.

—— 'Die beiden Tholoi zu Delphi', ibid., iv (1911), 171–213.

Robertson, C. M., 'Greek Mosaics', *JHS* lxxxv (1965), 72–89.

—— 'Greek Mosaics: A Postscript', *JHS* lxxxvii (1967) 133–6.

Von Rohden, H., 'Die Götterbilder des Dipoenos und Skyllis in Sikyon', *AZ* xxxiv (1876), 122–3.

Roux, G., *Pausanias en Corinthie*, Annales de l'Université de Lyon, Paris, 1958.

Skalet, C. H., *Ancient Sicyon, with a Prosopographia Sicyonia*, Baltimore, 1928.

Sordi, M., 'La Prima Guerra Sacra', *Riv. Fil.* xxxi (1953), 320–46.

Stikas, E., 'Περὶ τῶν ἐν θέσει 'Τζαμὶ' τῆς Σικυωνίας ἀνασκαφῶν *PAE* 1941–4, 61–4.

Ure, P. N., *The Origins of Tyranny*, Cambridge, 1922.

Vollgraff, W., and Beyen, H. G., *Argos et Sicyone*, The Hague, 1947.

Votsis, K., 'Nouvelle mosaique de Sicyone', *BCH* c (1976), 572–88.

White, M. E., 'The Dates of the Orthagorids', *Phoenix* xii (1950), 2–14.

INDEX

1. Theatre: ramps and side wall from E

2. Archaic temple from SW

3. Gymnasion: lower courtyard from NE

4. Gymnasion: south fountain

5. Gymnasion: north fountain

6. 'Akropolis' from Vasiliko

7. Tyche head (324)

8. Head of Demetrios (329)

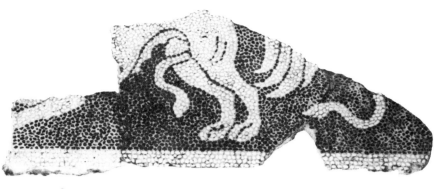

9. Mosaic (2872) (Plates 9-12 all show fragments of the same mosaic)

10. Mosaic (2874)

11. Mosaic (2872)

12. Mosaic (2872)

13. Griffin door panel from the 'Pausian floral' mosaic (2875) also illustrated in
Plates 14-16

14. Mosaic (2875): centre

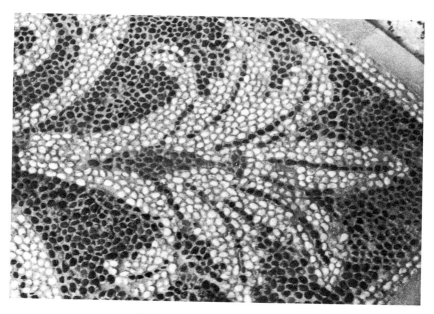

15. Mosaic (2875): corner flower

16. Mosaic (2875): flower at centre of side

17. Centaur mosaic (2873)